Ready® Classroom
Mathematics

Grade K • Volume 2

Curriculum Associates®

978-1-4957-8031-8
©2020–Curriculum Associates, LLC
North Billerica, MA 01862
5 6 7 8 9 10 11 12 13 14 15   21 20

BTS20

Contents

Contents (continued)

Contents (continued)

Contents (continued)

Show What You Know

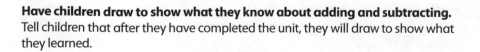

Have children draw to show what they know about adding and subtracting.
Tell children that after they have completed the unit, they will draw to show what they learned.

Build Your Vocabulary

Review

add

equal

minus

plus

subtract

My Math Words

Equation	*Plus* or *Minus*?	*Add* or *Subtract*?
$2 + 1 = 3$	plus minus	add subtract
$3 - 1 = 2$	plus minus	add subtract

My Academic Words

☐ collect   ☐ discover

_____

- - - - - - - - - - - - - - - - - - - -

We _____ flowers and leaves for science class.

_____

- - - - - - - - - - - - - - - - - - - -

I like to _____ new ways to learn how to add.

Have children draw two circles, then have them draw one more. Ask children to describe how they got from two circles to three using the *Review* words. Ask children to erase or cross out one of the circles. Have them describe subtraction using the *Review* words. Then ask children to circle the words that describe the equations. Review *My Academic Words* and complete the activity with children.

Understand Addition

Dear Family,

This week your child is exploring addition.

This lesson explores the idea of what it means to **add**. It also introduces the **plus sign** and the **equal sign** as a way to represent the joining together of two groups of objects into a single group. Your child will use connecting cubes as physical models and drawings as visual models to show adding two groups.

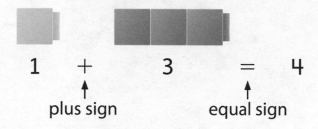

$$1 \quad + \quad 3 \quad = \quad 4$$

plus sign   equal sign

The lesson also introduces different problem situations.

Add To: There are 2 birds in a tree. 3 more birds join them.
How many birds are in the tree now?

Put Together: 2 oranges and 3 apples are in a bowl.
How many pieces of fruit are in the bowl?

Physically modeling addition, drawing pictures, and exploring different problem situations will help your child make connections to how addition is used in everyday life.

Invite your child to share what he or she knows about addition by doing the following activity together.

Activity   Adding

Do this activity with your child to explore what it means to add.

Materials 8 small objects of 2 different types or colors (such as pretzels and crackers, dried pasta pieces in 2 different shapes, or buttons in 2 different colors)

- Give your child two groups of objects that have a combined total of 5 or less. For example, place snack items such as 3 pretzels and 2 crackers in two groups.

- Ask how many objects are in each group. After your child counts, ask an addition problem about the groups, such as: *There are 3 pretzels and 2 crackers. How many snacks are there in all?*

- Your child puts the groups together and counts to find the total. You might also ask your child to write an equation, for example, $3 + 2 = 5$.

- Repeat at least 3 more times, each time using different quantities but keeping the total 5 or less.

- Ask your child addition problems about small groups of objects whenever you can. For example, have your child add apples and bananas, big spoons and small spoons, or yellow blocks and orange blocks.

Explore Addition

Try It

_____

- - - - - - - - - -   and   - - - - - - - - - -

_____   _____

- - - - - - - - - -   and   - - - - - - - - - -

_____   _____

- - - - - - - - - -   and   - - - - - - - - - -

_____   _____

- - - - - - - - - -   and   - - - - - - - - - -

_____   _____

Learning Target

- Represent addition and subtraction with objects, fingers, mental images, drawings, sounds, acting out situations, verbal explanations, expressions, or equations.

SMP 1, 2, 3, 4, 5, 6

Children explore the meaning of addition by making connections between concrete and verbal representations. Have 3 children come to the front of the room. Ask: *How many children are there? What can I do to make 5?* Write "3 and 2" on the board and have children write the numbers. Repeat, starting with 2, 1, and 4 children, having children write the number pair each time. Introduce *add* as a word for joining numbers.

Connect It

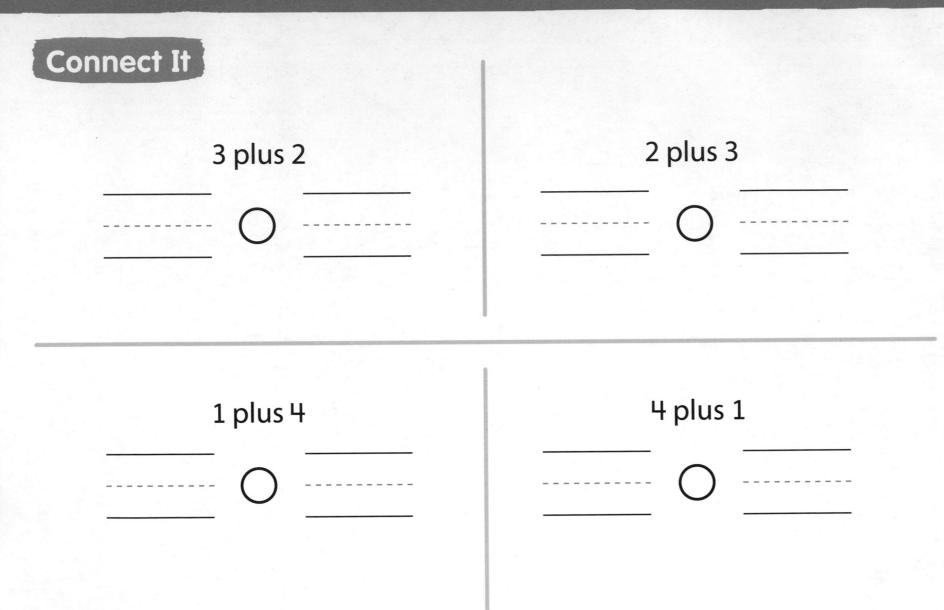

3 plus 2

○

2 plus 3

○

1 plus 4

○

4 plus 1

○

Introduce children to the plus sign to represent addition. Tell children that *plus* is another word that can be used instead of *and* when joining numbers. Read each number pair aloud using the word *and,* then again, replacing the word *and* with *plus.* Introduce the plus sign as the symbol that stands for *plus.* Have children write each number pair using the plus sign. Then have children model each expression using fingers.

Prepare for Addition

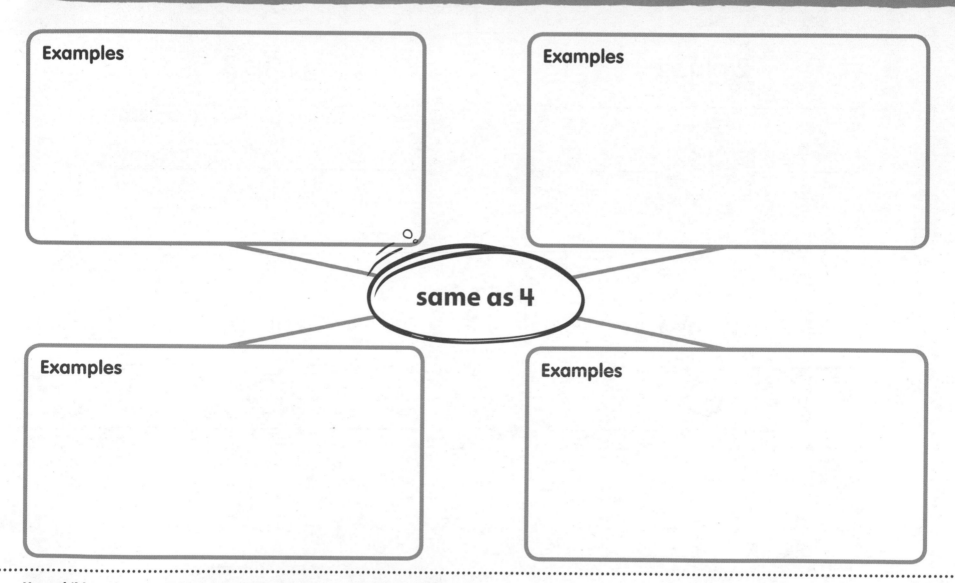

Examples

Examples

same as 4

Examples

Examples

Have children show quantities that are the same as 4. Tell children to fill in each box. Tell them to use pictures, words, and numbers. Encourage children to show as many ways as they can.

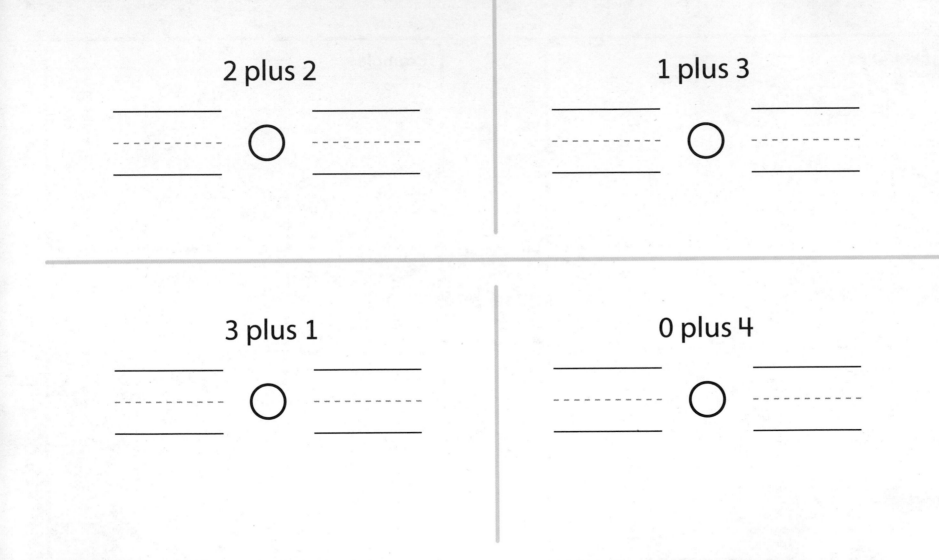

2 plus 2

1 plus 3

3 plus 1

0 plus 4

Have children practice using the plus sign to represent addition. Read each number pair aloud using the word *and*, then again, replacing the word *and* with *plus*. Have children write each number pair using the plus sign. Then have children model each expression using fingers.

Develop Understanding of Addition

 **Model It**

2 + 1

What can you add?

Ask children to draw a picture of things they might add together to show 2 + 1. For example, they might draw 2 crayons and 1 more crayon. Have children share and discuss their drawings, using the terms *plus* and *add*.

Discuss It Tell a story about why you might want to add the objects in your drawing.

Connect It

$$1 + 3$$

$$3 + 3$$

$$2 + 3$$

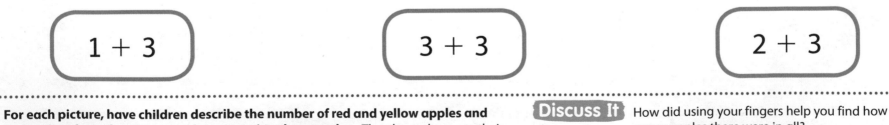

For each picture, have children describe the number of red and yellow apples and draw a line from the picture to the expression that matches. Then have them use their fingers to tell how many apples in all.

Discuss It How did using your fingers help you find how many apples there were in all?

Think About Addition

Show 1 + 4.

What can you add?

Have children draw a picture of objects they could add to show 1 + 4. For example, children might draw 1 large ball and 4 small balls.

Have children tell a story about the drawing. Encourage them to use the words *plus* and *add*.

©Curriculum Associates, LLC   Copying is not permitted.

Lesson 16 Understand Addition   **321**

| 3 + 3 | 2 + 2 | 1 + 1 |

Ask children to find the expression that describes the sum shown in each picture. Have children look at the first picture and tell how many cats and how many dogs there are. Read each expression aloud, and have children tell which one describes the first picture and then draw a line to match. Repeat for the second and third pictures.

Develop Understanding of Addition

Model It

Math Toolkit
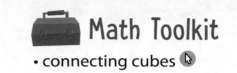
• connecting cubes

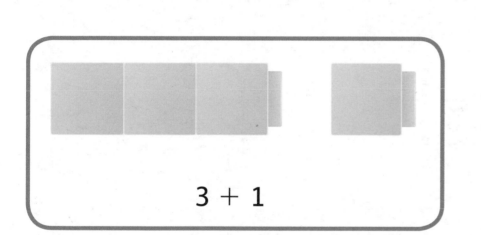

3 + 1

Children match two addends shown with connecting cubes to the total. Ask children which group of connecting cubes shows the same number as 3 and 1 put together. Have children draw a line from the expression 3 + 1 to the cubes that show a total of 4.

Discuss It How can you be sure of your answer?

Connect It

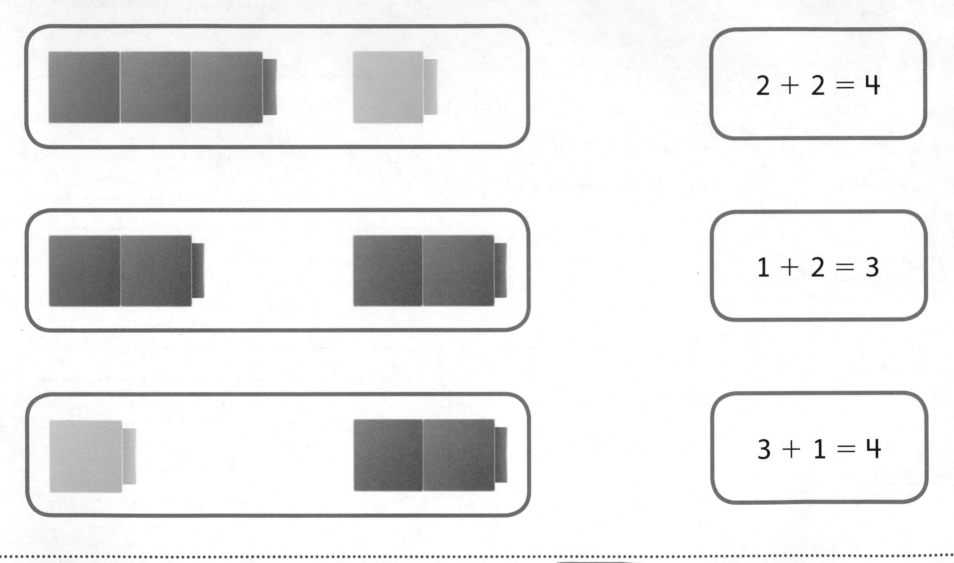

2 + 2 = 4

1 + 2 = 3

3 + 1 = 4

Have children match pictures to addition equations. Have children describe how many cubes are being added in each picture. Read each equation aloud together and discuss the meaning of each. Then have children draw lines to match.

Discuss It How can you find the total number of cubes in each picture?

Name: _____

Practice Addition

Example

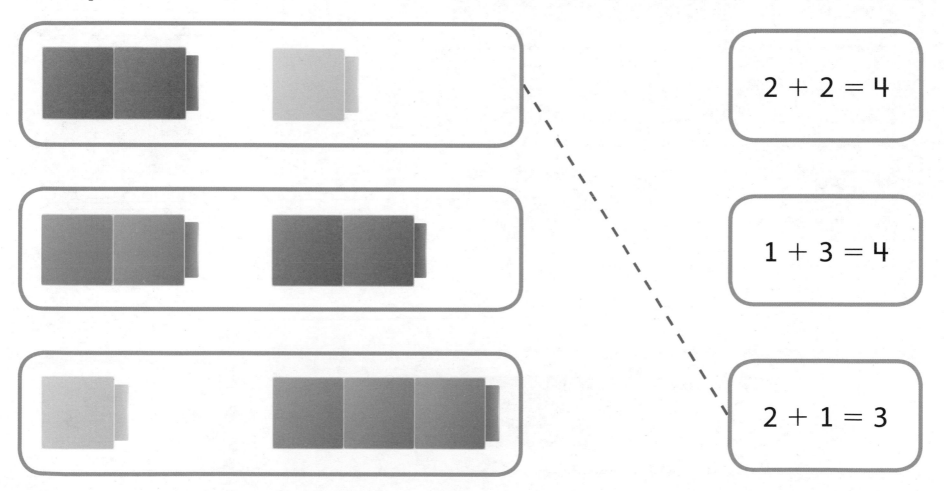

2 + 2 = 4

1 + 3 = 4

2 + 1 = 3

Have children match pictures to addition equations. Have children describe how many cubes are being added in each picture. Read each equation aloud together and discuss the meaning of each. Then have children draw lines to match each picture with its equation.

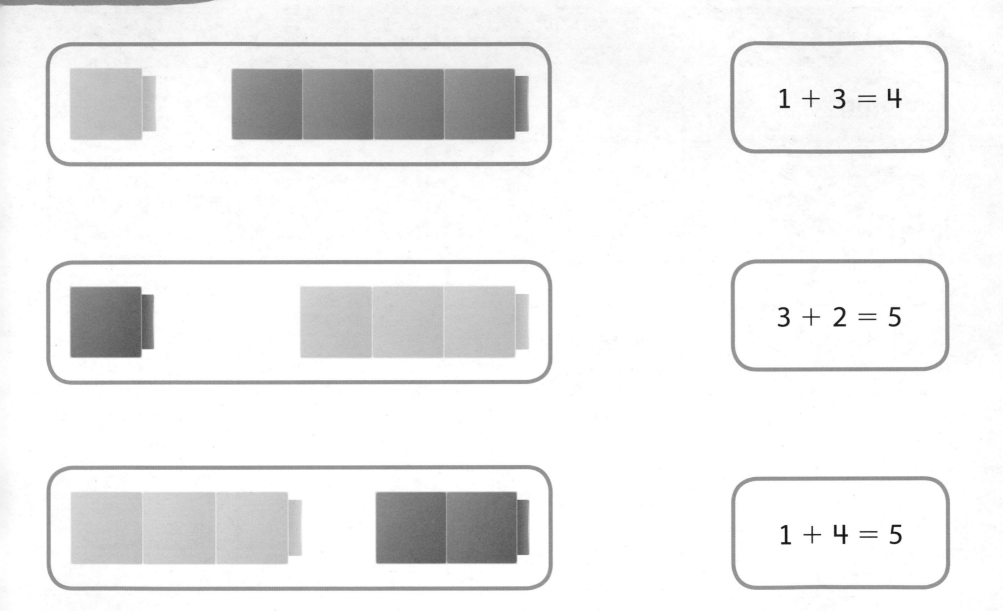

$$1 + 3 = 4$$

$$3 + 2 = 5$$

$$1 + 4 = 5$$

Have children match pictures to addition equations. Have children describe how many cubes are being added in each picture. Read each equation aloud together and discuss the meaning of each. Then have children draw lines to match each picture with its equation.

Refine Ideas About Addition

Apply It

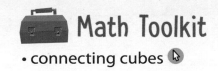
Math Toolkit

• connecting cubes

$2 + 1 =$ _____

$2 + 2 =$ _____

$2 + 3 =$ _____

Have children use cubes to model each expression you write on the board.
Then have children write the total for each.

Discuss It Did you use the same colors as your partner? Did you get the same total if you used different colors?

Connect It

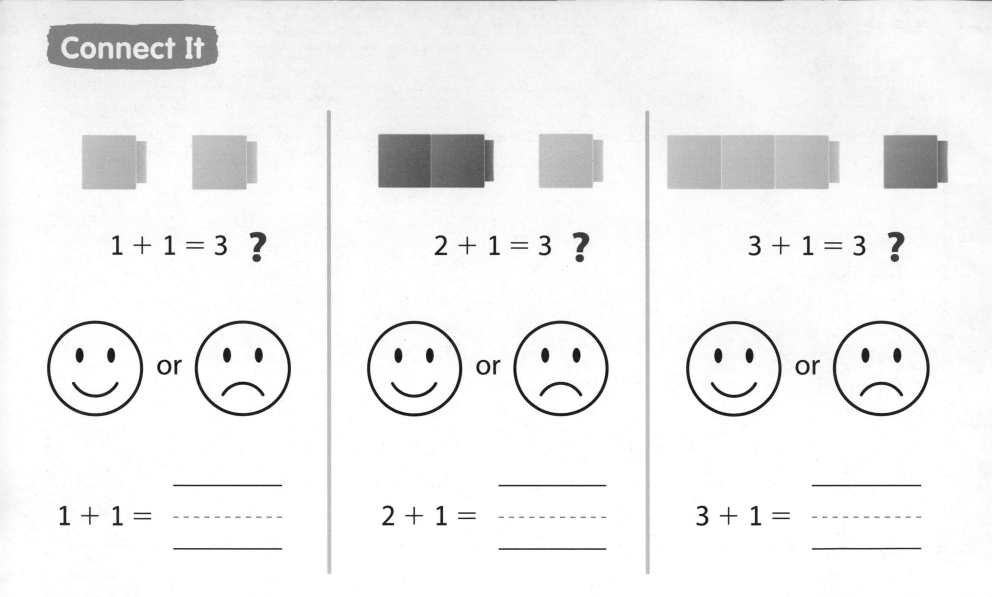

1 + 1 = 3 **?**

☺ or ☹

1 + 1 = _____

2 + 1 = 3 **?**

☺ or ☹

2 + 1 = _____

3 + 1 = 3 **?**

☺ or ☹

3 + 1 = _____

Have children check whether the equation matches the cubes. First, discuss the groups of cubes and then the equations below them. Have children color the happy face if they match or the sad face if they do not and write the total.

Discuss It Explain how you figured out where the mistakes are.

Add Within 5

Dear Family,

This week your child is learning to add within 5.

This lesson includes solving addition problems with totals up to 5. It also connects story problems to pictures, objects, 5-frames, and equations. This will provide your child with a strong foundation as he or she eventually moves from solving problems shown with pictures or models to solving problems shown only with numbers.

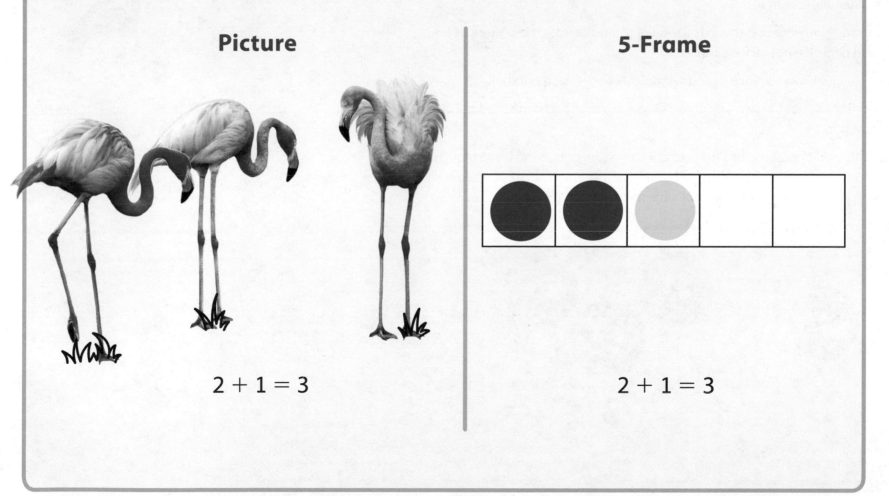

Picture	5-Frame
2 + 1 = 3	2 + 1 = 3

Activity Adding Within 5

Do this activity with your child to connect addition equations to concrete objects.

Materials 8 small objects of 2 different colors or types (such as buttons in 2 different colors or dried pasta pieces in 2 different shapes)

- Fold a sheet of paper in half.

- Write an addition equation that has a total of 5 or less across the bottom of the half-sized page. Do not include the total.

- Show your child how to place a group of objects above each number.

- Have your child count how many objects there are in all and write the total after the equal sign.

- Write other addition equations for your child to figure out on the three remaining sections of the folded paper (front and back). Each addition equation should have a total of 5 or less. Have your child use objects to find the totals.

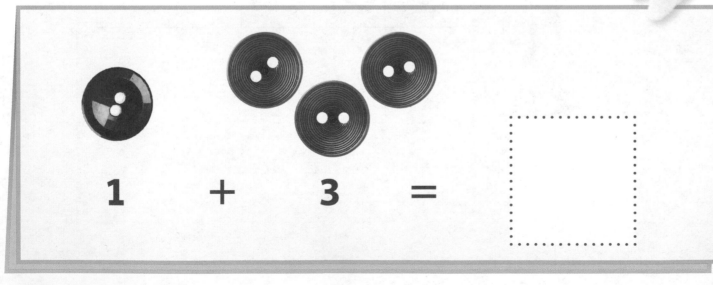

$$1 + 3 =$$

Explore Adding Within 5

Try It

Learning Target

- Solve addition and subtraction word problems, and add and subtract within 10.

SMP 1, 2, 3, 4, 5, 6, 7

🧰 **Math Toolkit**

- counters 🖰

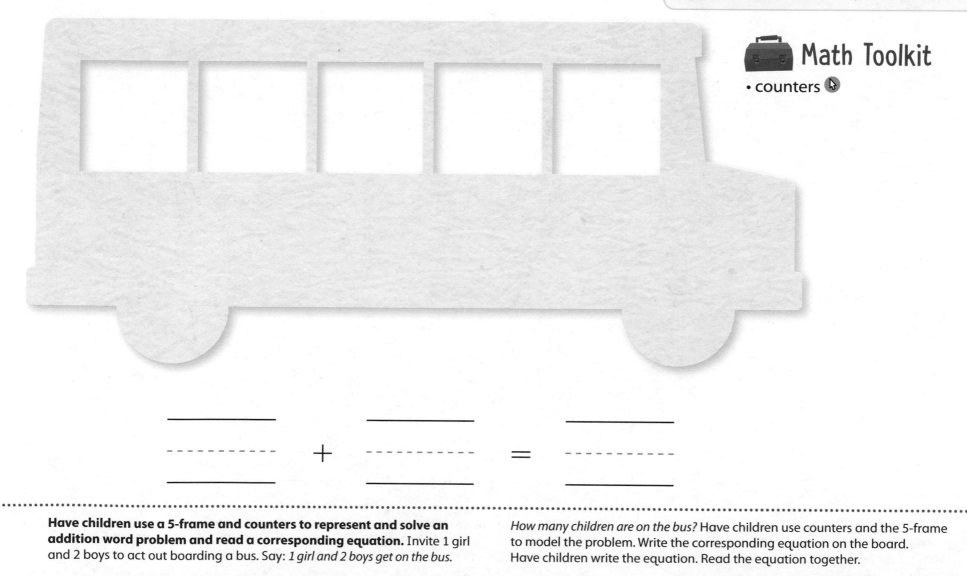

_____ + _____ = _____

Have children use a 5-frame and counters to represent and solve an addition word problem and read a corresponding equation. Invite 1 girl and 2 boys to act out boarding a bus. Say: *1 girl and 2 boys get on the bus.*

How many children are on the bus? Have children use counters and the 5-frame to model the problem. Write the corresponding equation on the board. Have children write the equation. Read the equation together.

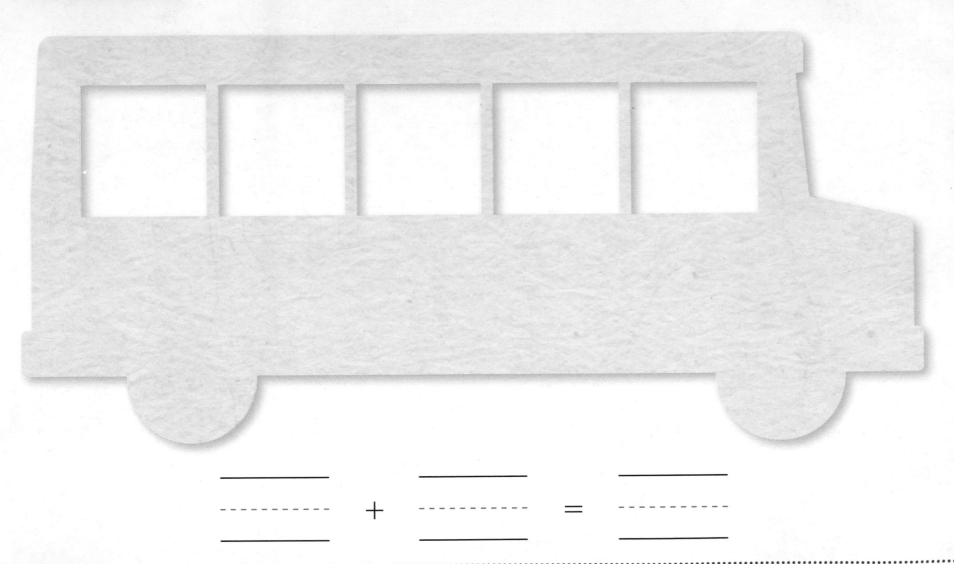

$$\underline{\hspace{4em}} + \underline{\hspace{4em}} = \underline{\hspace{4em}}$$

Have children use a 5-frame and counters to act out another addition problem and read a corresponding equation. Say: *There are 3 children on the bus. 1 girl gets on the bus. How many children are on the bus now?*

Have children use counters and the 5-frame to model the problem.
Have children help you complete the equation on the board. Then children write the equation. Read the equation aloud together.

Prepare for Adding Within 5

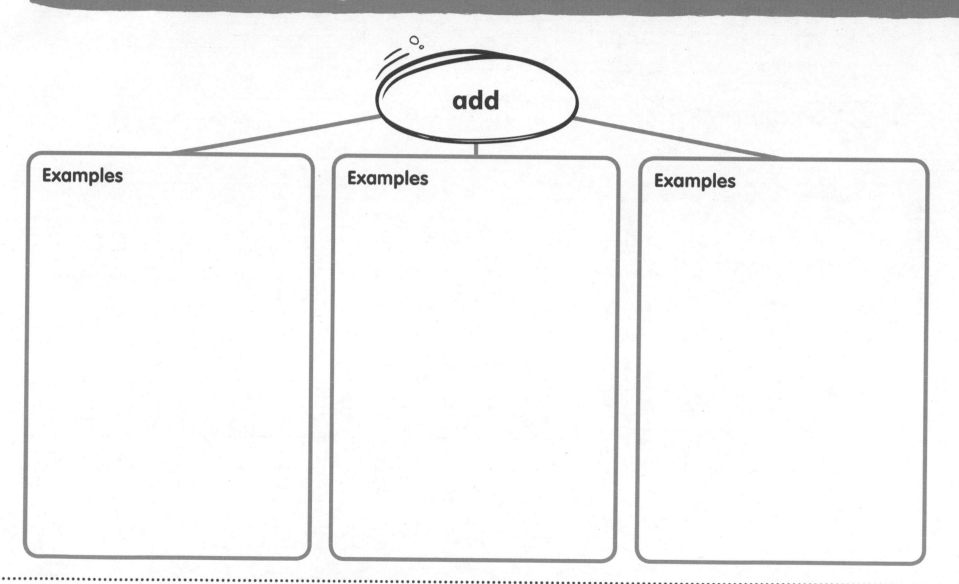

add

Examples

Examples

Examples

Have children show what it means to add. Have children fill in each of the boxes to show the meaning of addition (joining). Encourage them to use pictures, words, and numbers. Tell children to think of as many different ways as they can.

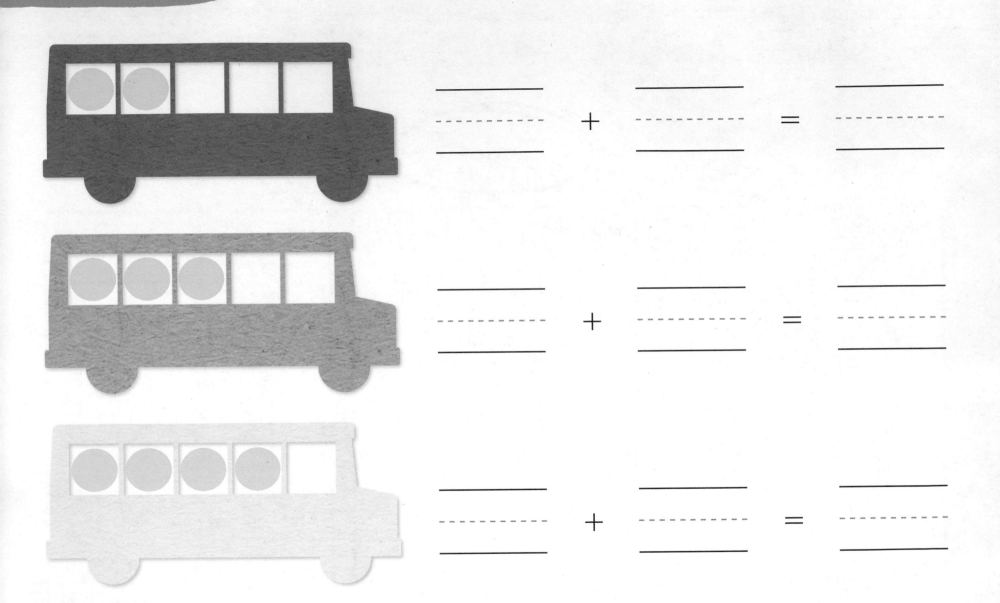

Have children complete 5-frames to represent addition problems and write the corresponding equations. Pose an addition story problem for the first bus. Say: *There are 2 girls on the bus. 3 boys get on the bus. How many children are on the bus now?* Have children draw counters to complete the 5-frame. Write 2 + 3 = 5 and have children write the equation. Repeat for the other two buses.

Develop Adding Within 5

Encourage children to describe addition problems for each group of animals. Provide an example, such as *3 little pigs and 1 big pig is 4 pigs*. Have children circle the two groups of animals that show 3 plus 1.

Discuss It How is the group of sheep like the group of pigs?

Connect It

Math Toolkit
• counters

$2 + 1 = 3$

$1 + 1 = 2$

$3 + 1 = 4$

Have children match pictures to equations. Have children tell the number of large and small animals and the total in each picture. Then have them say each equation aloud, use counters to model it, and draw a line from the picture to the equation that matches.

Discuss It How are the addition equations alike? How are they different?

Practice Adding Within 5

Have children use red and yellow crayons to color a group of animals or objects to show 3 + 1 and then tell the total. Then have children use two other colors to color a group of animals or objects to show 2 + 2. Have children color the rest of the picture.

$$2 + 1 = 3$$

$$4 + 1 = 5$$

$$1 + 1 = 2$$

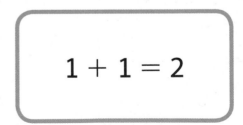

Have children match pictures to addition equations. Have children tell the number of large and small animals, as well as the total, in each picture. Read each addition equation aloud together. Then have children draw lines to match each picture to its addition equation.

338 **Lesson 17** Add Within 5

Develop Adding Within 5

Try It

Math Toolkit
• counters

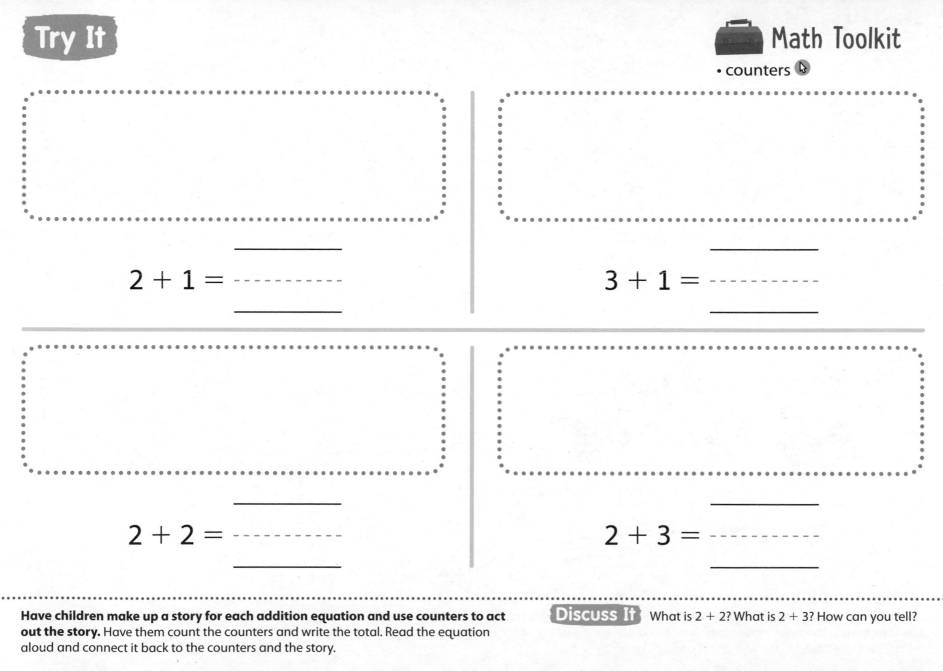

$2 + 1 =$ _____

$3 + 1 =$ _____

$2 + 2 =$ _____

$2 + 3 =$ _____

Have children make up a story for each addition equation and use counters to act out the story. Have them count the counters and write the total. Read the equation aloud and connect it back to the counters and the story.

Discuss It What is 2 + 2? What is 2 + 3? How can you tell?

Connect It

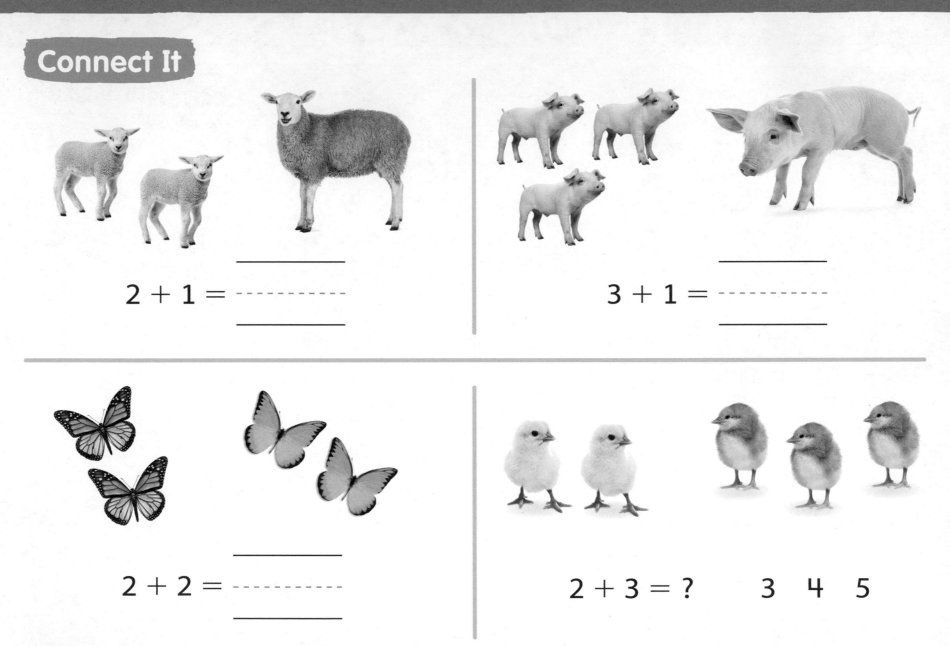

$2 + 1 =$ _____

$3 + 1 =$ _____

$2 + 2 =$ _____

$2 + 3 = ?$ 3   4   5

Have children compare each equation with the pictured addition problem and then count and write the total. Have them read the completed equation aloud. Have them relate the written total to the number of animals shown.

Discuss It Which is more, 2 + 1 or 3 + 1? How can you tell?

Practice Adding Within 5

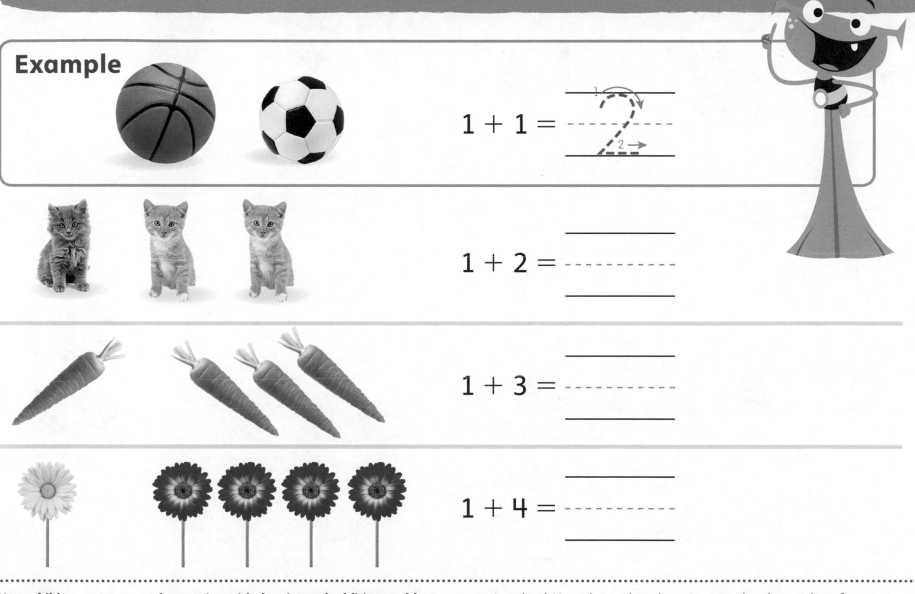

Example

$1 + 1 =$ _____

$1 + 2 =$ _____

$1 + 3 =$ _____

$1 + 4 =$ _____

Have children compare each equation with the pictured addition problem and then count and write the total. Have children read the completed equation aloud. Have them relate the written total to the number of objects shown.

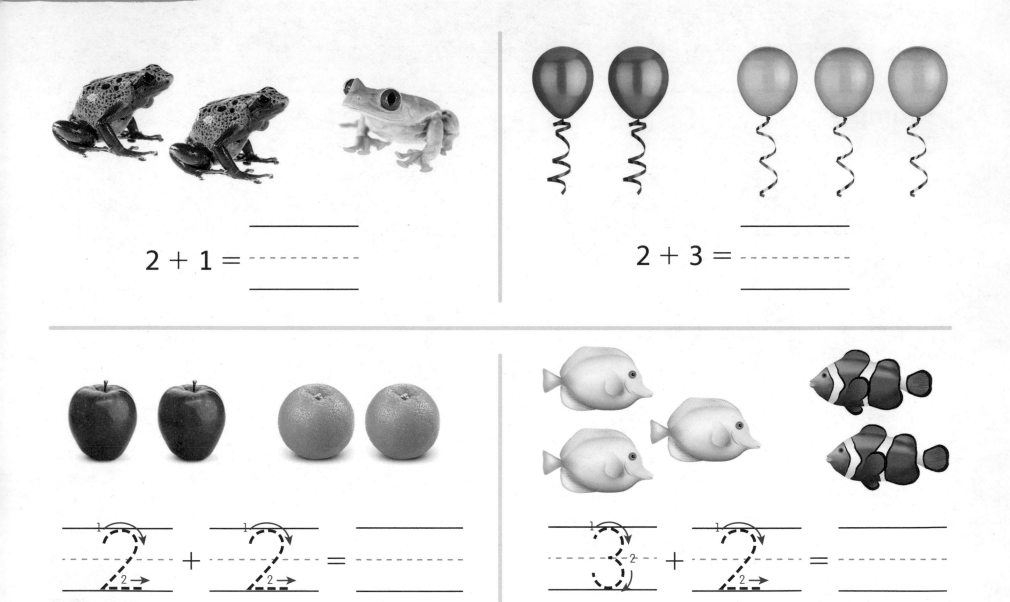

$2 + 1 = \underline{\hspace{3cm}}$

$2 + 3 = \underline{\hspace{3cm}}$

$2 + 2 = \underline{\hspace{3cm}}$

$3 + 2 = \underline{\hspace{3cm}}$

Have children compare each equation with the pictured addition problem and then complete the equation. Have children read the completed equation aloud. Have them relate the written total to the number of objects shown.

Refine Adding Within 5

Apply It

🧰 Math Toolkit
• counters
• crayons

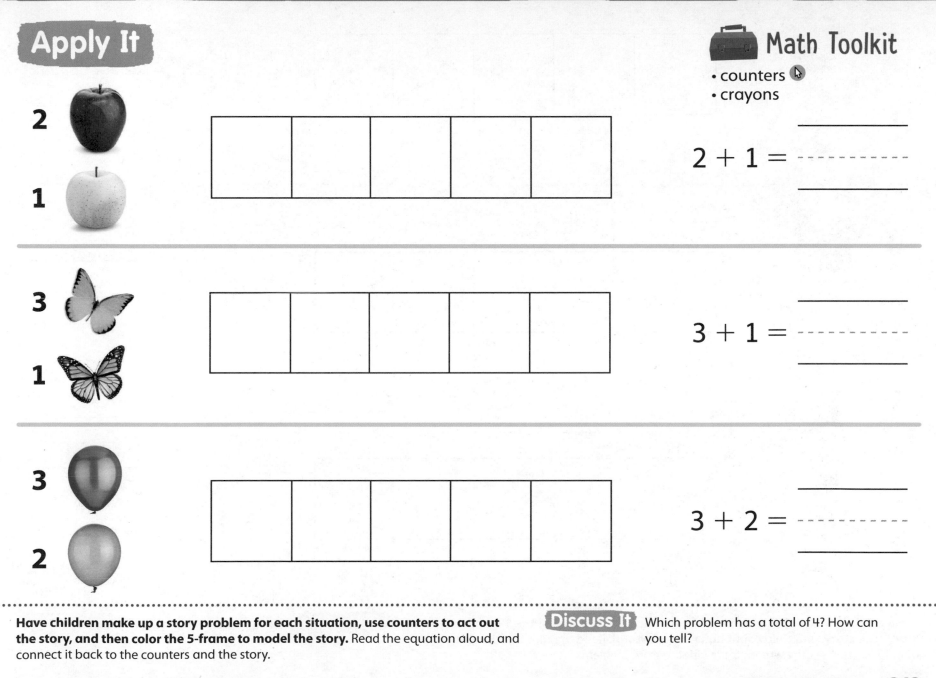

2
1

2 + 1 = _____

3
1

3 + 1 = _____

3
2

3 + 2 = _____

Have children make up a story problem for each situation, use counters to act out the story, and then color the 5-frame to model the story. Read the equation aloud, and connect it back to the counters and the story.

Discuss It Which problem has a total of 4? How can you tell?

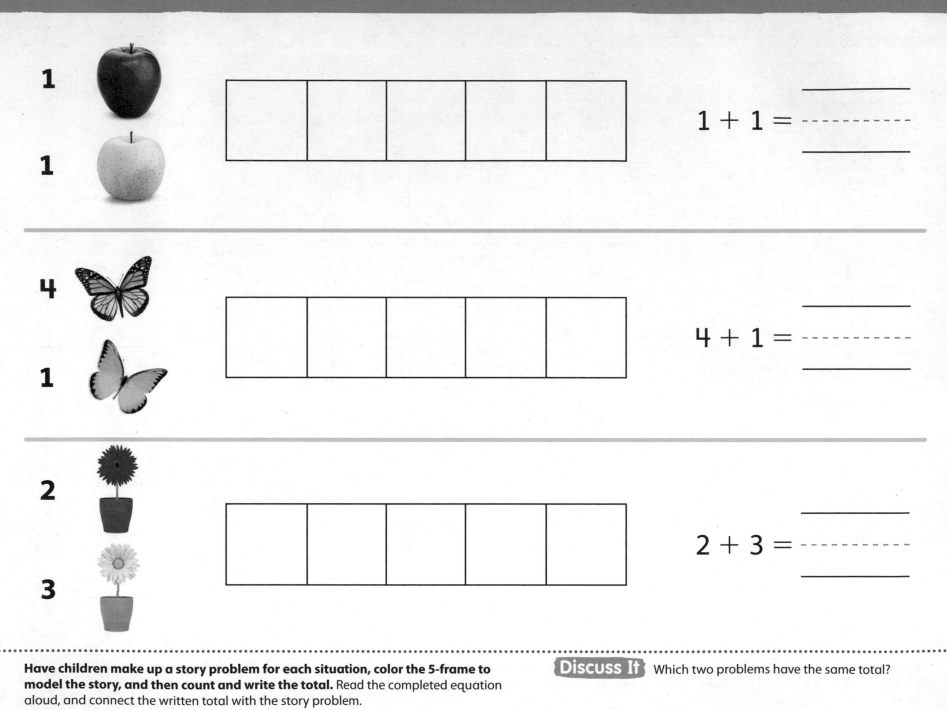

1

1

$1 + 1 =$ _____

_____

4

1

$4 + 1 =$ _____

_____

2

3

$2 + 3 =$ _____

_____

Have children make up a story problem for each situation, color the 5-frame to model the story, and then count and write the total. Read the completed equation aloud, and connect the written total with the story problem.

Discuss It Which two problems have the same total?

Practice Adding Within 5

Example

2
1

2 + 1 = 3

2
2

2 + 2 = _____

2
3

2 + 3 = _____

Have children make up a story problem for each set of pictures, color the 5-frame using two colors to model the story, and then write the total. For example, to tell a story for the first problem, children might say: *2 green frogs* *are in a pond. 1 blue frog joins them. Now 3 frogs are in the pond.* In each problem, after children color the 5-frame and complete the equation, read the equation aloud together and relate it to the story problem.

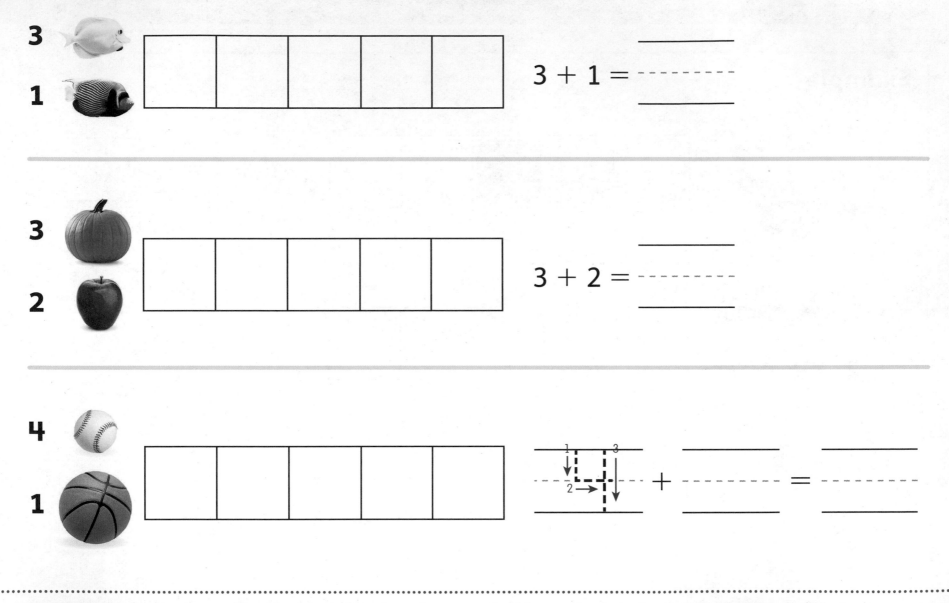

3

1

$3 + 1 =$ _____

3

2

$3 + 2 =$ _____

4

1

___ + ___ = ___

Have children make up a story problem for each set of pictures, color the 5-frame using two colors to model the story, and then complete the equation.

Read the completed equation aloud together and relate it to the story problem.

Refine Adding Within 5

Apply It

Math Toolkit
- two-color counters
- crayons

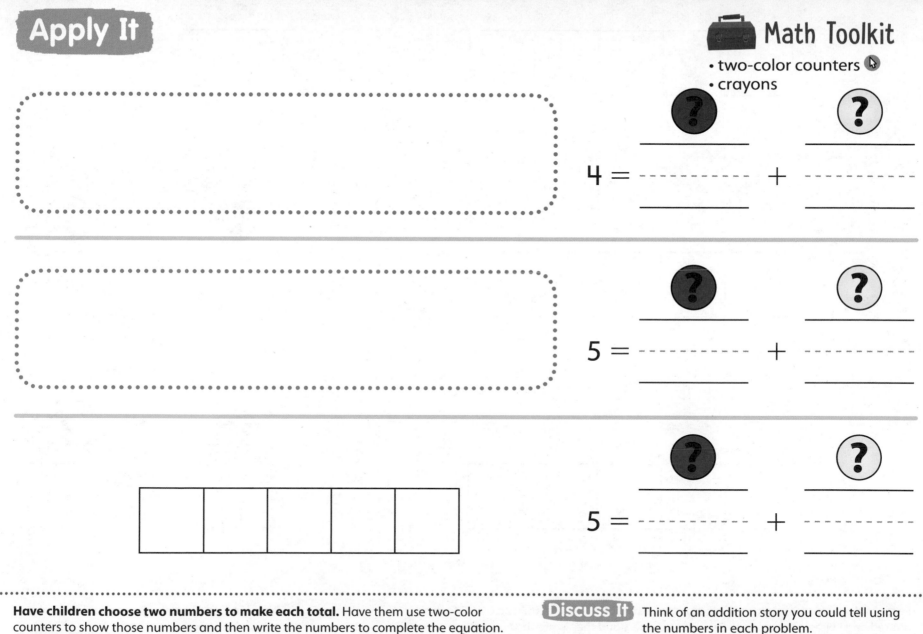

4 = _____ + _____

5 = _____ + _____

5 = _____ + _____

Have children choose two numbers to make each total. Have them use two-color counters to show those numbers and then write the numbers to complete the equation. Then have them color the 5-frame with red and yellow crayons and write the numbers.

Discuss It Think of an addition story you could tell using the numbers in each problem.

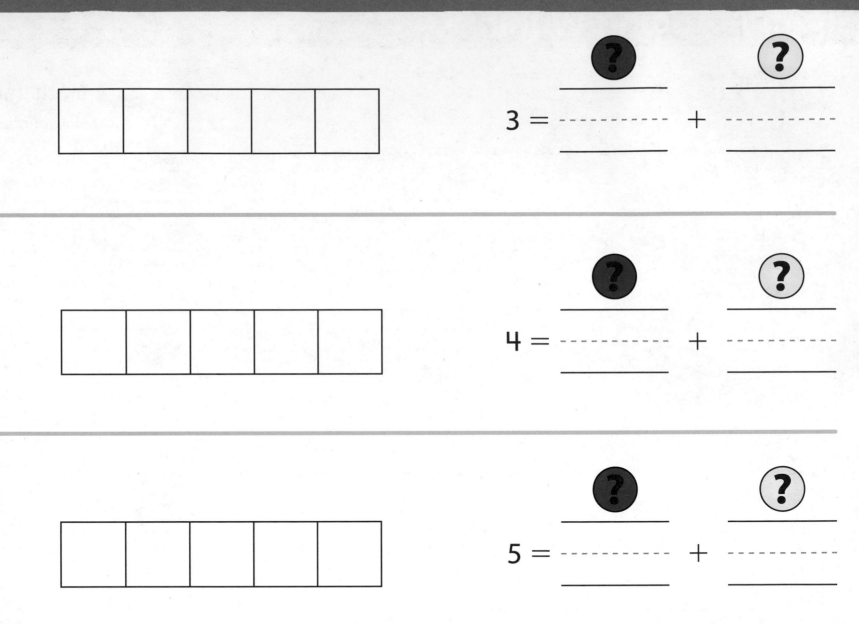

$$3 = \underline{} + \underline{}$$

$$4 = \underline{} + \underline{}$$

$$5 = \underline{} + \underline{}$$

Have children choose two numbers to make each total. Have them color the 5-frame with red and yellow crayons to show those numbers and then write the numbers to complete the equation. Explain that there are multiple correct answers.

Discuss It Think of an addition story you could tell using the numbers in each problem.

348   **Lesson 17** Add Within 5

Understand Subtraction

Dear Family,

This week your child is exploring subtraction.

This lesson explores the idea of what it means to **subtract** and introduces the **minus** sign and the equal sign as a way to represent taking away objects from a group. Your child will use counters and/or connecting cubes as physical models and drawings as visual models to show taking away from a group.

Modeling subtraction in these ways can help make connections to subtraction equations. For example, one side of a subtraction equation shows how many you start with and how many you take away. The other side shows how many are left.

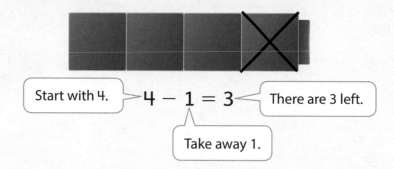

Start with 4. ⟩ $4 - 1 = 3$ ⟨ There are 3 left.

Take away 1.

This lesson also explores take-away problem situations.

Take-From Result Unknown: *There are 5 birds in a tree. 2 birds fly away. How many birds are in the tree now?*

Physically modeling subtraction, drawing pictures, and exploring subtraction problem situations will help your child make connections to how subtraction is used in daily life.

Invite your child to share what he or she knows about subtraction by doing the following activity together.

Activity   Subtracting

Do this activity with your child to explore subtraction.

Materials 5 animal-shape crackers or animal toys (or any small objects such as buttons or blocks)

Show your child groups of 2 to 5 animals. Tell subtraction stories such as the one below. Encourage your child to use the objects to act out each story and solve the problem.

- *4 ducks are in a pond.* (Have your child count the toy ducks.)

- *1 duck swims away.* (Remove 1 duck from the group.)

- *How many ducks are left?* (Have your child count and tell how many ducks are left.)

If you do not have small objects shaped like animals, you can use any small objects and explain that you will pretend they are ducks (or any animal that is your child's favorite).

Explore Subtraction

Try It

Learning Target

- Represent addition and subtraction with objects, fingers, mental images, drawings, sounds, acting out situations, verbal explanations, expressions, or equations.

SMP 1, 2, 3, 4, 5, 6

 **Math Toolkit**

- counters

Have children explore the meaning of subtraction by making connections between concrete and verbal representations. Invite 3 children to the front of the room. Have children act out 3 take away 2. Have children use counters to model the problem on the workmat. Write "3 take away 2" on the board. Repeat with other number pairs with totals within 5. Introduce *subtract* as a term for breaking apart numbers.

Connect It

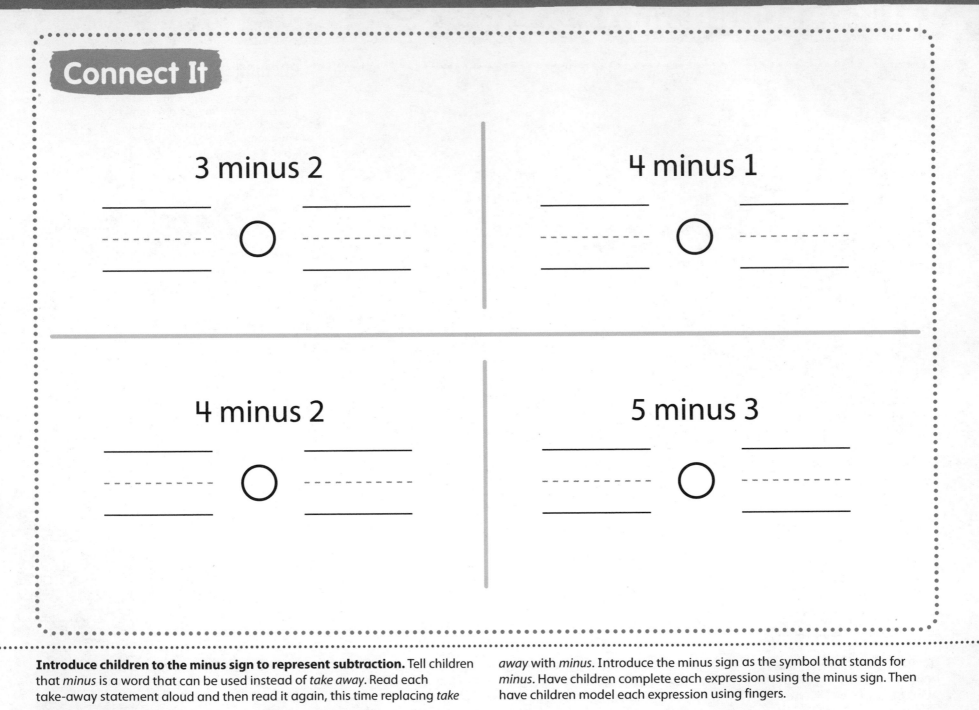

3 minus 2

4 minus 1

4 minus 2

5 minus 3

Introduce children to the minus sign to represent subtraction. Tell children that *minus* is a word that can be used instead of *take away*. Read each take-away statement aloud and then read it again, this time replacing *take away* with *minus*. Introduce the minus sign as the symbol that stands for *minus*. Have children complete each expression using the minus sign. Then have children model each expression using fingers.

Prepare for Subtraction

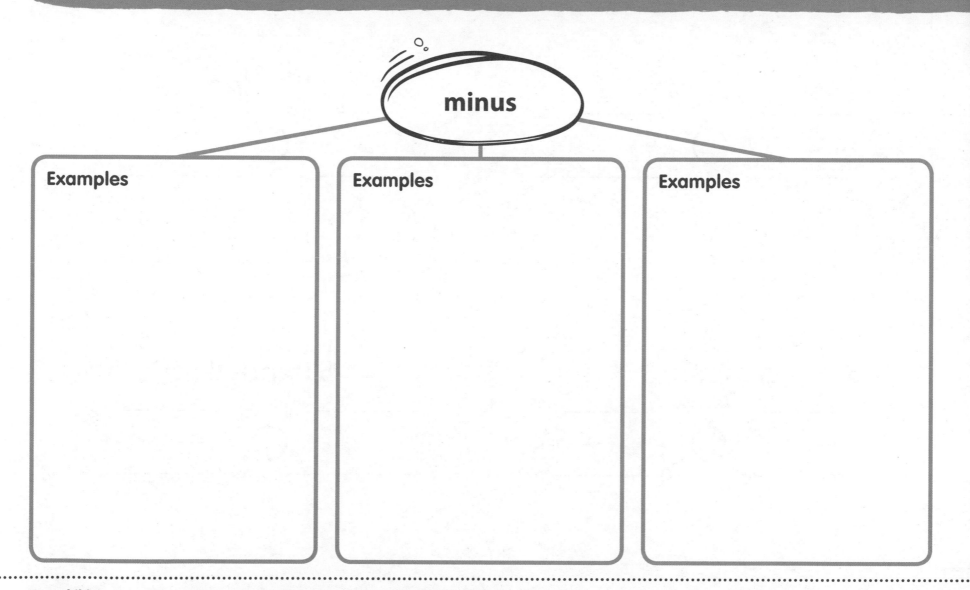

minus

Examples

Examples

Examples

Have children show the meaning of the word *minus*. Have children fill in each of the boxes to show the meaning of the word *minus*. Tell children that they can use words, numbers, and pictures. Encourage them to show as many ideas as they can.

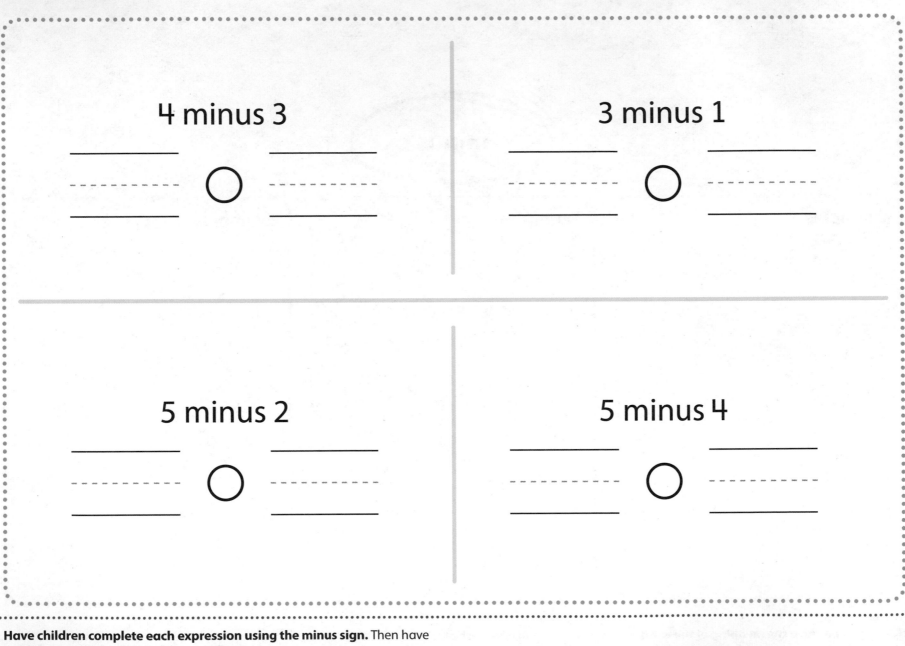

4 minus 3

3 minus 1

5 minus 2

5 minus 4

Have children complete each expression using the minus sign. Then have children model each expression using fingers.

Develop Understanding of Subtraction

Model It

3 − 1

What can you subtract?

Ask children to draw a picture that could show 3 take away 1. For example, they might draw 3 books with 1 book crossed out. Have children share and discuss their drawings, using the terms *take away*, *minus*, and *subtract*.

Discuss It Why did you take away one of the objects in your drawing?

Connect It

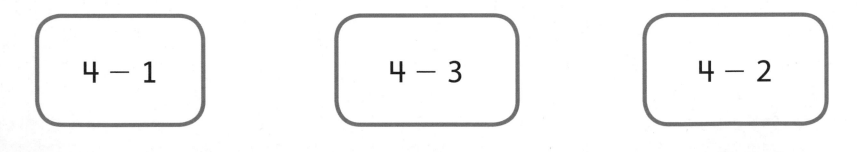

Ask children to match subtraction pictures with expressions. Have children describe each set of pictures. Remind children that the apples marked with an X are being taken away. Have children draw lines from the pictures to match the expressions.

Discuss It How are the sets of pictures the same? How are they different? What could you draw to show 4 − 4?

Think About Subtraction

4 − 1

What can you subtract?

Ask children to draw a picture that shows 4 take away 1. Give an example of subtracting, such as the following: *There are 4 books on the shelf. I take* *1 book. How many books are left on the shelf?* Encourage children to tell a similar story about their drawing.

2 − 1	5 − 1	3 − 1

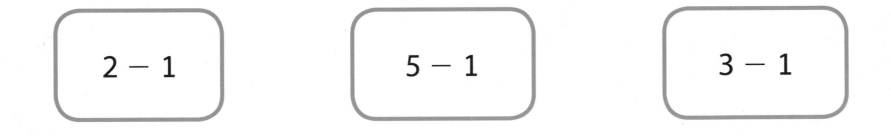

Ask children to match subtraction pictures with expressions. Have children describe each set of pictures. Remind children that the apples marked with an X are being taken away. Have children draw lines from the pictures to match the expressions.

Develop Understanding of Subtraction

Model It

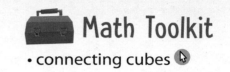 Math Toolkit

• connecting cubes

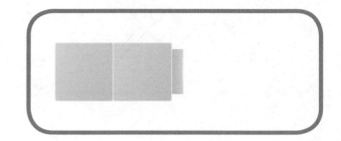

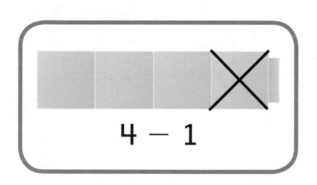

4 − 1

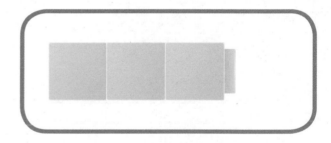

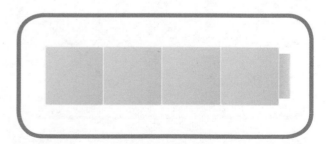

Children match a subtraction problem shown with connecting cubes to the difference.
Ask children which group of connecting cubes shows the same amount as 4 minus 1. Have children draw a line from the expression 4 − 1 to the cubes that show a difference of 3.

Discuss It How does the cube train with a cube marked with an X help you to solve 4 − 1?

Connect It

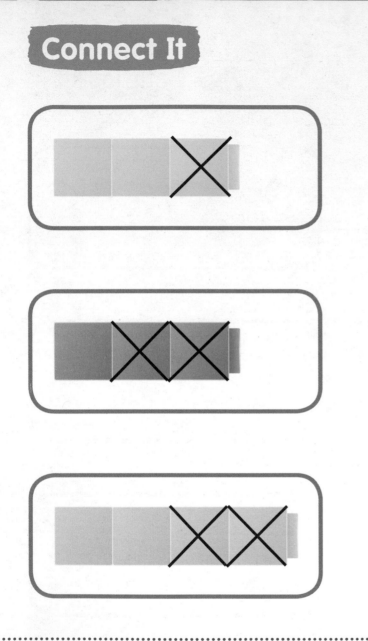

$3 - 2 = 1$

$4 - 2 = 2$

$3 - 1 = 2$

Ask children to match each picture with an equation. Discuss the number of cubes in each picture and how many are taken away. Read and discuss the meaning of each equation. Then have children draw lines to match.

Discuss It How can you check your answers to make sure the picture matches the equation you chose?

Practice Subtraction

Example

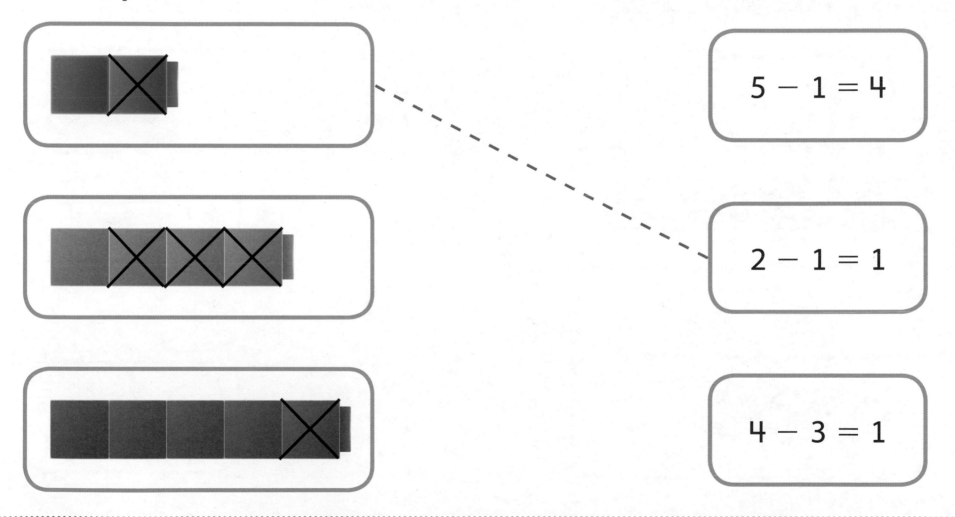

$$5 - 1 = 4$$

$$2 - 1 = 1$$

$$4 - 3 = 1$$

Ask children to match pictures to subtraction equations. Have children describe the number of cubes in each picture and how many are taken away.

Read each equation aloud together and discuss the meaning of each. Then have children draw lines to match each picture with its equation.

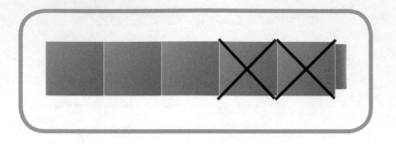

$$5 - 2 = 3$$

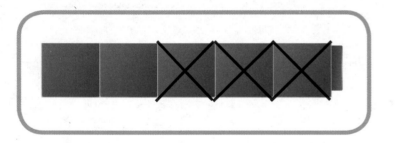

$$3 - 2 = 1$$

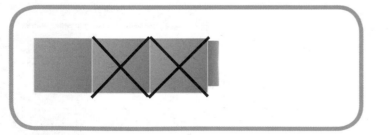

$$5 - 3 = 2$$

Ask children to match pictures to subtraction equations. Have children describe the number of cubes in each picture and how many are taken away.

Read each equation aloud together and discuss the meaning of each. Then have children draw lines to match each picture with its equation.

Refine Ideas About Subtraction

Apply It

🧰 **Math Toolkit**
• connecting cubes

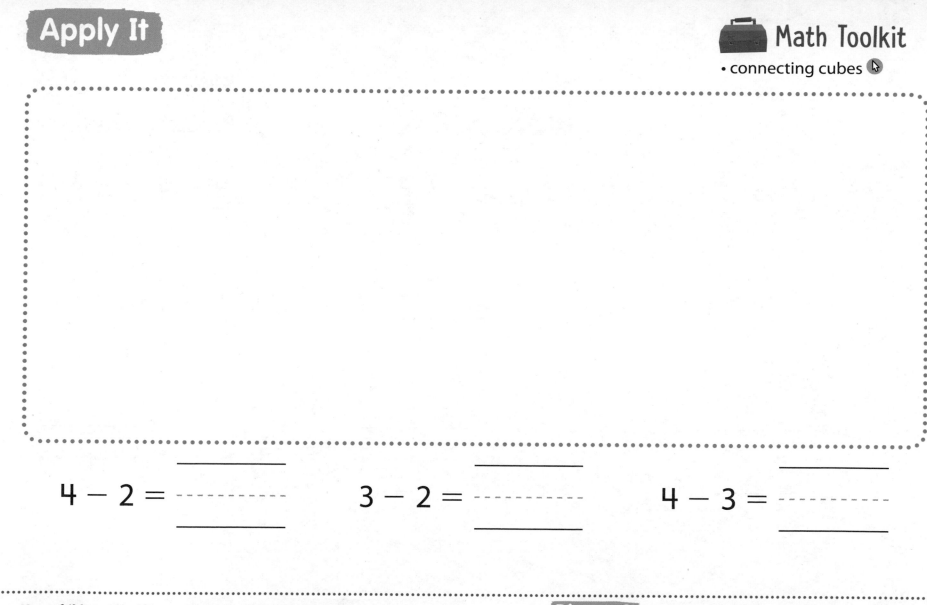

$4 - 2 = $ _____

$3 - 2 = $ _____

$4 - 3 = $ _____

Have children use cubes to model each problem. Then have them complete each equation.

Discuss It How could you solve 5 – 3? What could you use to help if you did not have cubes?

Connect It

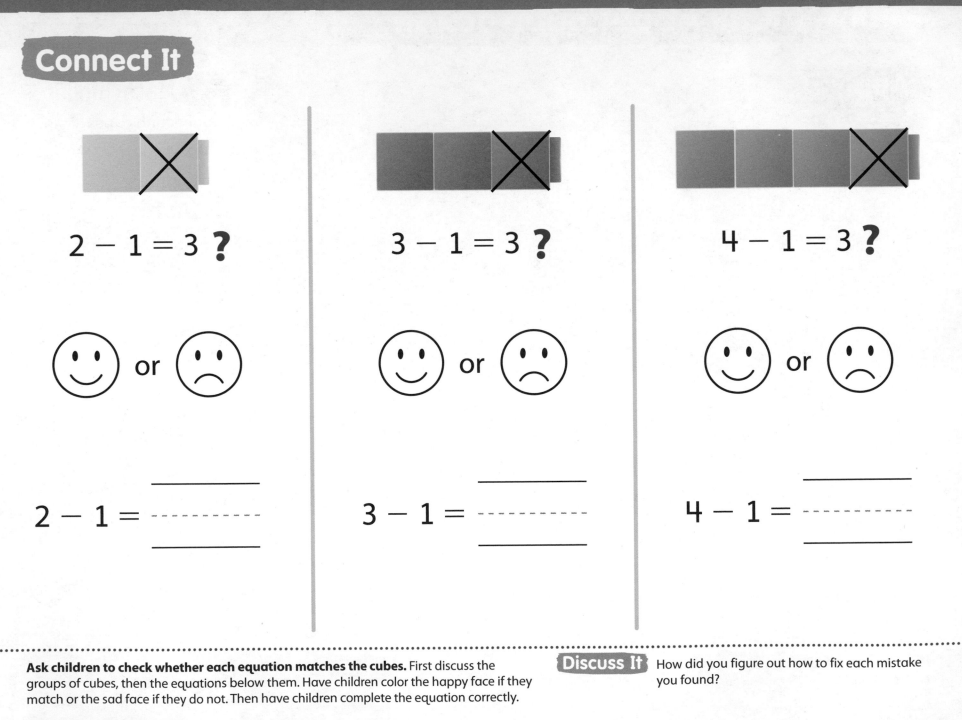

2 − 1 = 3 **?**

😊 or ☹️

2 − 1 = _____

3 − 1 = 3 **?**

😊 or ☹️

3 − 1 = _____

4 − 1 = 3 **?**

😊 or ☹️

4 − 1 = _____

Ask children to check whether each equation matches the cubes. First discuss the groups of cubes, then the equations below them. Have children color the happy face if they match or the sad face if they do not. Then have children complete the equation correctly.

Discuss It How did you figure out how to fix each mistake you found?

364   Lesson 18 Understand Subtraction

Subtract Within 5

Dear Family,

This week your child is learning to subtract within 5.

Subtraction problems in this lesson involve taking away part of a group of up to 5 objects and finding how many are left. In class, your child may use actual objects, connecting cubes, and/or counters on 5-frames to act out taking away part of a group.

When pictures of objects are shown with subtraction problems, you can cross out objects to show the action of taking away. Objects crossed out can be pictures of real-world objects, such as cups or balloons, or pictures of counters on 5-frames.

Connecting pictures, models, and subtraction stories to equations helps build a strong foundation for subtraction. Eventually your child will transition from solving problems shown with concrete objects or drawings to solving problems shown only with numbers.

Picture

$$4 - 2 = 2$$

5-Frame

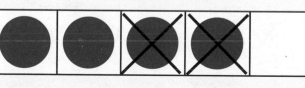

$$4 - 2 = 2$$

Invite your child to share what he or she knows about subtracting within 5 by doing the following activity together.

Activity Subtracting Within 5

Do this activity with your child to explore subtracting within 5.

Materials pencil, index cards or paper, 5 small objects (such as pennies, buttons, dried beans, or pasta shapes), cup

- On an index card or paper, write $5 - 3 = \boxed{}$.

- Place the subtraction problem and 5 pennies on the table.

- Point to the number 5 and say: *There are 5 pennies. How many do we need to take away?*

- Prompt your child to recognize that the minus sign and number 3 show that you need to take away 3. Have your child remove 3 pennies and place them in a cup.

- Ask: *How many pennies are left?* Have your child count the pennies on the table and write the answer in the box after the equal sign.

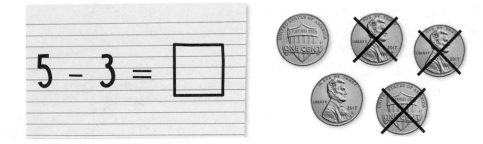

Repeat with other subtraction problems within 5, such as $3 - 1$, $5 - 2$, and $4 - 3$.

During your daily routine, encourage your child to use objects to model subtraction whenever you can. For example, when clearing the table, you might say: *There are 4 cups on the table. I am taking away 1. How many cups are left?* Model subtraction with up to 5 crayons, blocks, spoons, raisins, crackers, or other objects.

Explore Subtracting Within 5

Try It

Learning Target

- Solve addition and subtraction word problems, and add and subtract within 10.

SMP 1, 2, 3, 4, 5, 6

Math Toolkit

- counters
- index cards

Have children act out subtraction word problems. Pose the problem: *In a parking lot, there are 5 cars parked in a row. 1 car leaves. How many cars are still in the row?* Act out the subtraction. Model the subtraction. Solve another problem: *There are 4 cars in a row. 2 cars leave the row. How many cars are still in the row?*

Connect It

Children use counters and their fingers to model other subtraction problems. Say: *Adam has 4 crayons. He gives 1 to his sister. How many crayons does Adam have left?* Ask children to use counters to show the subtraction.

Repeat, saying: *Adam has 5 crayons. He gives 2 to his sister. How many crayons does Adam have left now?* Ask children to use their fingers to model and solve the problem.

Prepare for Subtracting Within 5

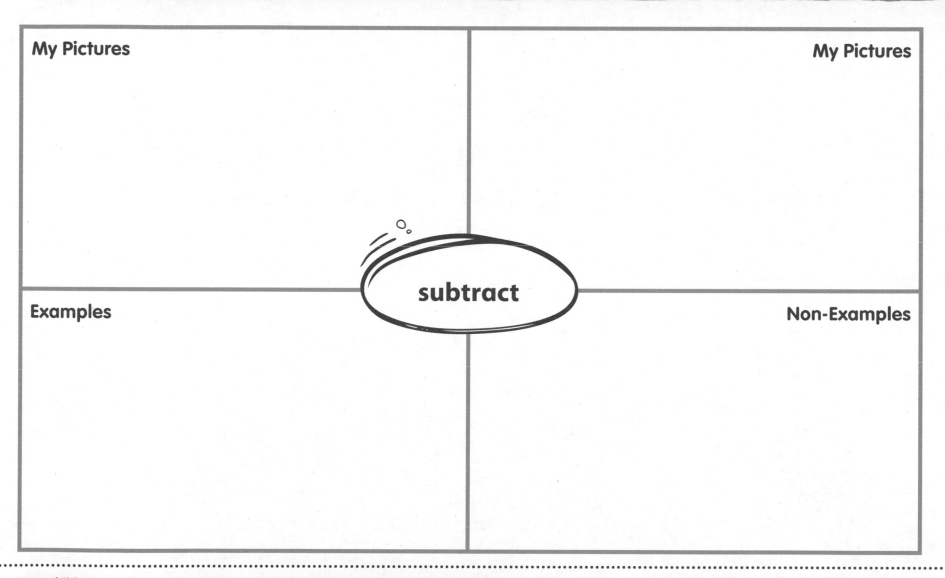

My Pictures	My Pictures
Examples	**Non-Examples**

subtract

Have children complete as many boxes as they can. Have children draw pictures to show the meaning of the word *subtract*. Then have children draw or write examples and non-examples of the word *subtract*.

Children use small objects and their fingers to model subtraction problems. Say: *Carmen has 5 markers. She gives 3 to her brother. How many markers does Carmen have left?* Ask children to use objects to show the subtraction. Repeat, saying: *Carmen has 4 markers. She gives 2 to her brother. How many markers does Carmen have left now?* Ask children to use their fingers to model and solve the problem.

Encourage children to describe subtraction problems for groups of objects. Provide an example: *There were 5 candles, but 4 are gone. Now there is only 1 candle left.* Then have children circle the groups of objects that show 5 minus 2.

Discuss It If somebody eats another slice of cake, how many will be left?

Connect It

Math Toolkit
• connecting cubes

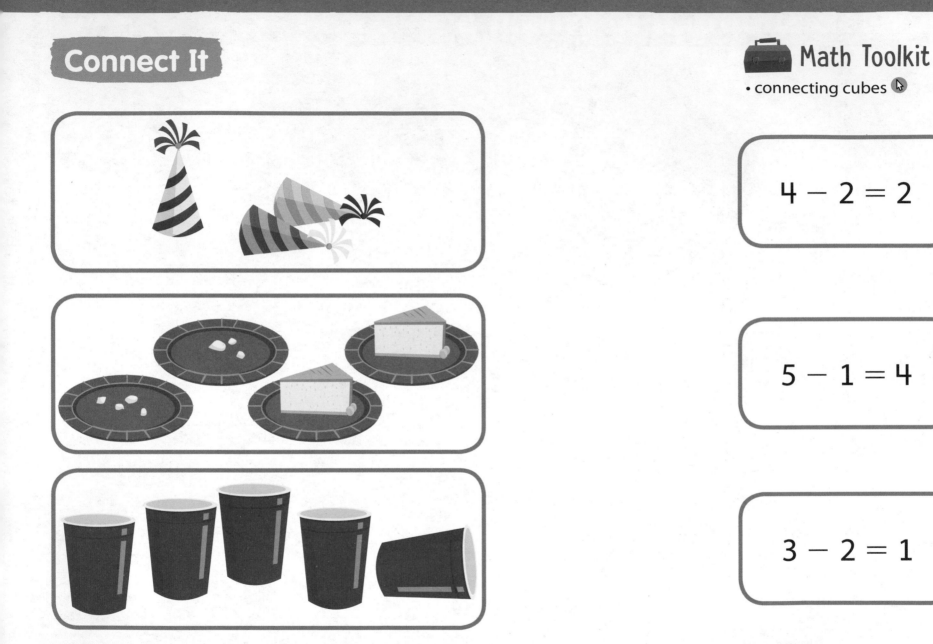

$4 - 2 = 2$

$5 - 1 = 4$

$3 - 2 = 1$

Have children match pictures to equations. Have children tell a subtraction story for each picture and read each equation aloud. Then have children draw lines to match each picture to its equation.

Discuss It What is a subtraction story? Why do the equations match the pictures?

Practice Subtracting Within 5

Have children color the 5 plates and 3 pieces of cake and tell a subtraction story about this part of the picture. Then have children color a part of the picture that shows 5 take away 1 and tell a story about that. Have children color the rest of the picture.

$$4 - 3 = 1$$

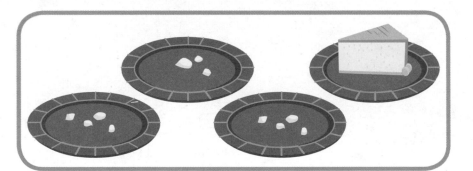

$$5 - 3 = 2$$

$$2 - 1 = 1$$

Have children match pictures to equations. Have children tell a subtraction story for each picture. Read each equation aloud together. Then have children draw lines to match each picture to its equation.

Develop Subtracting Within 5

Try It

🧰 Math Toolkit
• counters

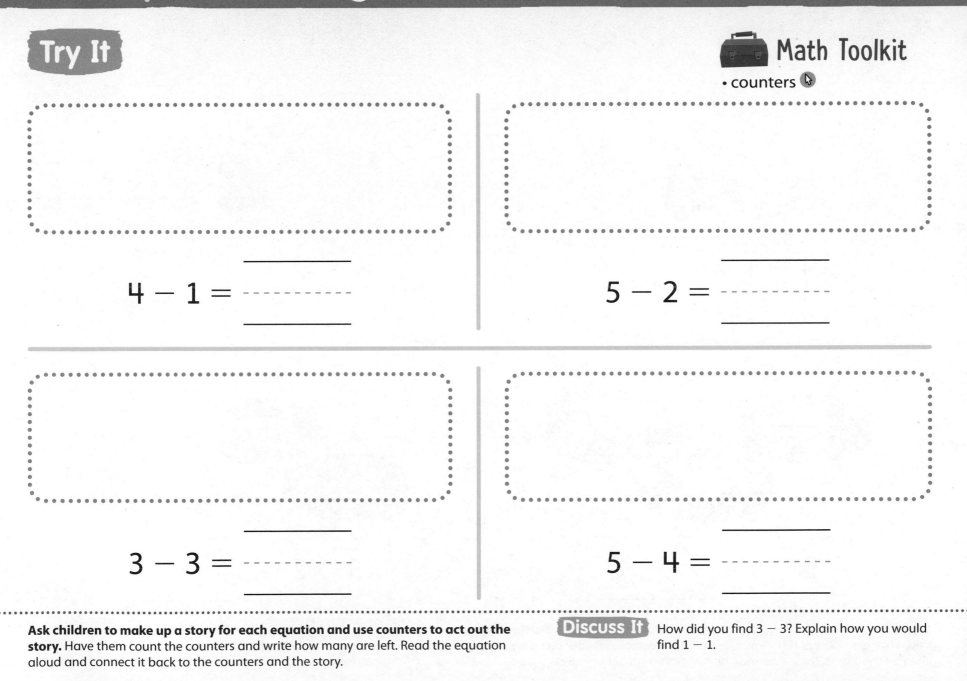

$$4 - 1 = \underline{}$$

$$5 - 2 = \underline{}$$

$$3 - 3 = \underline{}$$

$$5 - 4 = \underline{}$$

Ask children to make up a story for each equation and use counters to act out the story. Have them count the counters and write how many are left. Read the equation aloud and connect it back to the counters and the story.

Discuss It How did you find 3 − 3? Explain how you would find 1 − 1.

Connect It

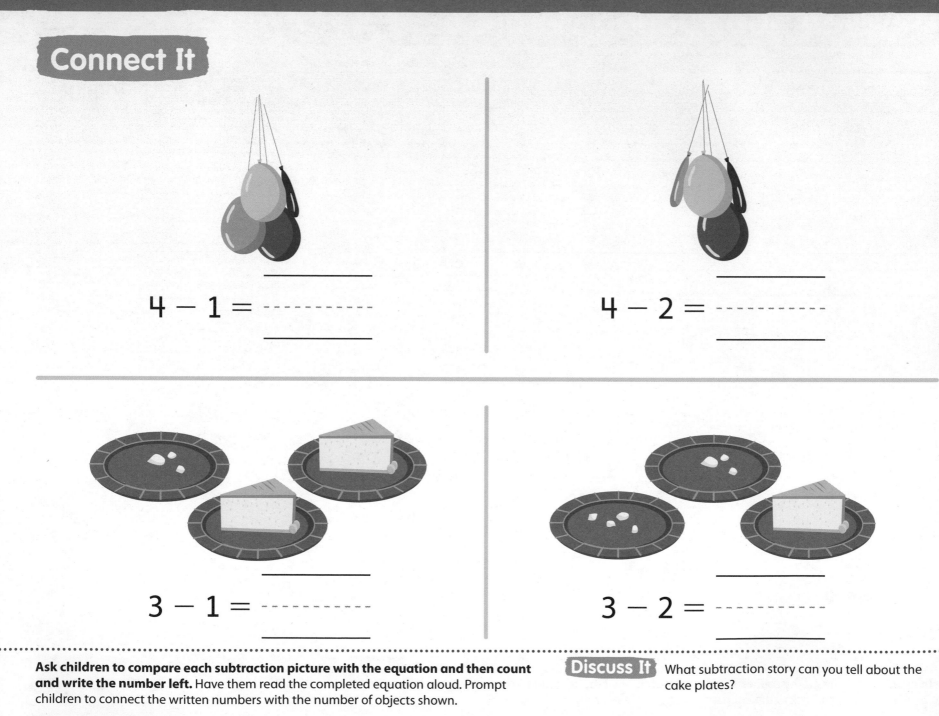

$4 - 1 =$ _____

$4 - 2 =$ _____

$3 - 1 =$ _____

$3 - 2 =$ _____

Ask children to compare each subtraction picture with the equation and then count and write the number left. Have them read the completed equation aloud. Prompt children to connect the written numbers with the number of objects shown.

Discuss It What subtraction story can you tell about the cake plates?

Practice Subtracting Within 5

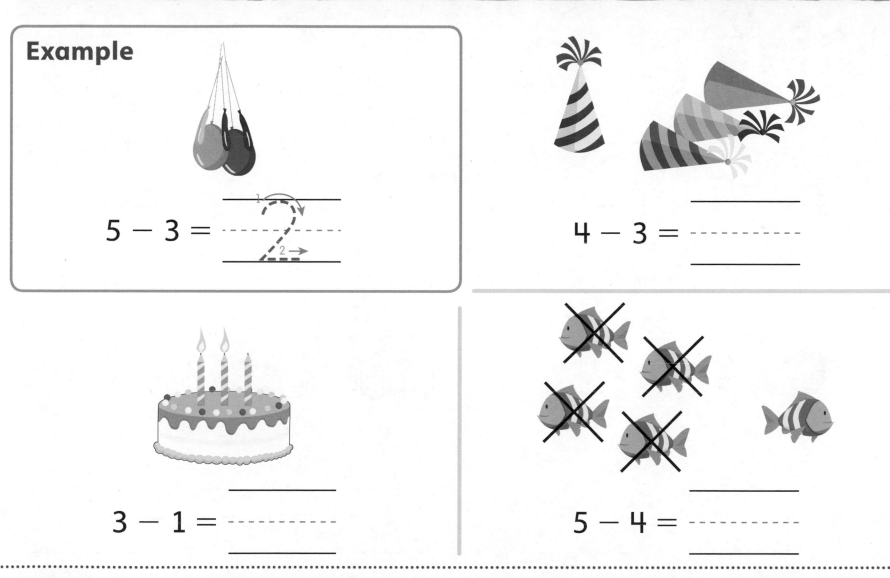

Example

$5 - 3 =$ _2_

$4 - 3 =$ _____

$3 - 1 =$ _____

$5 - 4 =$ _____

Ask children to compare each subtraction picture with the equation and then count and write the number left. Have children read the completed equation aloud. Prompt them to connect the written numbers with the number of objects shown.

5 − 1 = _____

4 − 2 = _____

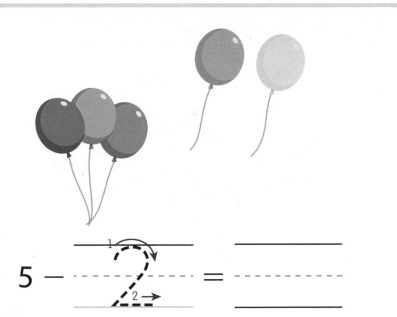

5 − 2 = _____

_____ − _____ = _____

Ask children to compare each subtraction picture with the equation and then complete the equation. Have children read the completed equation aloud. Prompt them to connect the written numbers with the number of objects shown.

Refine Subtracting Within 5

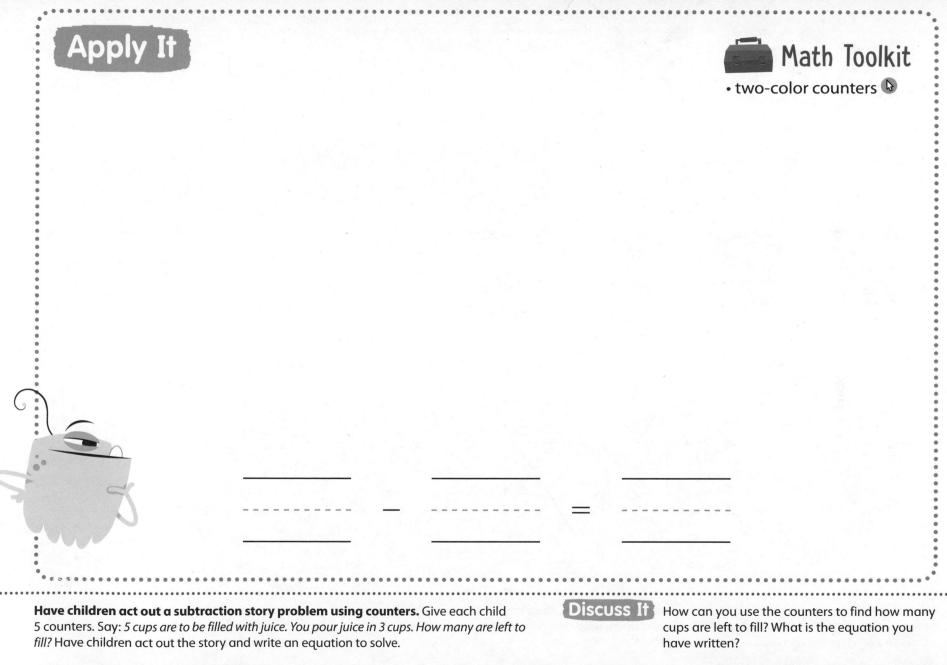

Apply It

🧰 **Math Toolkit**
• two-color counters

_____   _____   _____

‒ ‒ ‒ ‒ ‒ – ‒ ‒ ‒ ‒ ‒ = ‒ ‒ ‒ ‒ ‒

_____   _____   _____

Have children act out a subtraction story problem using counters. Give each child 5 counters. Say: *5 cups are to be filled with juice. You pour juice in 3 cups. How many are left to fill?* Have children act out the story and write an equation to solve.

Discuss It How can you use the counters to find how many cups are left to fill? What is the equation you have written?

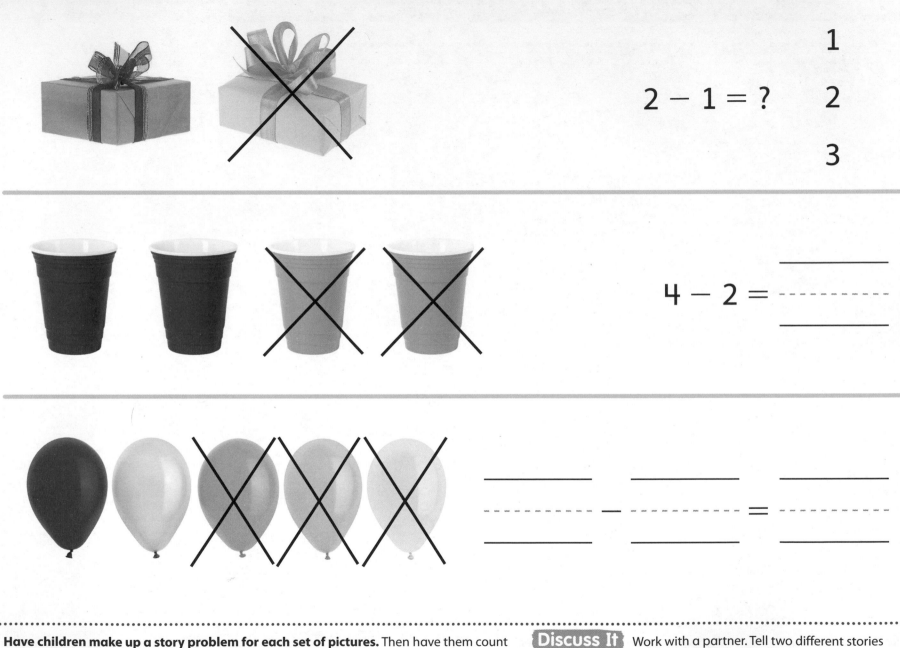

$2 - 1 = ?$

1

2

3

$4 - 2 = $ _____

_____ − _____ = _____

Have children make up a story problem for each set of pictures. Then have them count and circle or write to complete the equation. Have children read the completed equation aloud and connect the numbers with the story problem.

Discuss It Work with a partner. Tell two different stories about the balloon problem.

Practice Subtracting Within 5

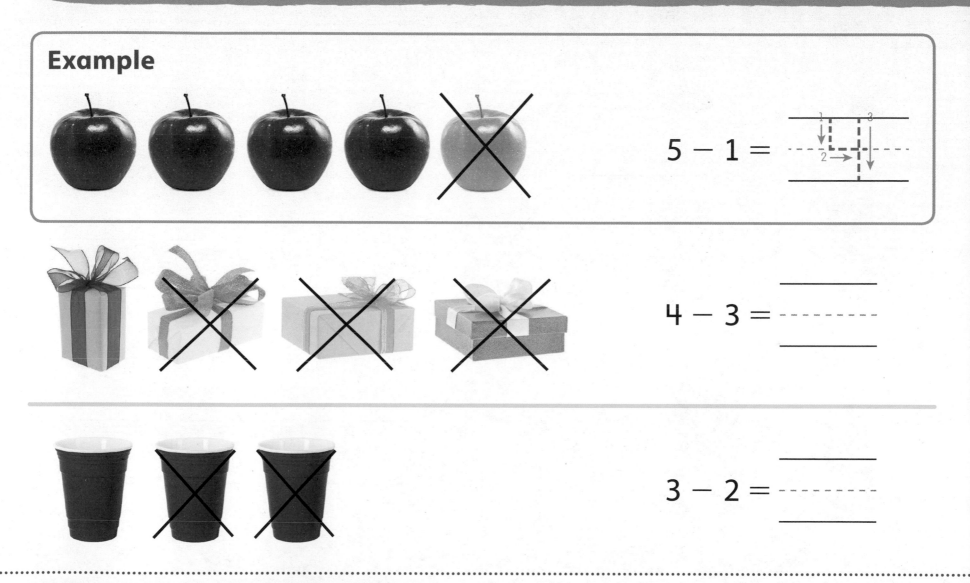

Example

$5 - 1 =$ _____

$4 - 3 =$ _____

$3 - 2 =$ _____

Ask children to make up a story problem for each set of pictures.
Then have them count and write the number left. Have children read
the completed equation aloud and connect it with the story problem.

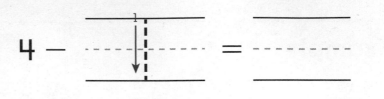

$4 -$ ___ $=$ ___

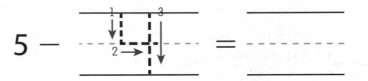

$5 -$ ___ $=$ ___

___ $-$ ___ $=$ ___

Ask children to make up a story problem for each set of pictures.
Then have them complete the equation. Have children read the completed
equation aloud and connect it with the story problem.

Refine Subtracting Within 5

Apply It

🧰 **Math Toolkit**
· counters

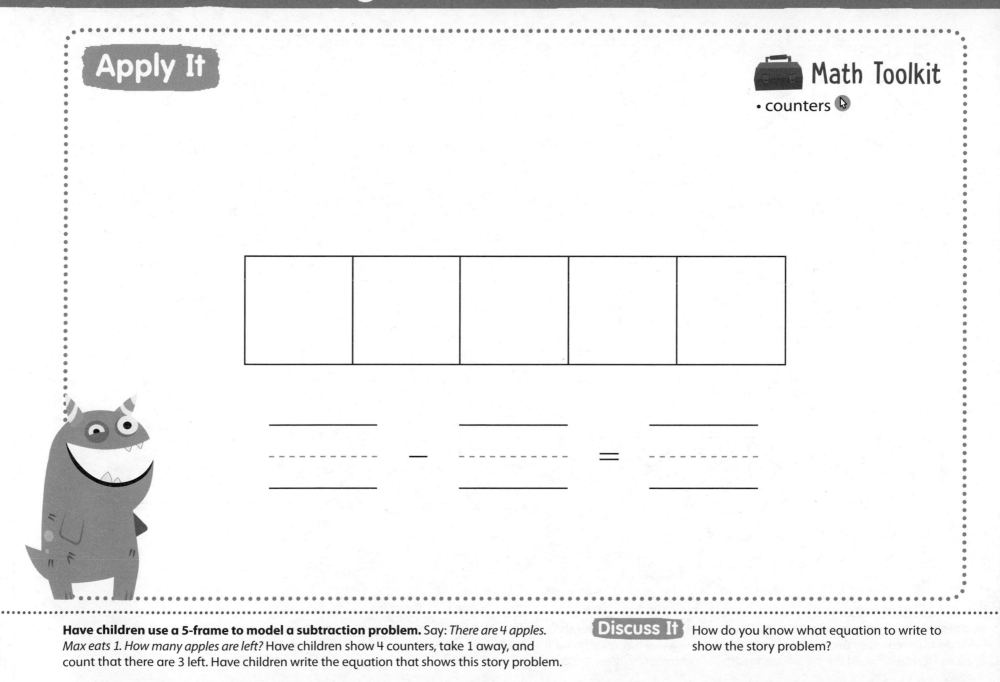

Have children use a 5-frame to model a subtraction problem. Say: *There are 4 apples. Max eats 1. How many apples are left?* Have children show 4 counters, take 1 away, and count that there are 3 left. Have children write the equation that shows this story problem.

Discuss It How do you know what equation to write to show the story problem?

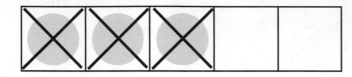

_____ _ _____ = _____

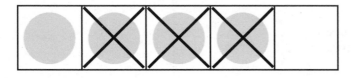

_____ _ _____ = _____

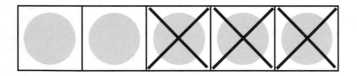

_____ _ _____ = _____

Have children write each equation. The counters show how many to start, and the Xs show how many are taken away. Then, ask children to tell how they found the answers. Some may have used the pictures, and some may have used other strategies.

Discuss It What pattern do you see when you look at your equations? What pattern do you see when you look at the pictures?

Practice Facts to 5

Dear Family,

This week your child is reviewing both addition and subtraction facts within 5 and moving from problems shown with pictures to problems shown only with numbers.

This lesson begins to show how addition and subtraction facts relate to each other. For example, knowing that 3 + 1 = 4 can help you find that 4 − 1 = 3. And knowing that 3 + 2 = 5 can help you find that 5 − 2 = 3. Focusing on the relationships between math facts will help your child build strong problem-solving skills, as well as solve addition and subtraction problems more quickly and accurately.

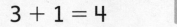

$$3 + 1 = 4$$

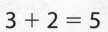

$$3 + 2 = 5$$

This week's lesson progresses from solving problems shown with pictures to solving problems shown only with numbers. Even with numbers-only problems, your child will be encouraged to use any strategy he or she likes for solving, such as modeling with fingers.

Invite your child to share what he or she knows about practicing addition and subtraction facts to 5 by doing the following activity together.

Activity Addition and Subtraction Facts to 5

Do this activity with your child to practice addition and subtraction facts to 5.

Materials 20 index cards or pieces of paper, 1 cup, at least 60 small objects (such as pennies, dried beans, or pasta shapes)

- Write the addition and subtraction facts below on index cards or pieces of paper. Mix the cards and place them facedown in a pile.

- Your child turns over the top card and uses any strategy (such as modeling with fingers or objects) to find the answer. Then he or she counts out the same number of objects as the answer and places them in a cup.

- Have your child continue to turn over cards, find the answer, and add that number of objects to the cup. See how full the cup can get! Continue until all cards have been used.

$1 + 1$	$2 + 2$	$5 - 1$	$4 - 2$
$1 + 2$	$2 + 3$	$5 - 2$	$4 - 3$
$1 + 3$	$3 + 1$	$5 - 3$	$3 - 1$
$1 + 4$	$3 + 2$	$5 - 4$	$3 - 2$
$2 + 1$	$4 + 1$	$4 - 1$	$2 - 1$

Explore Facts to 5

Try It

Learning Target
- Fluently add and subtract within 5.
SMP 1, 2, 3, 4, 5, 6, 7

$1 + 1 =$ _____

$1 + 2 =$ _____

$1 + 3 =$ _____

$1 + 4 =$ _____

Children act out addition facts within 5, model with fingers, and write the total. Review the plus and equal signs. Write "1 + 1 = __" on the board. Invite 1 child to the front of the class. Ask: *How many more children should stand to model this problem? What does the number of children standing show?* Complete the addition fact on the board. Repeat, adding 2, 3, and 4 to 1. Have children complete each equation and model each addition fact using fingers.

Connect It

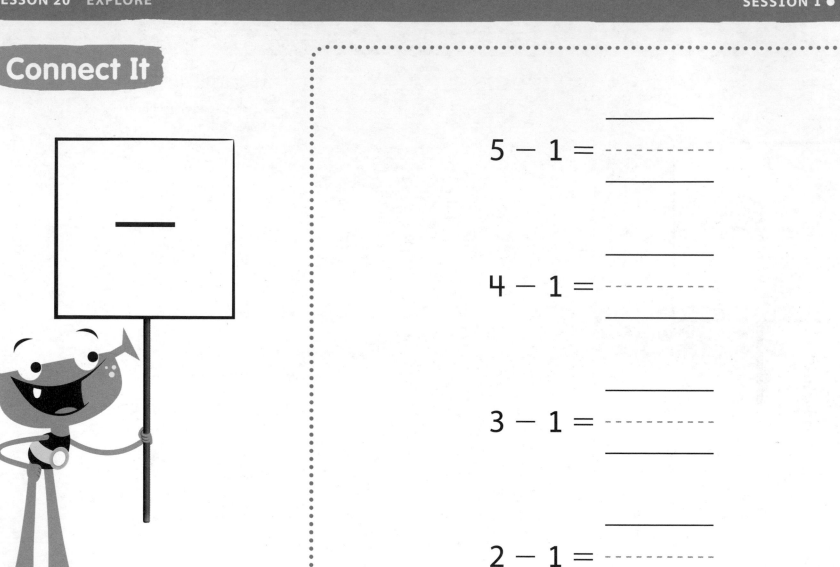

$$5 - 1 =$$

$$4 - 1 =$$

$$3 - 1 =$$

$$2 - 1 =$$

Children act out subtraction facts within 5, model with fingers, and write the difference. Invite 5 children to the front of the class. Write "5 − 1 = ___" on the board. Ask: *What does this say? How many are left if we take 1 away from 5?*

Have children act out the problem. Complete the subtraction fact on the board. Repeat, subtracting 1 from 4, 3, and 2. Then children complete each equation and model each subtraction fact using fingers.

Prepare for Facts to 5

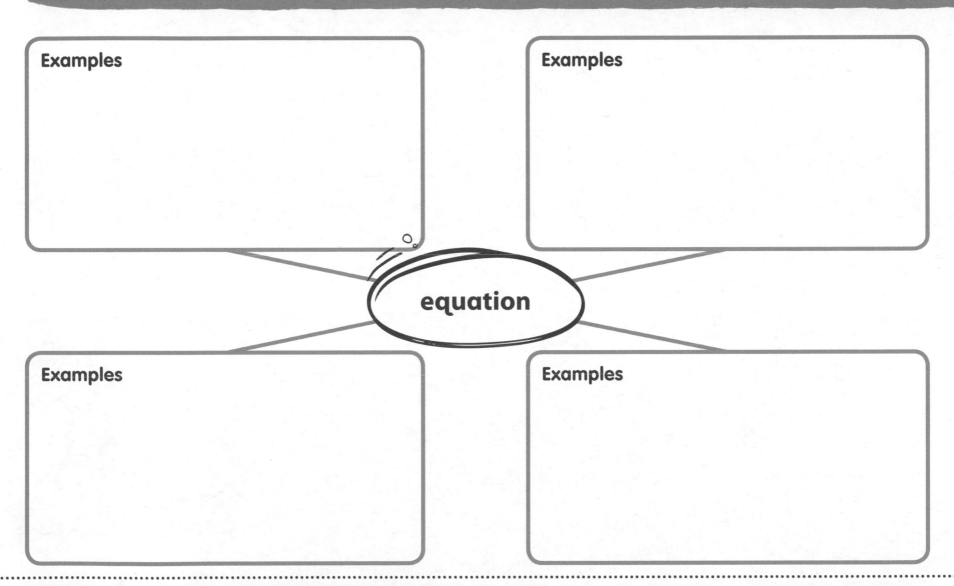

Examples

Examples

equation

Examples

Examples

Have children show the meaning of the word *equation*. Have children fill in each of the boxes to show the meaning of the word *equation*. Tell children that they can use words, numbers, and pictures. Encourage them to show as many ideas as they can.

$$2 + 2 = \underline{\hspace{3cm}}$$

$$3 + 2 = \underline{\hspace{3cm}}$$

$$4 - 2 = \underline{\hspace{3cm}}$$

$$5 - 2 = \underline{\hspace{3cm}}$$

Have children solve addition and subtraction problems. Review the plus, minus, and equal signs. Ask children to model addition and subtraction facts within 5 with fingers and write the total or difference.

Develop Facts to 5

Have children tell story problems using addition and subtraction. Provide an example, such as: *The castle has 2 windows on top plus 3 below. How many windows are there in all?* Have children mark an X on objects they take away and circle the number left.

Discuss It What different number facts for 5 can you find?

Connect It

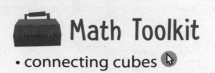 **Math Toolkit**
• connecting cubes

$$2 + 3 = 5$$

$$3 - 2 = 1$$

$$4 - 2 = 2$$

Have children match pictures to equations. Read each equation aloud together. Then have children draw lines to connect each picture to a matching equation.

Discuss It How can a picture tell a subtraction story or an addition story?

Practice Facts to 5

Have children color the 5 children in the picture. Then have them tell an addition story and a subtraction story about the 5 children. For example, *3 girls and 2 boys are at the beach. How many children are at the beach?* and

There are 5 friends playing. 1 friend leaves. How many friends are playing now? As children color the rest of the picture, encourage them to share an addition story and a subtraction story for each group of objects.

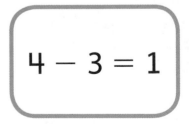

$$2 + 2 = 4$$

$$5 - 2 = 3$$

$$4 - 3 = 1$$

Have children match pictures to equations. Read each equation aloud together. Then have children draw lines to connect each picture to a matching equation.

Try It

Math Toolkit
• two-color counters

$$5 - 4 = \rule{2cm}{0.4pt}$$

$$1 + 4 = \rule{2cm}{0.4pt}$$

$$4 + 0 = \rule{2cm}{0.4pt}$$

$$4 - 0 = \rule{2cm}{0.4pt}$$

Have children use counters to solve addition and subtraction problems. Give children 5 two-color counters. Have them choose an equation, place the first number of counters on the workmat, and then either add to or take away to find the answer.

Discuss It What happens to the total number of counters when you add or take away 0? Why?

Connect It

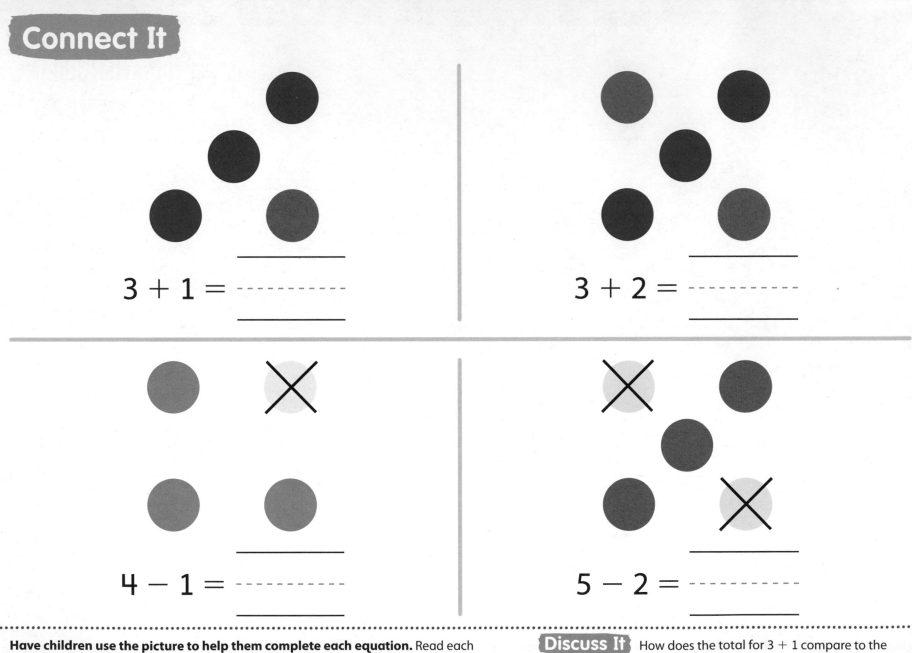

$3 + 1 =$ _____

$3 + 2 =$ _____

$4 - 1 =$ _____

$5 - 2 =$ _____

Have children use the picture to help them complete each equation. Read each equation. Encourage children to look for patterns as they compare the equations. For example, $3 + 1 = 4$, so if you start with 4 and take away 1, you get 3.

Discuss It How does the total for $3 + 1$ compare to the total for $3 + 2$? How do the addends compare?

Practice Facts to 5

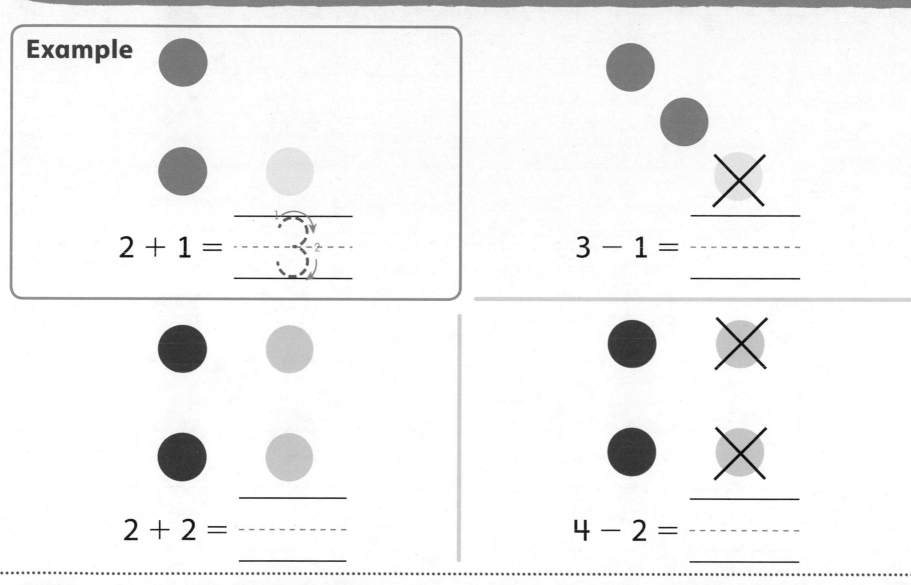

Example

$2 + 1 = 3$

$3 - 1 = $ ____

$2 + 2 = $ ____

$4 - 2 = $ ____

Have children use the picture to help complete each equation. Read each equation aloud together. Encourage children to compare the equations and look for patterns. For example, $2 + 1 = 3$, so if you start with 3 and take away 1, you have 2 left.

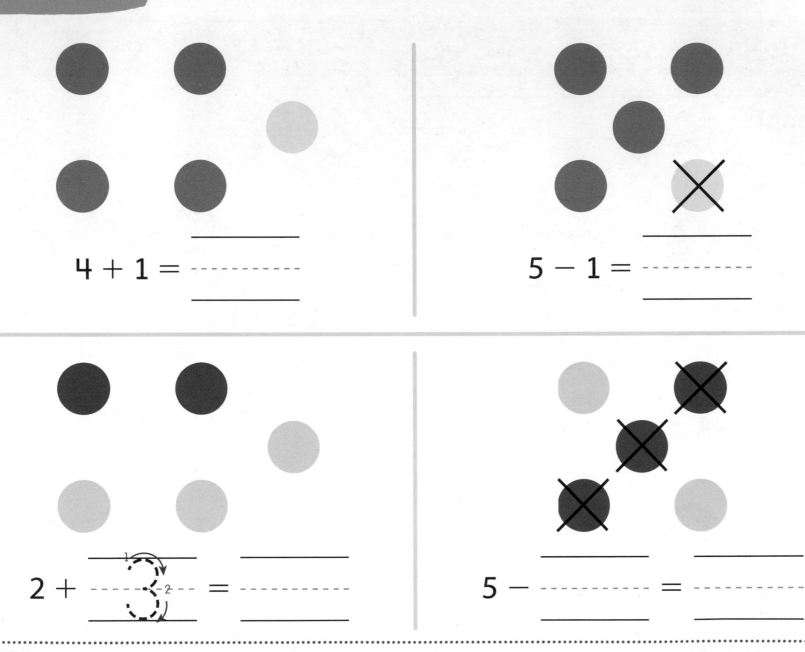

$4 + 1 = $ _____

$5 - 1 = $ _____

$2 + 3 = $ _____

$5 - $ _____ $ = $ _____

Have children use the picture to help complete each equation.
Read each equation aloud together. Encourage children to compare the equations and look for patterns. For example, $4 + 1 = 5$, so if you start with 5 and take away 1, you have 4 left.

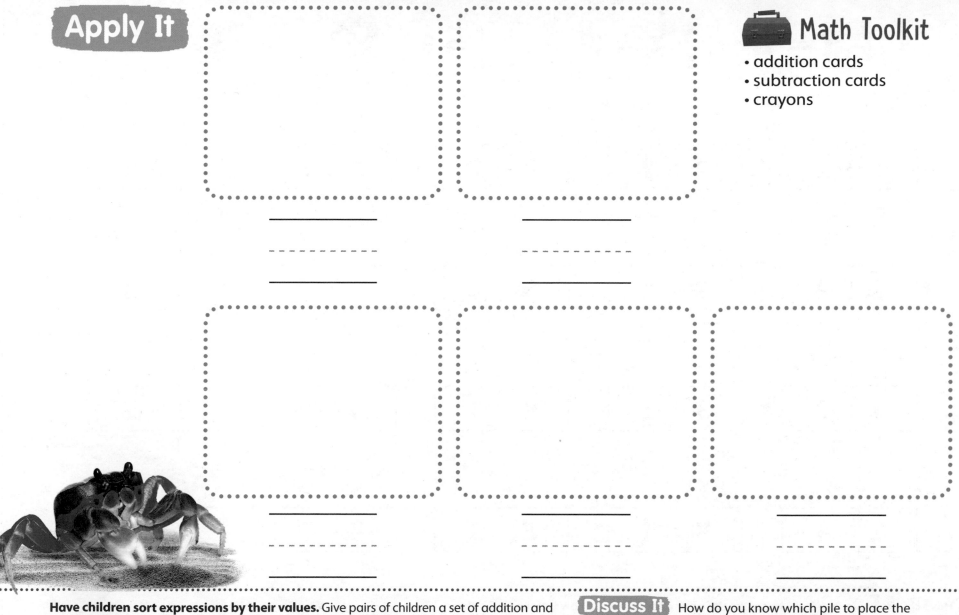

Math Toolkit
- addition cards
- subtraction cards
- crayons

Have children sort expressions by their values. Give pairs of children a set of addition and subtraction expression cards. Have them write the numbers 1 to 5 on the page and then sort the set of cards into piles that equal those numbers.

Discuss It How do you know which pile to place the addition and subtraction cards on?

☒ = 1   ☒ = 2   ☐ = 3   ☒ = 4   ☒ = 5

$1 + 1$	$2 + 2$	$4 - 2$	$2 + 3$	$5 - 2$
$1 + 2$	$2 + 1$	$3 - 1$	$3 + 2$	$5 - 3$
$1 + 3$	$3 + 1$	$4 - 1$	$5 - 4$	$3 - 2$
$1 + 4$	$4 + 1$	$5 - 1$	$4 - 3$	$2 - 1$

Have children color the facts based on the color of the answer shown at the top of the page. Discuss any number patterns in the rows and columns. Have children draw lines to connect the facts that have the same addends but in a different order.

Discuss It Why do you think that $4 + 1$ is the same color as $1 + 4$? What else is alike? Can you find some other facts that look like $4 + 1$ and $1 + 4$?

Practice Facts to 5

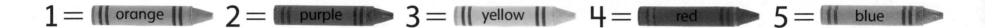

$1 =$ orange $2 =$ purple $3 =$ yellow $4 =$ red $5 =$ blue

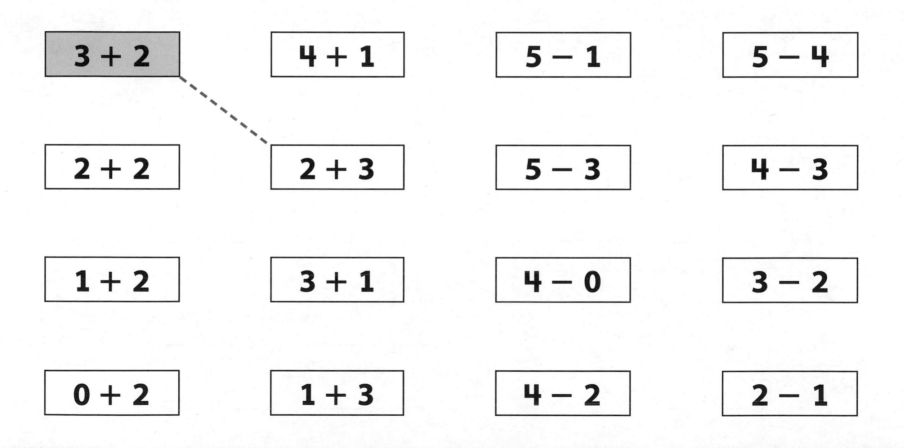

3 + 2	4 + 1	5 − 1	5 − 4
2 + 2	2 + 3	5 − 3	4 − 3
1 + 2	3 + 1	4 − 0	3 − 2
0 + 2	1 + 3	4 − 2	2 − 1

Have children color the facts based on the color of the answer shown at the top of the page. Discuss any number patterns in the rows and columns.

Have children draw lines to connect the facts that have the same addends but in a different order.

$$1 + 1 = \underline{}$$

$$3 + 1 = \underline{}$$

$$5 - 3 = \underline{}$$

$$4 - 0 = \underline{}$$

$$4 - 2 = \underline{}$$

$$4 = \underline{} + \underline{}$$

$$3 - 1 = \underline{}$$

$$4 = \underline{} - \underline{}$$

Have children complete each fact. Ask children to complete each fact in the first column. Discuss any patterns children notice. Then have children complete the first two facts in the second column. Discuss patterns they notice. Next, have children write one addition and one subtraction fact that equal 4 and are different from those above.

Refine Facts to 5

Apply It

🧰 Math Toolkit
- two-color counters

5 − 3	2 + 1	3 + 1	4 − 3	3 − 2
2 + 3	3 − 1	1 + 4	3 − 0	5 − 0
1 + 0	2 + 2	5 − 2	1 + 1	4 − 1
5 − 1	2 + 0	5 − 4	1 + 3	3 + 2

Have children match expressions with the same value. Give partners 20 two-color counters to cover each expression. Have them take turns to look under two counters. If the expressions have the same value, they keep the counters. Repeat until the board is clear.

Discuss It Which addition and subtraction facts are easiest for you to remember? How can you figure out a fact that you do not remember?

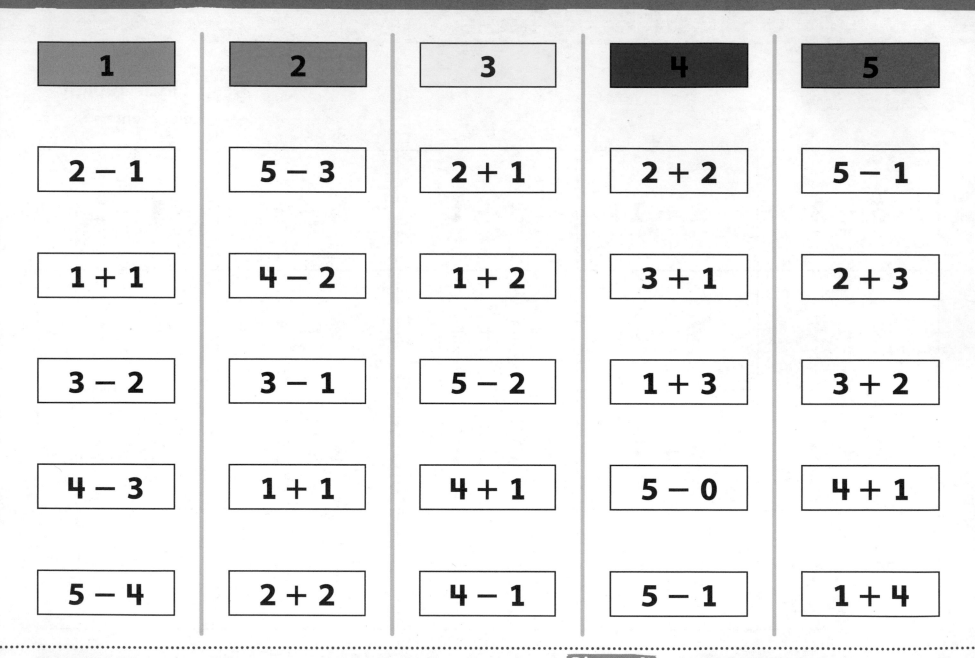

1	2	3	4	5
2 − 1	5 − 3	2 + 1	2 + 2	5 − 1
1 + 1	4 − 2	1 + 2	3 + 1	2 + 3
3 − 2	3 − 1	5 − 2	1 + 3	3 + 2
4 − 3	1 + 1	4 + 1	5 − 0	4 + 1
5 − 4	2 + 2	4 − 1	5 − 1	1 + 4

Have children look at the facts in each column and color all those that equal the number at the top. Have children draw an X on the facts that do not belong in each column. Discuss any patterns children notice about the facts that have the same answer.

Discuss It   How did you decide which facts did not belong with the others?

Add Within 10

Dear Family,
This week your child is learning to add within 10.

This lesson includes addition problems with totals from 6 to 10 and continues to connect story problems to pictures, objects, models, and equations. In class, your child may also model addition problems with fingers, which are useful and easily available tools for adding.

Your child will find two numbers that add up to a given total using counters on 10-frames. He or she will also add two numbers that have a sum up to 10. Repeated work with 10-frames leads to the ability to quickly visualize numbers as amounts, which is important for building addition skills. Also, because a 10-frame is made up of 10 boxes arranged in 2 rows of 5, it can help your child see how the numbers being added and the total relate to both 5 and 10—a useful understanding for later work with greater numbers.

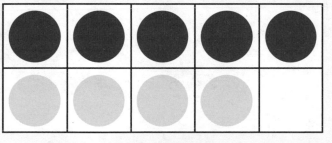

$$5 + 4 = 9$$

Invite your child to share what he or she knows about adding within 10 by doing the following activity together.

Activity   Adding Within 10

Do this activity with your child to add within 10.

Have your child use fingers to solve the addition problems below and tell you each total. You may want to present the problems in a story context. Your child may add with fingers in any way he or she prefers.

If your child needs assistance, have him or her mirror you as you use your fingers to find 5 + 4.

- Say: *There are 5 cups in the sink and 4 cups on the counter. How many cups are there in all?* Show 5 fingers on one hand.

- Say: *Now, let us add 5 and 4.* Hold up 4 fingers on the other hand.

- Ask: *How many fingers are up now?* Have your child count the 9 fingers that are up.

Follow a similar procedure to solve the other addition problems below.

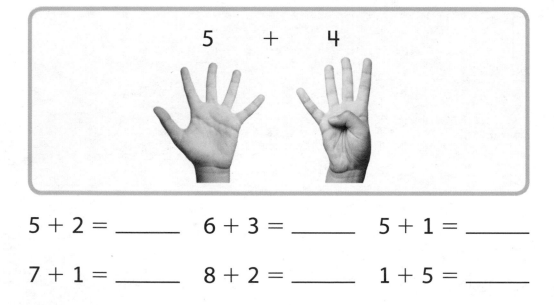

5   +   4

$5 + 2 =$ _____ $6 + 3 =$ _____ $5 + 1 =$ _____

$7 + 1 =$ _____ $8 + 2 =$ _____ $1 + 5 =$ _____

Explore Adding Within 10

Try It

Learning Target

- Solve addition and subtraction word problems, and add and subtract within 10.

SMP 1, 2, 3, 4, 5, 6

 Math Toolkit

- counters

_____   _____   _____

_ _ _ _ _ + _ _ _ _ _ = _ _ _ _ _

_____   _____   _____

Have children act out and solve an addition problem and write a corresponding equation. Say: *4 children are sitting at a table. 2 more children join them. How many children are sitting at the table now?*

Have children act out the problem and then model the problem with counters. Discuss how to show this as an equation. Write 4 + 2 = 6 on the board and have children write it.

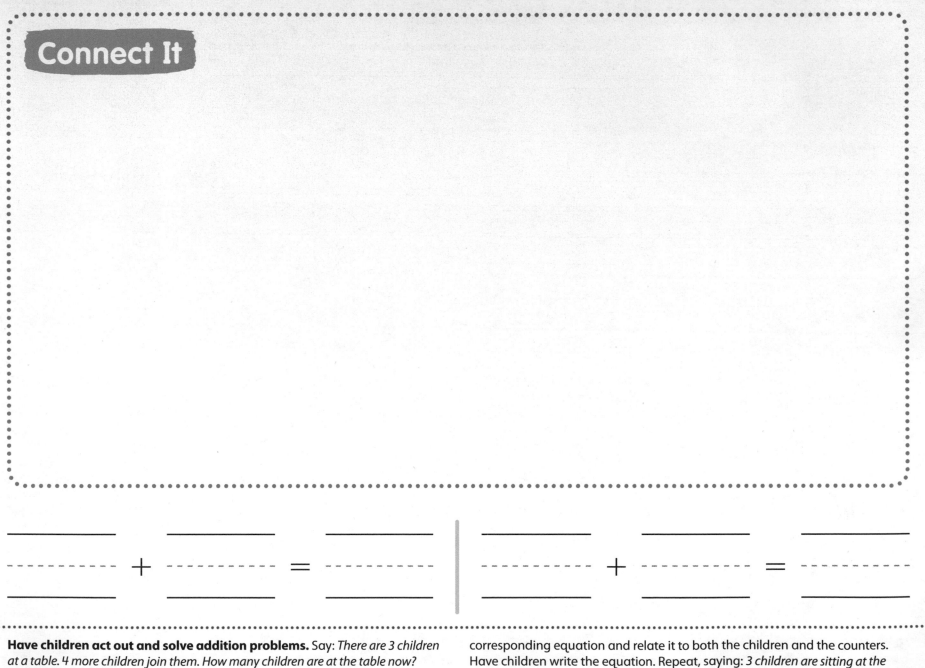

Connect It

_____ + _____ = _____ | _____ + _____ = _____

Have children act out and solve addition problems. Say: _There are 3 children at a table. 4 more children join them. How many children are at the table now?_ Have children act out the problem and then use counters to model it. Write the corresponding equation and relate it to both the children and the counters. Have children write the equation. Repeat, saying: _3 children are sitting at the table. 2 children are standing at the table. How many children are at the table in all?_

Prepare for Adding Within 10

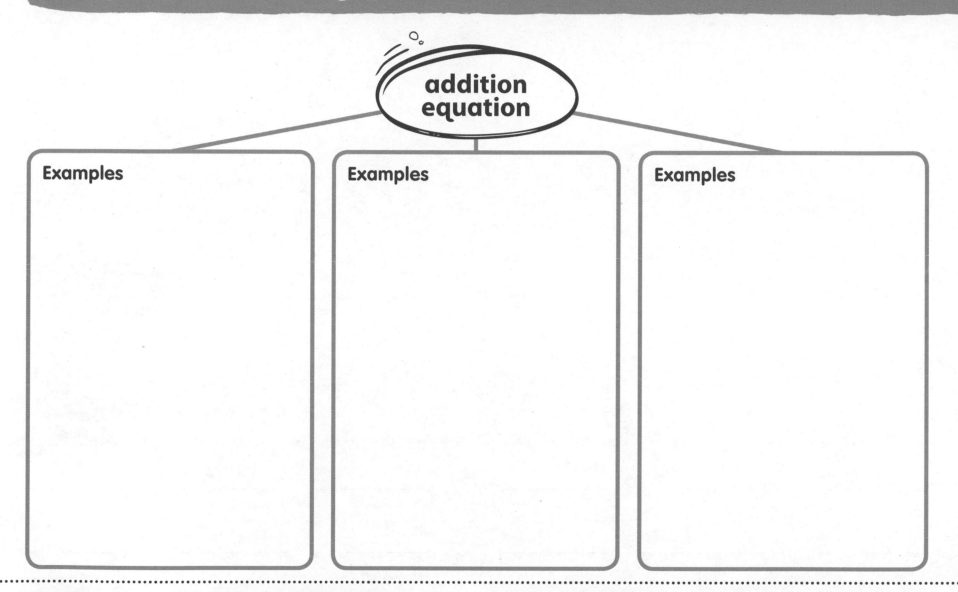

addition
equation

Examples

Examples

Examples

Have children show the meaning of the term *addition equation.*
Have children fill in each of the boxes to show the meaning of the term

addition equation. Tell children that they can use words, numbers, and pictures. Encourage them to show as many ideas as they can.

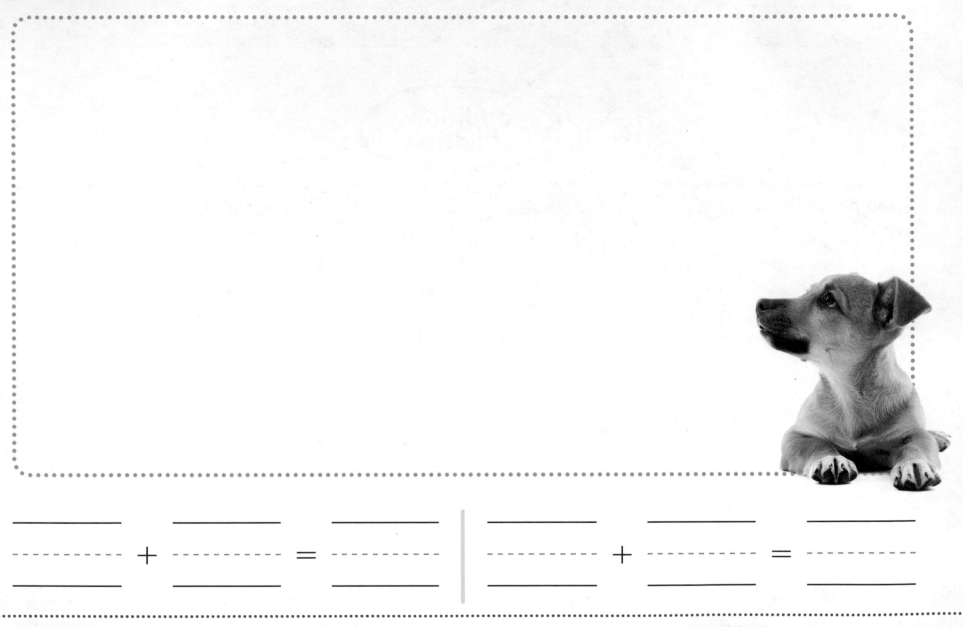

———— + ———— = ———— | ———— + ———— = ————

Have children solve addition problems. Say: *There are 5 dogs at a park. 2 more dogs join them. How many dogs are at the park?* Have children use their fingers and then small objects to model the problem. Write the corresponding equation and relate it to both the fingers and the objects. Have children write the equation. Repeat, saying: *4 dogs at a park are on leashes. 4 dogs are not on leashes. How many dogs are at the park in all?*

410   Lesson 21 Add Within 10

Develop Adding Within 10

Encourage children to tell addition story problems for various groups of objects. Ask children to discuss the addition facts shown by each group of objects, in more than one way if possible. Have children circle the group that shows $4 + 3 = 7$.

Discuss It How many dogs will there be if one more comes into the store? How do you know?

Connect It

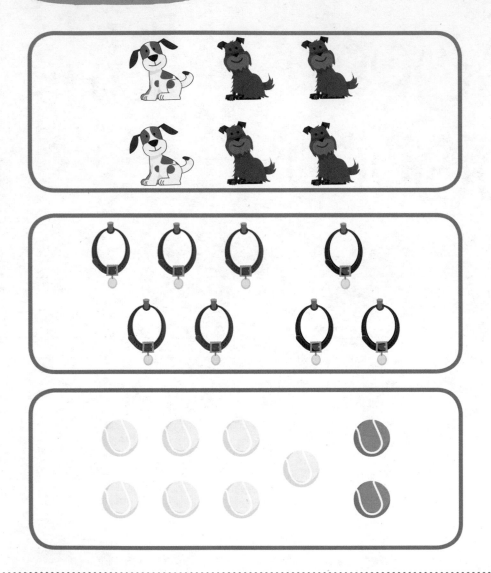

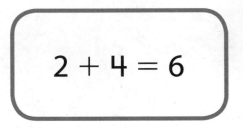

$$7 + 2 = 9$$

$$2 + 4 = 6$$

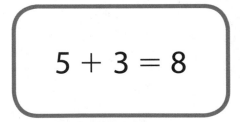

$$5 + 3 = 8$$

Have children match pictures to equations. Have children describe the two groups and the total in each picture. Have them read the equations aloud. Then have children draw lines to match each picture to an equation.

Discuss It How did you know which picture matches each equation?

Practice Adding Within 10

Have children use red and yellow to color a group of related objects and describe an addition problem. For example, they might color the 4 large collars red and the 6 small collars yellow and demonstrate that 4 + 6 = 10.

Then have children use two other colors to color another group of related objects and describe an addition problem. Have children color the rest of the picture.

$$5 + 1 = 6$$

$$6 + 2 = 8$$

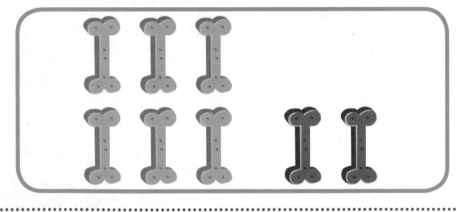

$$3 + 4 = 7$$

Have children match pictures to equations. Have children describe the two groups and the total in each picture. Read each equation aloud together. Then have children draw lines to match each picture to an equation.

414   **Lesson 21** Add Within 10

Develop Adding Within 10

 Try It

 Math Toolkit
- two-color counters

$$5 + 3 = \underline{\hspace{2cm}}$$ $$4 + 5 = \underline{\hspace{2cm}}$$

Have children model addition problems. Give each child 10 counters. Tell an addition story for $5 + 3 = 8$. Ask children to model the problem with counters. Have them count the counters to find how many and write to complete the equation. Repeat for $4 + 5 = 9$.

Discuss It How do the counters match the equations?

Connect It

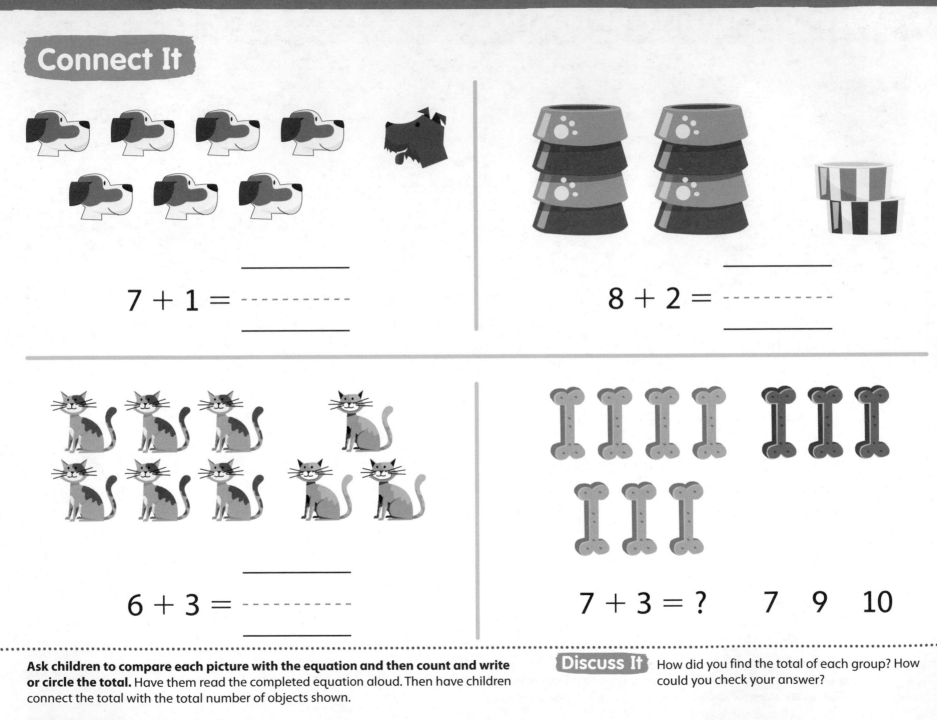

$7 + 1 =$ ____

$8 + 2 =$ ____

$6 + 3 =$ ____

$7 + 3 = ?$ 7   9   10

Ask children to compare each picture with the equation and then count and write or circle the total. Have them read the completed equation aloud. Then have children connect the total with the total number of objects shown.

Discuss It How did you find the total of each group? How could you check your answer?

Practice Adding Within 10

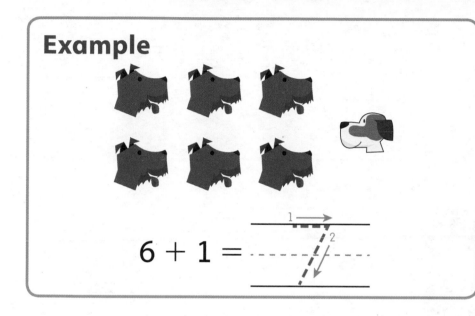

Example

6 + 1 = 7

4 + 2 = _____

5 + 3 = _____

9 + 1 = _____

Ask children to compare each picture with the equation and then count and write the total. Have children read the completed equation aloud. Then have them connect the written total with the total number of objects shown.

$$5 + \rule{2cm}{0.4pt} = \rule{2cm}{0.4pt}$$

$$6 + \rule{2cm}{0.4pt} = \rule{2cm}{0.4pt}$$

$$3 + \rule{2cm}{0.4pt} = \rule{2cm}{0.4pt}$$

Ask children to compare each picture with the equation and then complete the equation. Have children read the completed equation aloud. Then have them connect the written total with the total number of animals shown.

Refine Adding Within 10

 Apply It

 Math Toolkit

• two-color counters

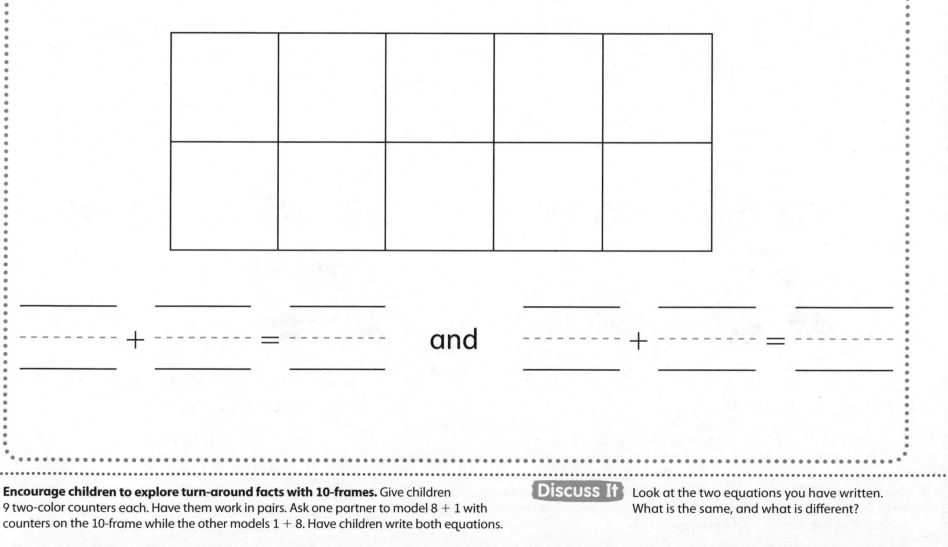

___ ___ ___
—— + —— = —— and
___ ___ ___

___ ___ ___
—— + —— = ——
___ ___ ___

Encourage children to explore turn-around facts with 10-frames. Give children 9 two-color counters each. Have them work in pairs. Ask one partner to model $8 + 1$ with counters on the 10-frame while the other models $1 + 8$. Have children write both equations.

Discuss It Look at the two equations you have written. What is the same, and what is different?

$7 + 2 =$ _____

$2 + 7 =$ _____

$5 + 5 =$ _____

$6 + 4 =$ _____

Ask children to compare each picture with the equation and count and write the total. Have them read the completed equation aloud. Then have children connect the written total with the total number of animals shown.

Discuss It Compare the two problems about rabbits. What is the same, and what is different?

Practice Adding Within 10

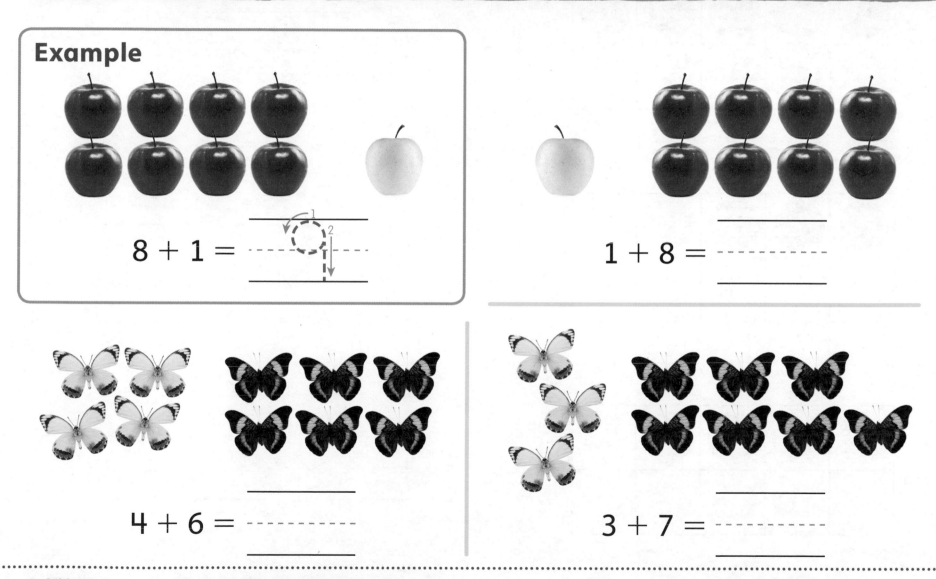

Example

$8 + 1 =$ _____

$1 + 8 =$ _____

$4 + 6 =$ _____

$3 + 7 =$ _____

Ask children to compare each picture with the equation and then count and write the total. Have children read the completed equation aloud. Then have them connect the written total with the total number of objects shown.

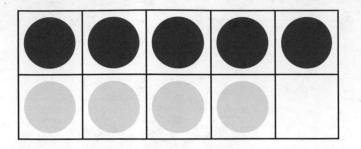

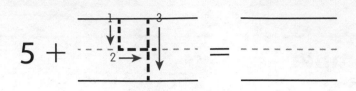

$$5 +$$

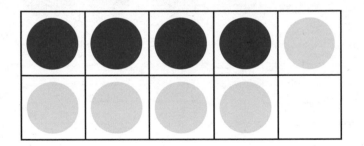

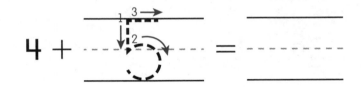

$$4 +$$

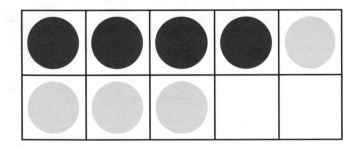

$$\underline{\hspace{2cm}} + \underline{\hspace{2cm}} = \underline{\hspace{2cm}}$$

Ask children to compare each picture with the equation and then complete the equation. Have children read the completed equation aloud. Then have them connect the written total with the total number of counters shown.

Refine Adding Within 10

Apply It

Math Toolkit
- two-color counters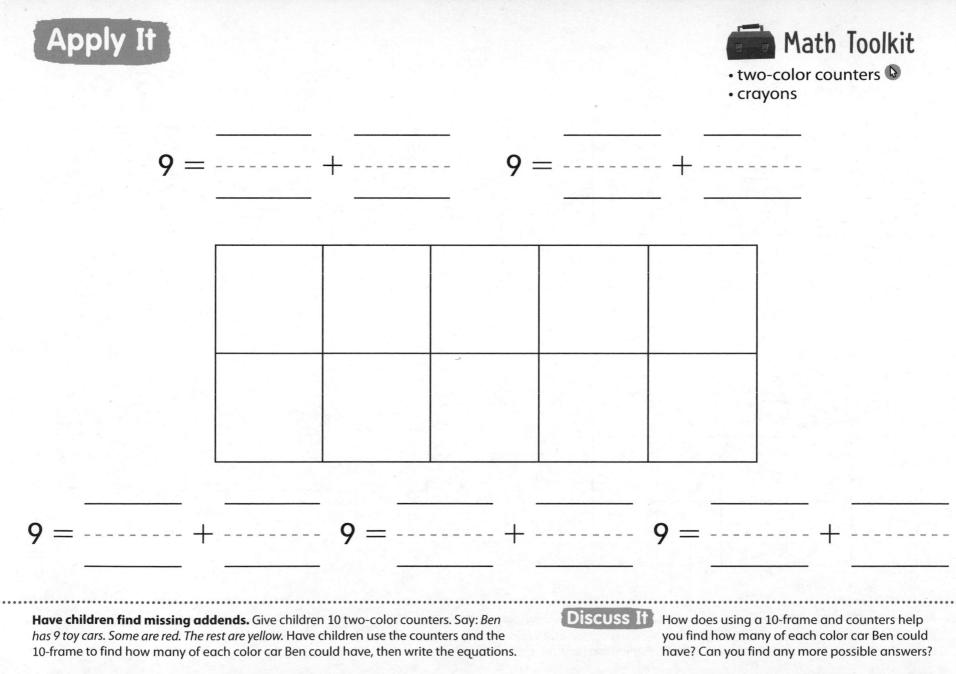
- crayons

$$9 = \underline{\hspace{2cm}} + \underline{\hspace{2cm}} \qquad 9 = \underline{\hspace{2cm}} + \underline{\hspace{2cm}}$$

$$9 = \underline{\hspace{1.5cm}} + \underline{\hspace{1.5cm}} \qquad 9 = \underline{\hspace{1.5cm}} + \underline{\hspace{1.5cm}} \qquad 9 = \underline{\hspace{1.5cm}} + \underline{\hspace{1.5cm}}$$

Have children find missing addends. Give children 10 two-color counters. Say: *Ben has 9 toy cars. Some are red. The rest are yellow.* Have children use the counters and the 10-frame to find how many of each color car Ben could have, then write the equations.

Discuss It How does using a 10-frame and counters help you find how many of each color car Ben could have? Can you find any more possible answers?

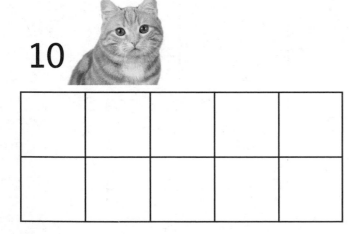

8

$8 =$ 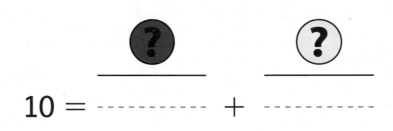 _____ + _____

10

$10 =$ _____ + _____

For each model, tell a problem aloud, such as: *There are 8 dogs. Some are playing. The rest are napping.* Have children find two numbers to make the given total and color the 10-frame with red and yellow to show their numbers. Then have them complete the equation.

Discuss It Work with a partner. Are your equations the same? Are both your equations correct?

424   Lesson 21 Add Within 10

Find the Missing Part of 10

Dear Family,

This week your child is learning to find the missing part of 10.

This skill involves learning the number pairs that make 10 and applying these facts to solve problems where part of the 10 is missing. For example, when shown a group of 10 shapes where some of them are covered and 7 are showing, children can figure out how many are missing using the fact that 7 and 3 make 10. So, 3 shapes must be missing.

Your child will be given 1 to 9 objects, or a number from 1 to 9, and then he or she will find the number of objects or the number needed to make 10 altogether. Your child will use drawings and equations to find and show the missing part. This builds on skills your child learned earlier when he or she was making groups of 10.

$$6 + 4 = 10$$

Invite your child to share what he or she knows about finding the missing part of 10 by doing the following activity together.

Activity ▸ Finding the Missing Part of 10

Do this activity with your child to find the missing part of 10.

Materials 10 small objects, such as craft sticks, pennies, cotton balls, or buttons

- Place the 10 objects on the table or floor and have your child count them to check that there are 10.

- Have your child close his or her eyes or look away while you remove some of the objects and hide them behind your back.

- Have your child look and count the number of objects remaining.

- Ask your child how many objects you are hiding behind your back. Encourage him or her to try to say the number without counting on first.

- Have your child say the equation: ___ + ___ = 10.

- Switch roles and repeat with a different number of objects taken away.

- Repeat until all the number pairs that make 10 have been used.

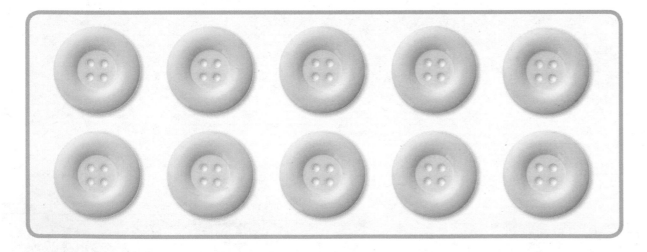

Explore Finding the Missing Part of 10

Try It

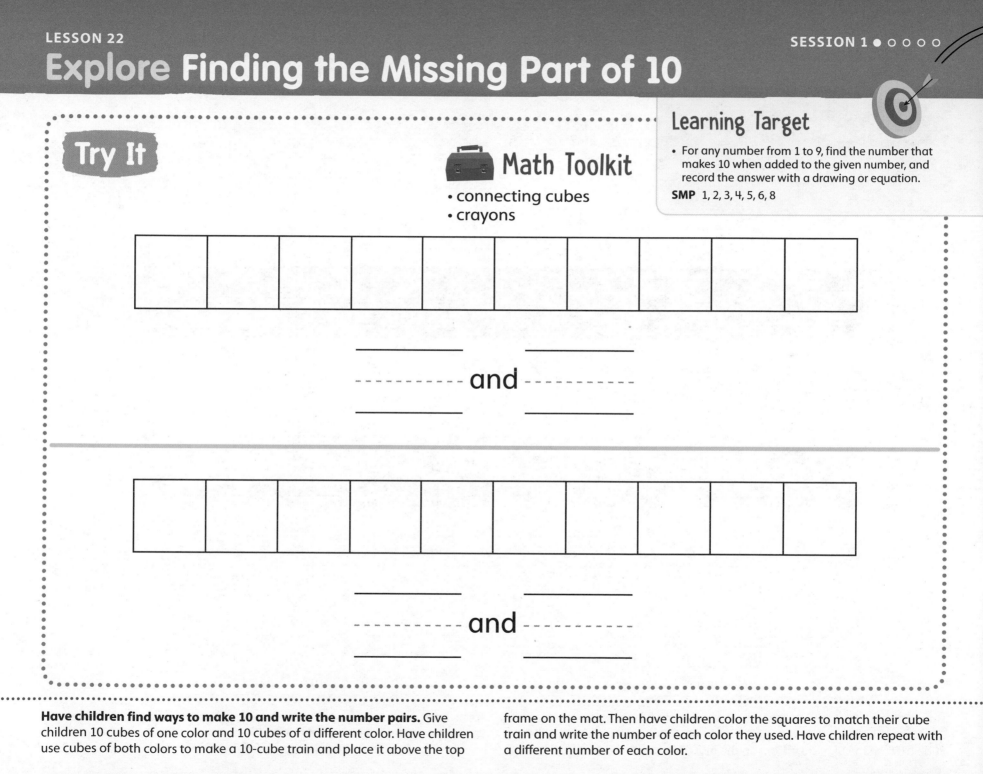

Math Toolkit
- connecting cubes
- crayons

Learning Target
- For any number from 1 to 9, find the number that makes 10 when added to the given number, and record the answer with a drawing or equation.

SMP 1, 2, 3, 4, 5, 6, 8

_____ _____

- - - - - **and** - - - - -

_____ _____

_____ _____

- - - - - **and** - - - - -

_____ _____

Have children find ways to make 10 and write the number pairs. Give children 10 cubes of one color and 10 cubes of a different color. Have children use cubes of both colors to make a 10-cube train and place it above the top frame on the mat. Then have children color the squares to match their cube train and write the number of each color they used. Have children repeat with a different number of each color.

Connect It

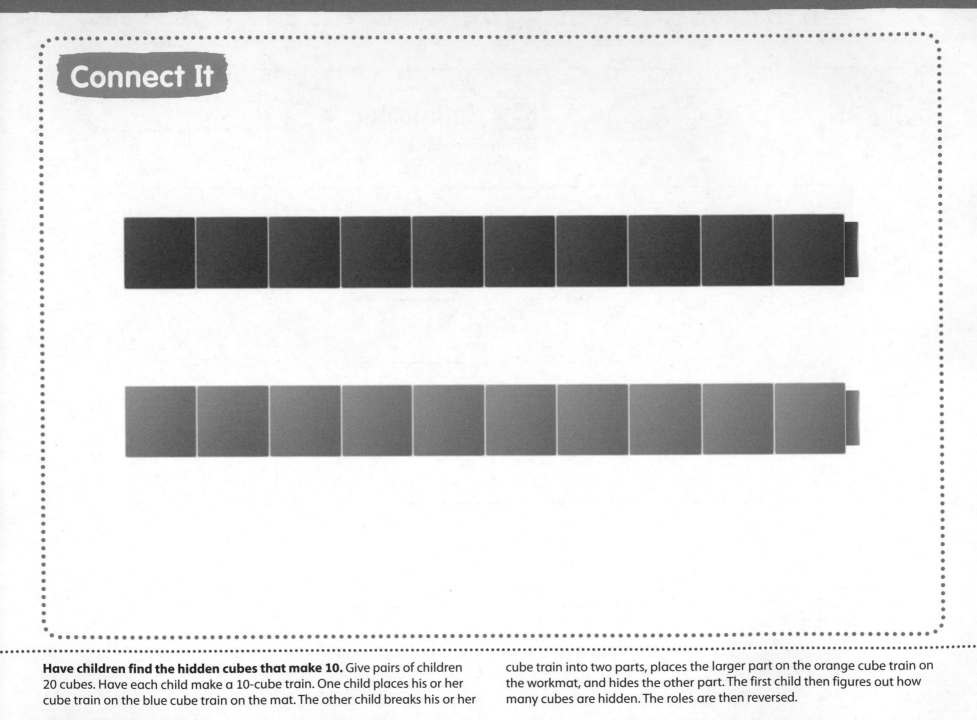

Have children find the hidden cubes that make 10. Give pairs of children 20 cubes. Have each child make a 10-cube train. One child places his or her cube train on the blue cube train on the mat. The other child breaks his or her cube train into two parts, places the larger part on the orange cube train on the workmat, and hides the other part. The first child then figures out how many cubes are hidden. The roles are then reversed.

Prepare for Finding the Missing Part of 10

number pairs for 10

Examples	Examples	Examples

Have children show the meaning of the term *number pairs for 10*. Have children fill in each of the boxes to show the meaning of the term *number pairs for 10*. Tell children to use words, numbers, and pictures. Encourage them to show as many ideas as they can.

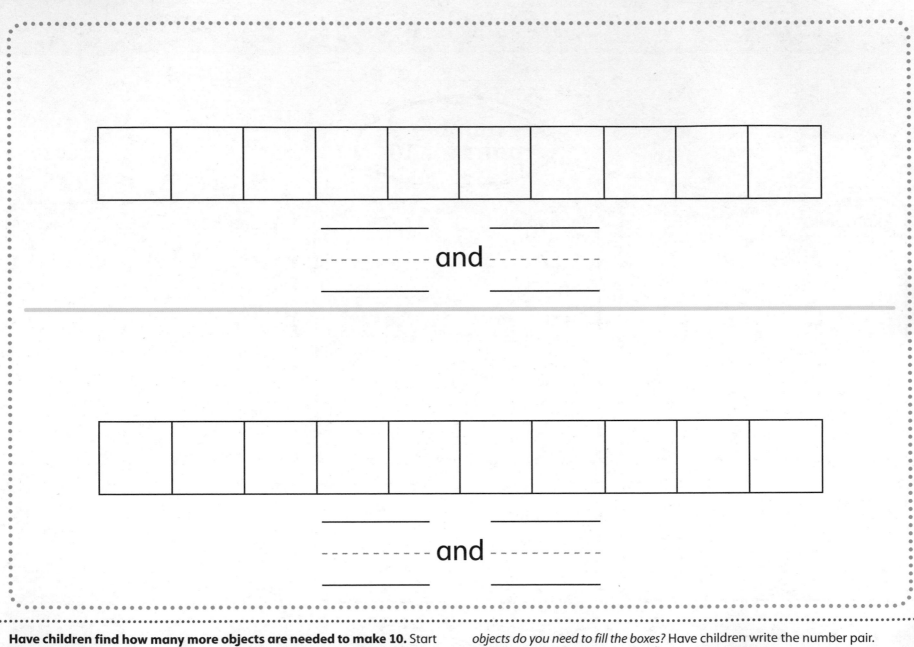

_____ and _____

_____ and _____

Have children find how many more objects are needed to make 10. Start with at least 10 small objects. Give children 7 small objects and have them place the objects in the boxes in the first workspace. Ask: *How many more objects do you need to fill the boxes?* Have children write the number pair. Repeat, giving children 6 small objects to fill the boxes.

Develop Finding the Missing Part of 10

Seeds

Have children find how many of each item make 10. Have children look at each group of 10 and say how many of each item make the group of 10. Then have children circle the box of red peppers and the bottles of water and have them find how many are missing.

Discuss It How can you tell how many items are missing in a group? Do any of the groups have the same number of each item?

Connect It

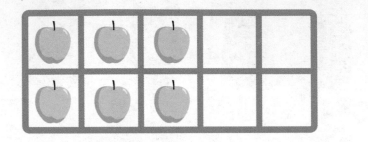

6 and ----------- make

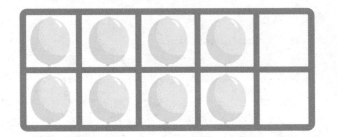

8 and ----------- make

3 and ----------- make

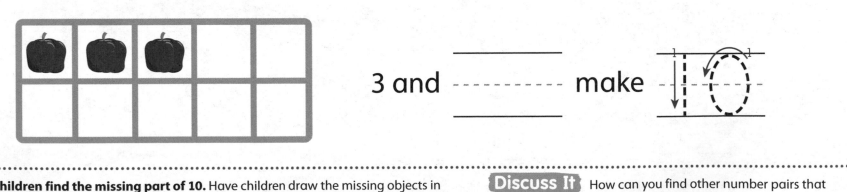

Have children find the missing part of 10. Have children draw the missing objects in each box of 10. Then have children write how many objects were missing. Have children read aloud the number pairs that make 10.

Discuss It How can you find other number pairs that make 10?

Practice Finding the Missing Part of 10

Have children use the picture to find number pairs that make 10. Have children use two colors to color the flowers. Then have them say how many of each color there are to name a number pair that makes 10. Repeat with other groups in the market stall. Have children choose different number pairs to make 10.

_____
2 and --------- make 10
_____

_____
5 and --------- make 10
_____

_____
9 and --------- make 10
_____

Have children find the missing part of 10. Have children draw the missing objects in each set of 10. Then have children write how many objects were missing. Have children read aloud the number pairs that make 10.

Develop Finding the Missing Part of 10

Try It

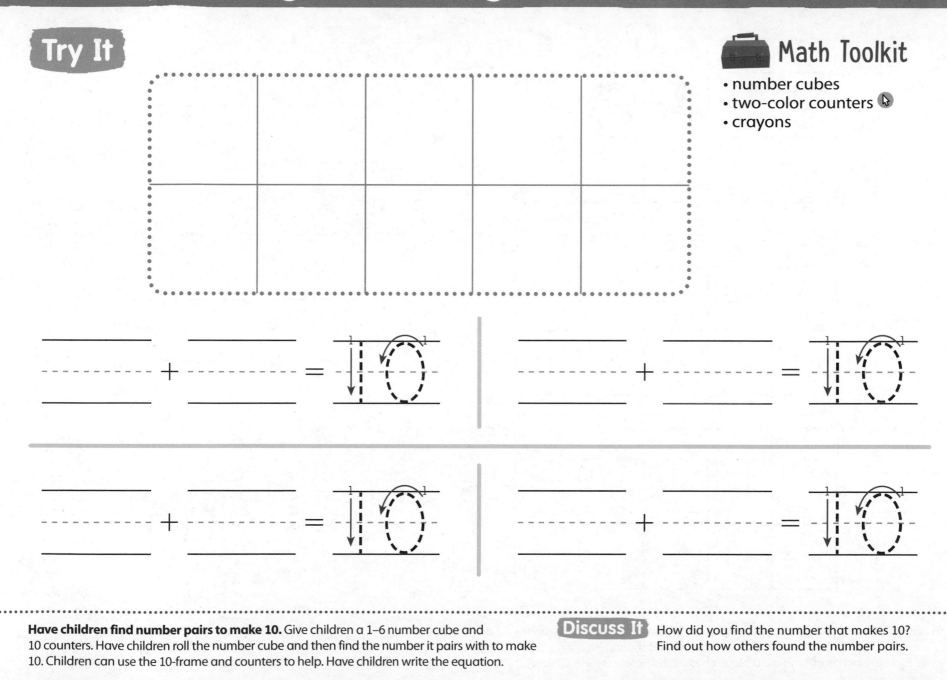

Math Toolkit
- number cubes
- two-color counters
- crayons

_____ + _____ = 10   _____ + _____ = 10

_____ + _____ = 10   _____ + _____ = 10

Have children find number pairs to make 10. Give children a 1–6 number cube and 10 counters. Have children roll the number cube and then find the number it pairs with to make 10. Children can use the 10-frame and counters to help. Have children write the equation.

Discuss It How did you find the number that makes 10? Find out how others found the number pairs.

Connect It

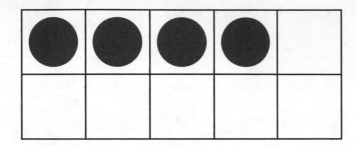

$$4 + \underline{\hspace{2cm}} = \underline{\hspace{1cm}}$$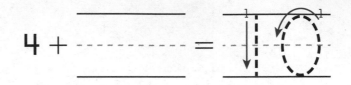

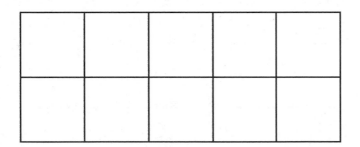

$$1 + \underline{\hspace{2cm}} = \underline{\hspace{1cm}}$$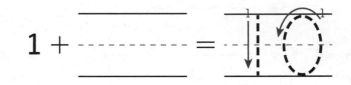

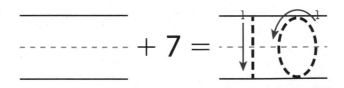

$$\underline{\hspace{2cm}} + 7 = \underline{\hspace{1cm}}$$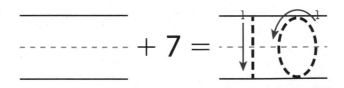

....

Have children use drawings to help find number pairs to make 10. Have children draw the given number of counters in the 10-frame and then use a different color to draw the remaining counters to make 10. Have children complete the equations.

Discuss It How can you use a 10-frame to help you find number pairs that make 10?

Practice Finding the Missing Part of 10

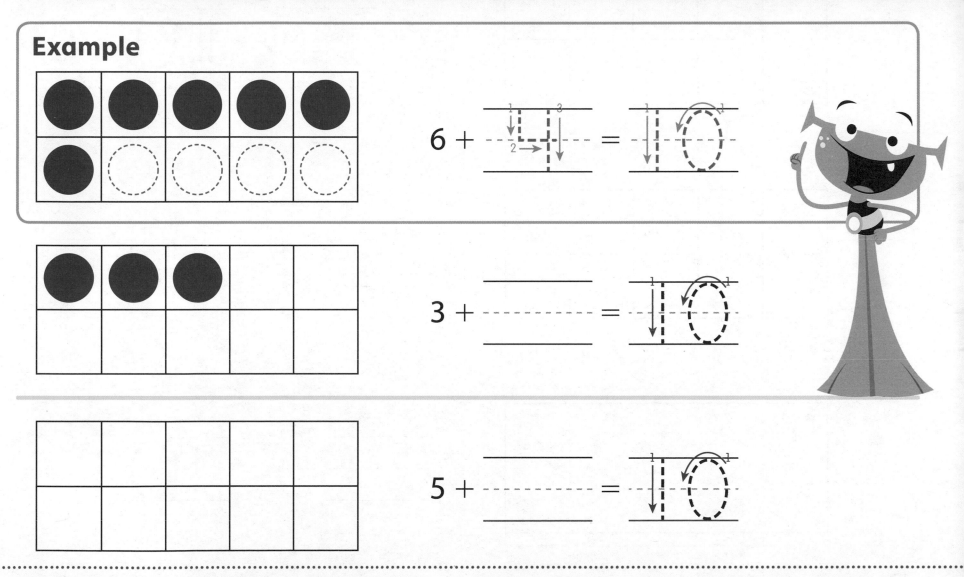

Example

$$6 +$$ ___ $$=$$ 10

$$3 +$$ ___ $$=$$ 10

$$5 +$$ ___ $$=$$ 10

Have children use drawings to help find number pairs to make 10. Have children draw the given number of counters in the 10-frame and then use a different color to draw the remaining counters to make 10. Have children complete the equations.

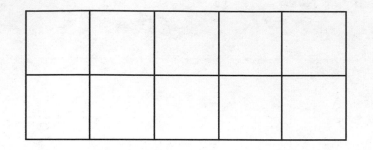

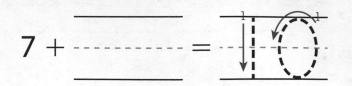

$7 +$ _____ $=$ 10

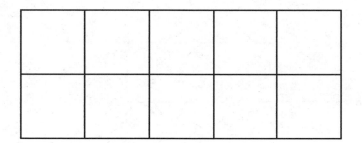

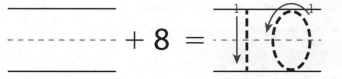

_____ $+ 8 =$ 10

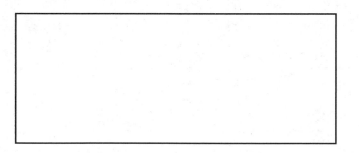

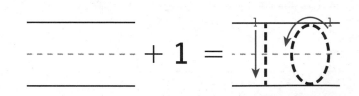

_____ $+ 1 =$ 10

Have children use drawings to help find number pairs to make 10. Have children draw the given number of counters in the 10-frame and then use a different color to draw the remaining counters to make 10. Have children complete the equations. For the last problem, have children use their own drawings to help find the missing number to make 10.

 **Apply It**

 **Math Toolkit**

• counters

Have children find the missing part of 10. Have children work in pairs. Give each pair 10 counters to place on the workmat. One child looks away, and the other child hides some of the counters. The first child then figures out how many are hidden. Switch roles and repeat.

Discuss It What number pairs do you know that make 10?

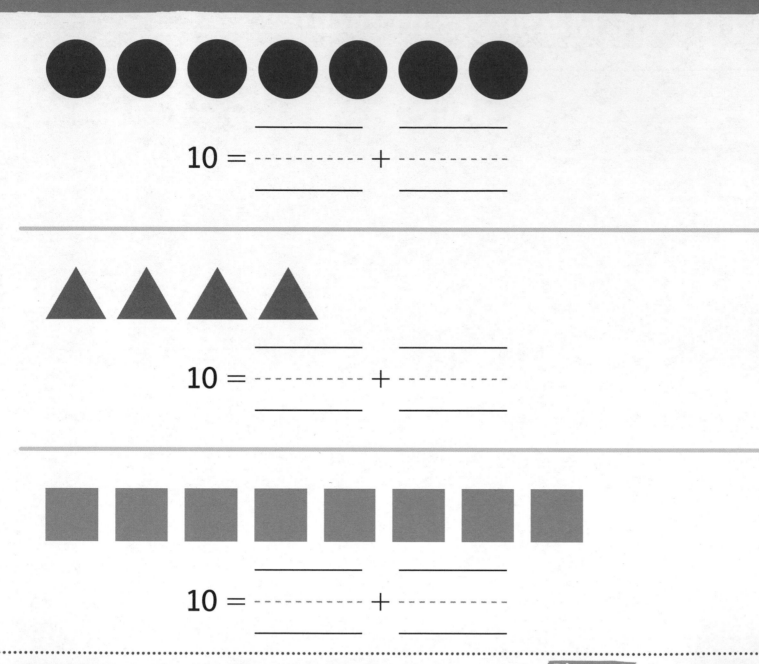

$$10 = \underline{\hspace{2cm}} + \underline{\hspace{2cm}}$$

$$10 = \underline{\hspace{2cm}} + \underline{\hspace{2cm}}$$

$$10 = \underline{\hspace{2cm}} + \underline{\hspace{2cm}}$$

Have children use drawings and equations to find missing parts of 10. Ask children to draw more of each shape to make 10 in each group. Then have them complete the equation. Encourage children to read the equations aloud.

Discuss It How can you figure out how many shapes to draw without counting on?

Practice Finding the Missing Part of 10

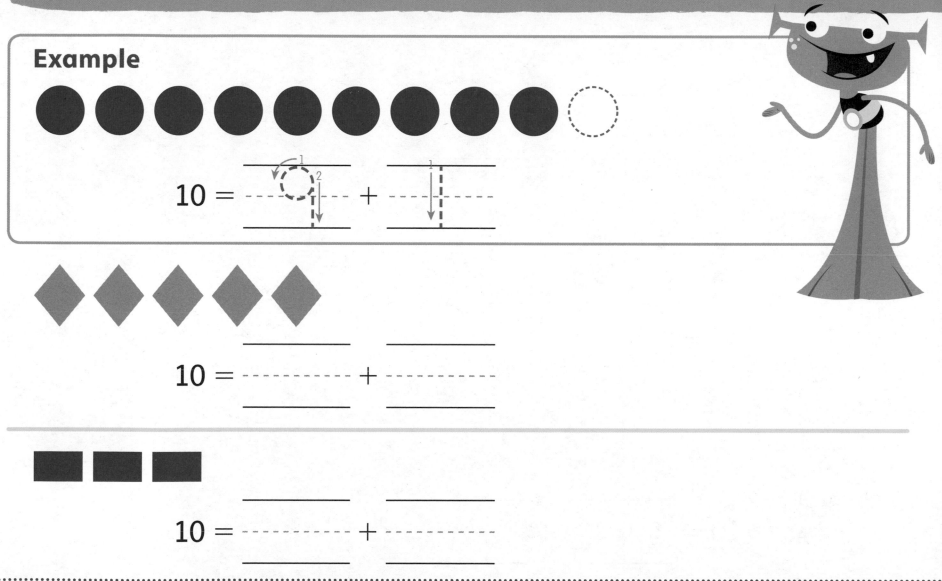

Example

$$10 = \underline{\hspace{3cm}} + \underline{\hspace{3cm}}$$

$$10 = \underline{\hspace{3cm}} + \underline{\hspace{3cm}}$$

$$10 = \underline{\hspace{3cm}} + \underline{\hspace{3cm}}$$

Have children use drawings and equations to find missing parts of 10. Ask children to draw more of each shape to make 10 in each group. Then have them complete the equation. Encourage children to read the equations aloud.

$$10 = \underline{\hspace{2cm}} + \underline{\hspace{2cm}}$$

$$10 = \underline{\hspace{2cm}} + \underline{\hspace{2cm}}$$

$$10 = \underline{\hspace{2cm}} + \underline{\hspace{2cm}}$$

Have children use drawings and equations to find missing parts of 10. Ask children to draw more of each shape to make 10 in each group. Then have them complete the equation. Encourage children to read the equations aloud.

442   Lesson 22 Find the Missing Part of 10

Refine Finding the Missing Part of 10

Apply It

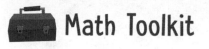

Math Toolkit

• number cards

$$10 = \underline{\hspace{2cm}} + \underline{\hspace{2cm}}$$

Have children play a memory game to match number pairs to 10. Give pairs of children number cards 1 to 5 and 5 to 9 to lay facedown. Have them take turns to turn cards over to find number pairs to 10. Then have them choose one of the pairs, draw it, and write the equation.

Discuss It How many different number pairs did you find?

_____ = _____ + _____

_____ = _____ + _____

Have children make 10 to solve story problems. Say: _Coach Joe needs 10 soccer balls for practice. He has these 3 soccer balls. How many more does he need so that he has 10 in all?_ Have children draw a picture and write an equation. Repeat for 1 soccer ball.

Discuss It When making 10, how does knowing the number you need for 1, 2, 3, and 4 help to find the number you need for 6, 7, 8, and 9?

Subtract Within 10

Dear Family,

This week your child is learning to subtract within 10.

This lesson includes subtraction problems that involve taking away part of a group of up to 10 objects and finding how many are left. There is a continued focus on connecting story problems about subtraction to pictures, objects, models, and equations.

Your child will also examine pictures of hands as models for subtracting and will practice modeling subtraction problems with fingers. Counters on 10-frames will be used to model and solve subtraction problems. Exploring these various models will allow your child to continue developing a strong understanding of what it means to subtract. These models also emphasize the relationship between the numbers in each subtraction problem and 5 or 10. This is useful both for subtraction within 10 and for subtraction with greater numbers.

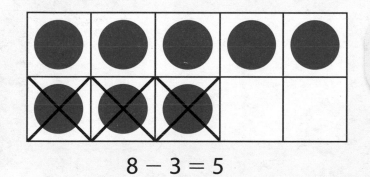

$8 - 3 = 5$

Start with 8 counters. Then take away 3.

Invite your child to share what he or she knows about subtracting within 10 by doing the following activity together.

Activity Subtracting Within 10

Do this activity with your child to subtract within 10.

Have your child use fingers to solve the subtraction problems below and tell you the answer. You may want to present the problems in a story context. Your child may subtract with fingers in any way he or she prefers.

If your child needs assistance, have him or her mirror you as you use fingers to solve $8 - 3$.

- Say: *I had 8 grapes, and I ate 3 of them. How many grapes are left?* Show 8 with 5 fingers on one hand and 3 fingers on the other hand.

- Say: *Now let us take away 3.* Fold down 3 fingers.

- Ask: *How many fingers are still up?* Have your child count the 5 fingers that are up.

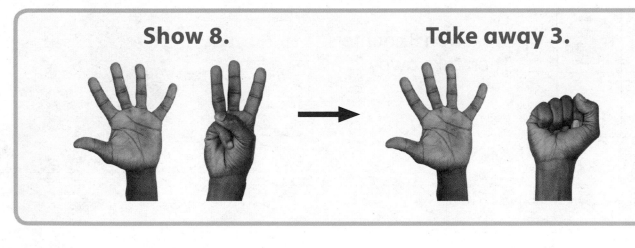

Show 8. → Take away 3.

$8 - 3 =$ _____ $7 - 2 =$ _____ $9 - 3 =$ _____

$10 - 4 =$ _____ $10 - 5 =$ _____ $6 - 4 =$ _____

Explore Subtracting Within 10

$$7 - 1 = \underline{\qquad}$$

$$7 - 2 = \underline{\qquad}$$

Have children act out subtraction word problems and write the corresponding equations. Say: *There are 7 birds sitting on a branch. 1 bird flies away. How many birds are still on the branch?* Have children cover 1 bird using an index card. Ask children to complete an equation to represent the story problem. Repeat with the problem: *There are 7 birds on a branch. 2 birds fly away. How many birds are still on the branch?*

Connect It

🧰 Math Toolkit
• counters
• index cards

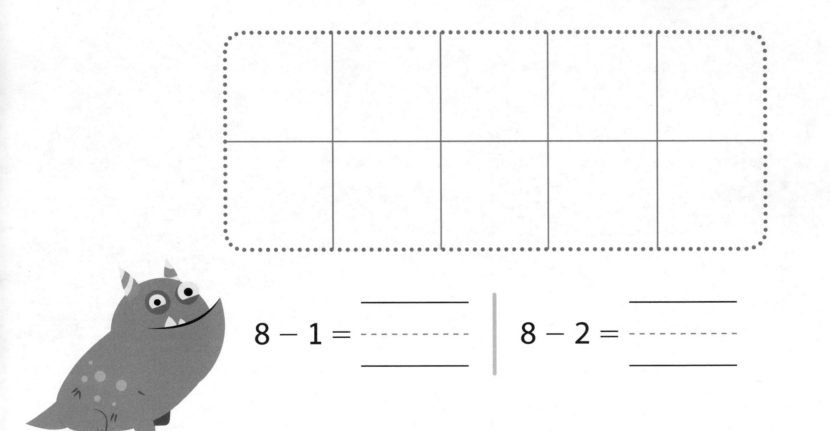

$8 - 1 = $ _____ | $8 - 2 = $ _____

Have children solve more subtraction word problems using counters and write corresponding equations. Say: *Katie has 8 stickers. She gives 1 to her brother. How many stickers does Katie have left for herself?* Have children show the problem with counters on the 10-frame and then complete the corresponding equation. Repeat with a new situation: *Will has 8 stickers. He gives 2 to his sister. How many stickers does Will have left for himself?*

Prepare for Subtracting Within 10

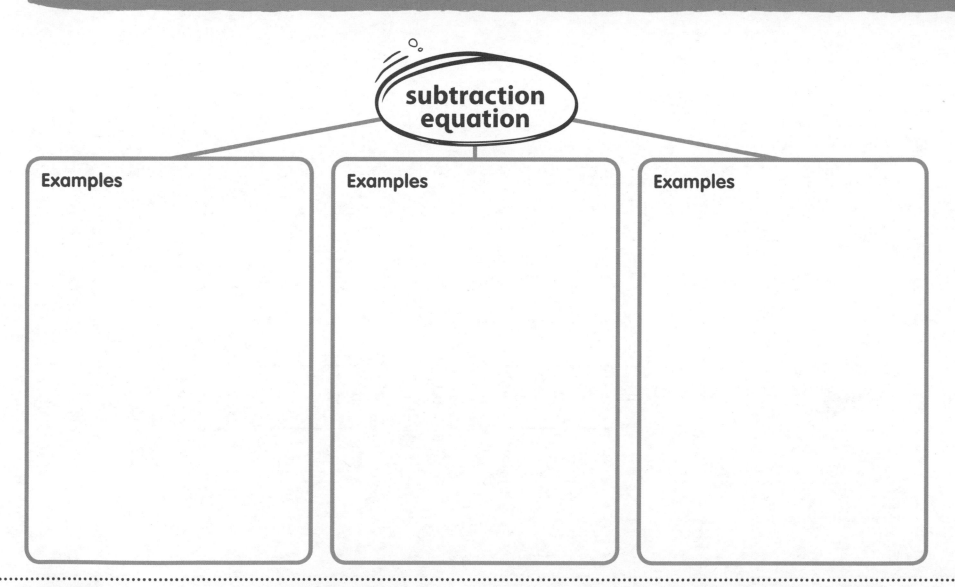

subtraction equation

Examples

Examples

Examples

Have children show the meaning of the term *subtraction equation*. Have children fill in each of the boxes to show the meaning of the term *subtraction equation*. Tell children that they can use words, numbers, and pictures. Encourage them to show as many ideas as they can.

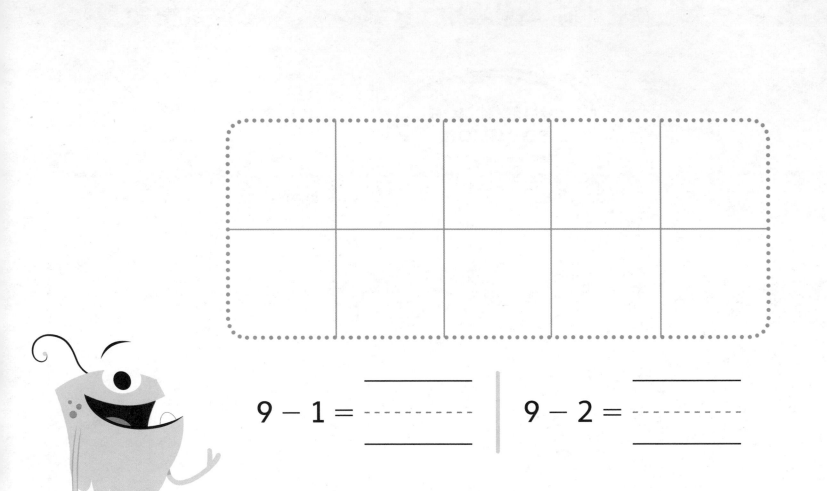

$$9 - 1 = \underline{\quad\quad}$$

$$9 - 2 = \underline{\quad\quad}$$

Have children solve subtraction word problems using counters and write corresponding equations. Say: *Jana has 9 balloons. She gives 1 to her brother. How many balloons does Jana have left for herself?* Have children show the problem with small objects on the 10-frame and then complete the corresponding equation. Repeat with a new situation: *Elijah has 9 balloons. He gives 2 to his sister. How many balloons does Elijah have left for himself?*

Develop Subtracting Within 10

Encourage children to describe take-away situations they see in the picture. For each group of items, have children circle the items that are left after some are taken away.

Discuss It How do the flowers show a take-away story?

Connect It

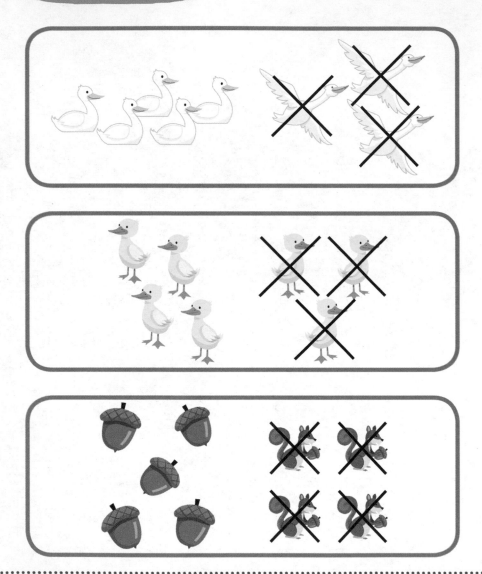

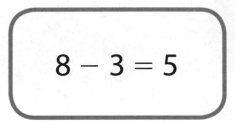

$$9 - 4 = 5$$

$$8 - 3 = 5$$

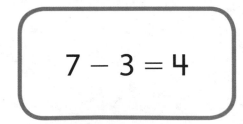

$$7 - 3 = 4$$

Have children match pictures to equations. Ask children to tell the total number of objects in each picture and then describe how many are being taken away. Have children find the equation that matches each picture and then draw a line to show the match.

Discuss It How can you find the total in each picture? How does looking at the picture tell you how many to subtract?

Name: _____

Practice Subtracting Within 10

Have children color the 4 standing flowers and the 2 drooping flowers and then tell a subtraction story about this part of the picture. Then have children color a part of the picture that shows 10 take away 1 and tell a story about that. For example: *The boy had 10 balloons. One balloon floated away. How many balloons does the boy have now?* Have children color the rest of the picture.

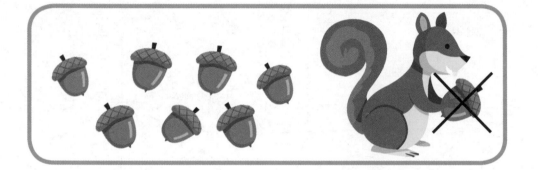

$$8 - 1 = 7$$

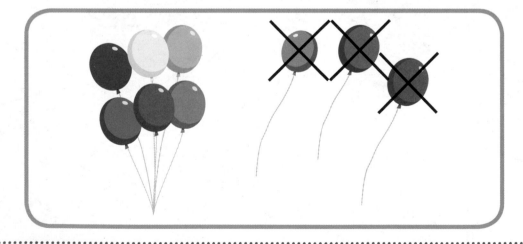

$$9 - 3 = 6$$

$$7 - 2 = 5$$

Have children match pictures to equations. Ask children to tell the total number of objects in each picture and then describe how many are being taken away. Have children find the equation that matches each picture and then read it aloud together while looking at the picture. Then have children draw a line to show the match.

Develop Subtracting Within 10

Try It

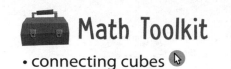 Math Toolkit
• connecting cubes

——————— ——————— ———————

- - - - - - - - — - - - - - - - - = - - - - - - - -

——————— ——————— ———————

Have children model a subtraction word problem. Give each child 10 cubes and have them use the cubes to act out a subtraction story. Say: *There were 10 balloons. 2 balloons popped. How many balloons are left?* Have children then say and write the equation.

Discuss It How did you use the cubes to model the subtraction story? What does each part of the equation show?

Connect It

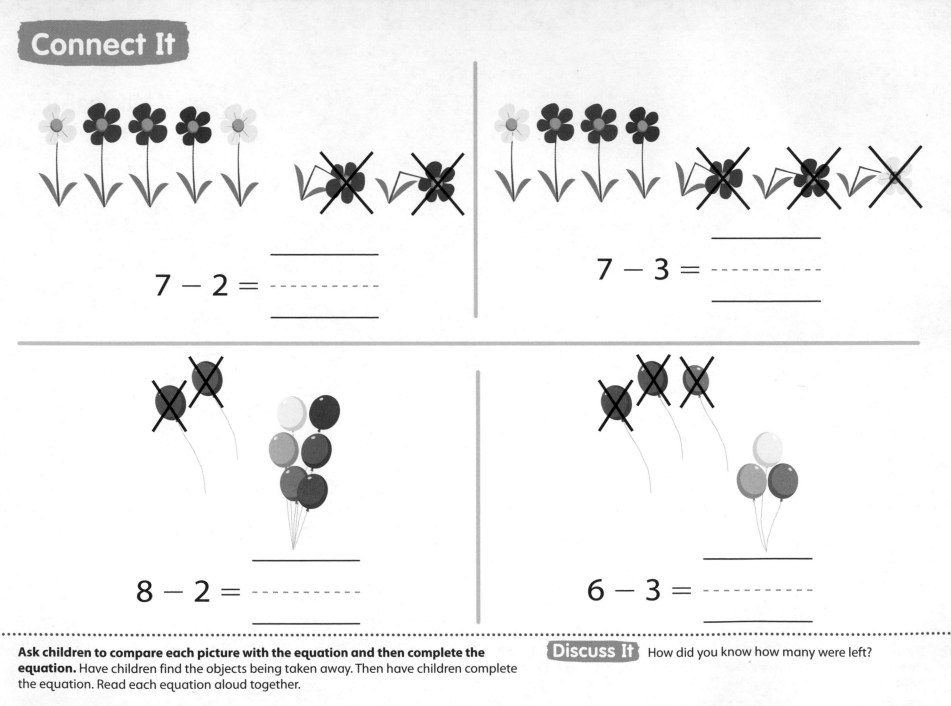

7 − 2 = _____

7 − 3 = _____

8 − 2 = _____

6 − 3 = _____

Ask children to compare each picture with the equation and then complete the equation. Have children find the objects being taken away. Then have children complete the equation. Read each equation aloud together.

Discuss It How did you know how many were left?

Practice Subtracting Within 10

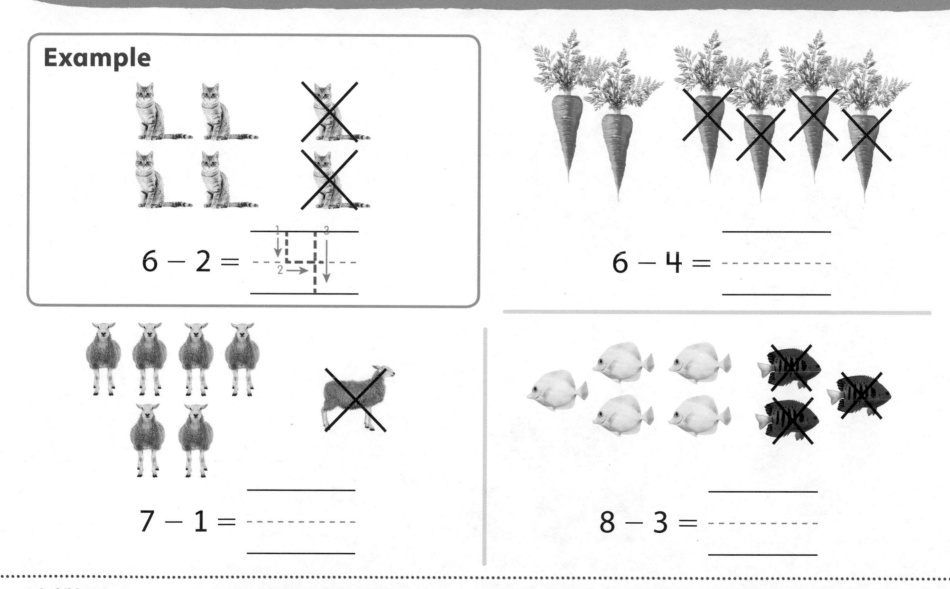

Example

$6 - 2 =$

$6 - 4 =$ _____

$7 - 1 =$ ------

$8 - 3 =$ ------

Ask children to compare each picture with the equation and then complete the equation. Have children find the animals or objects being taken away. Then have children complete the equation. Read each equation aloud together.

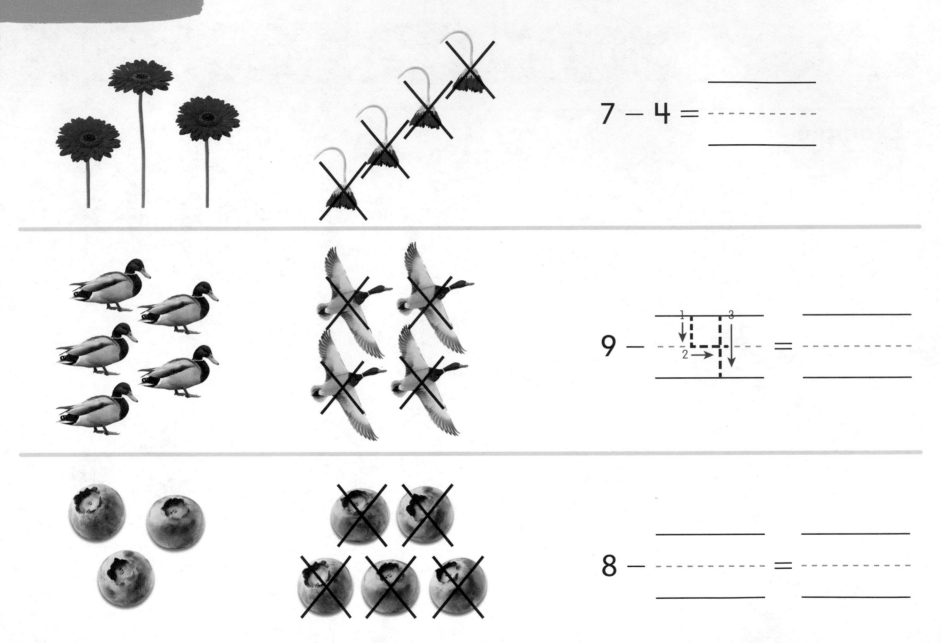

$$7 - 4 = \text{\_\_\_\_}$$

$$9 - \text{\_\_\_\_} = \text{\_\_\_\_}$$

$$8 - \text{\_\_\_\_} = \text{\_\_\_\_}$$

Ask children to compare each picture with the equation and then complete the equation. Have children find the animals or objects being taken away. Then have children complete the equation. Read each equation aloud together.

Refine Subtracting Within 10

Apply It

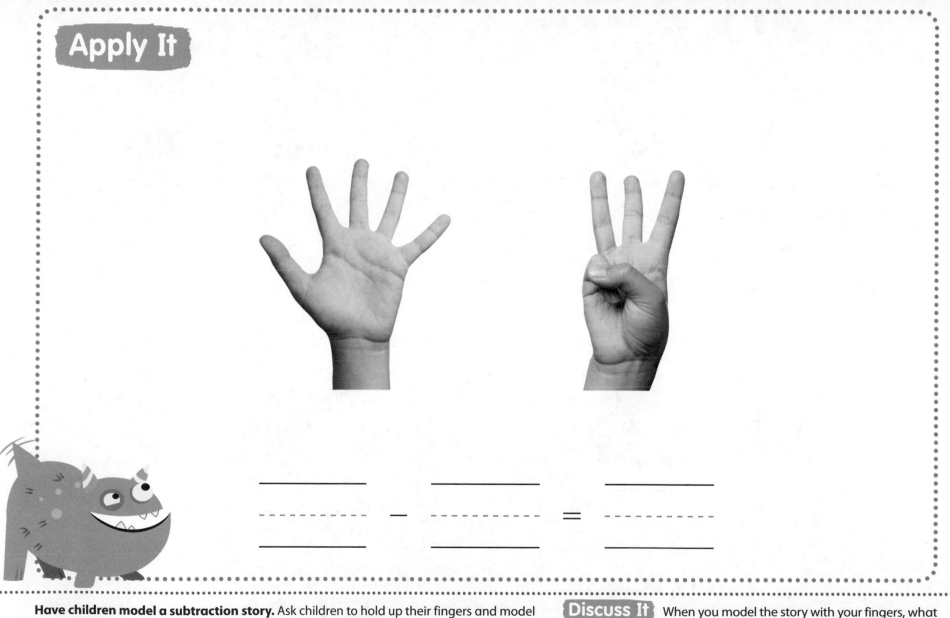

_____   _____   _____

- - - - - - - - - - - = - - - - - - - -

_____   _____   _____

Have children model a subtraction story. Ask children to hold up their fingers and model this story: _There are 8 crayons in a box. Jon takes out 5 crayons. How many are left in the box?_ Have children mark the fingers on the page to show the problem and write the equation.

Discuss It When you model the story with your fingers, what does each finger represent? How do you use your fingers to show the crayons being taken away?

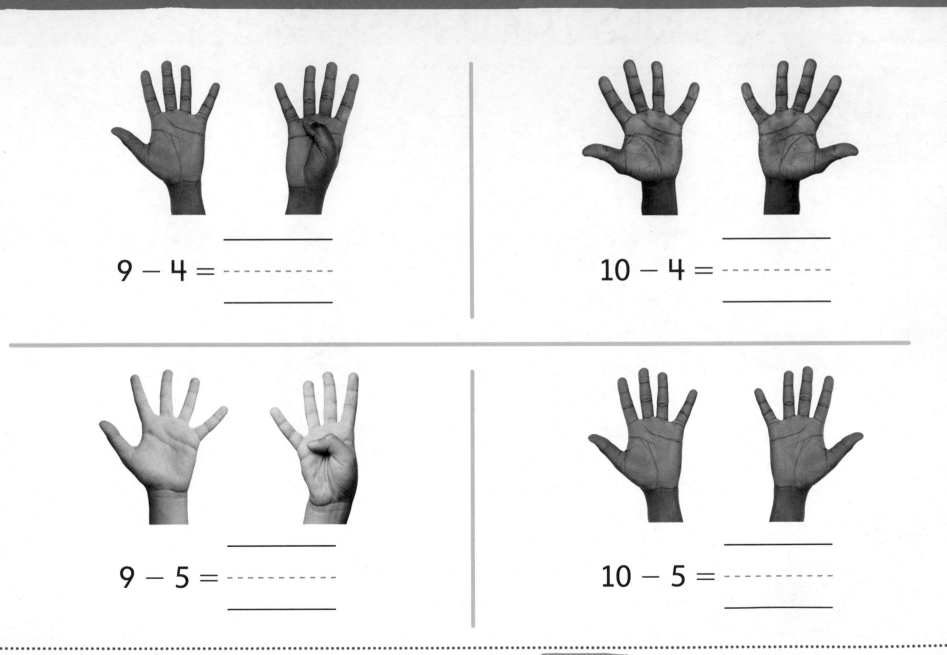

9 – 4 = _____

10 – 4 = _____

9 – 5 = _____

10 – 5 = _____

Ask children to compare the fingers showing the numbers with the equation to solve the subtraction problem. Have children mark an X on fingers being taken away. Then have children complete each equation. Read each equation aloud.

Discuss It How did you choose which fingers to "take away" in each problem?

Practice Subtracting Within 10

Example

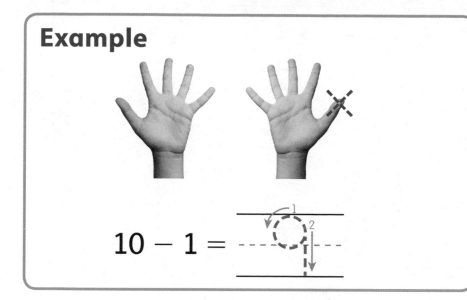

10 − 1 = _____

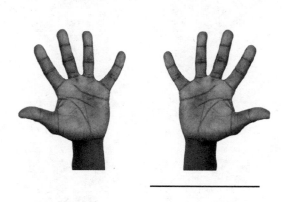

10 − 3 = _____

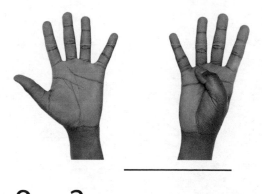

9 − 2 = _____

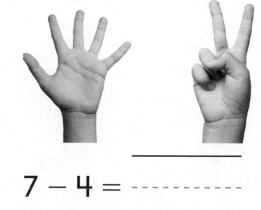

7 − 4 = _____

Ask children to compare each finger picture with the equation. Have children mark an X on fingers being taken away. Then have children complete each equation. Read each equation aloud together.

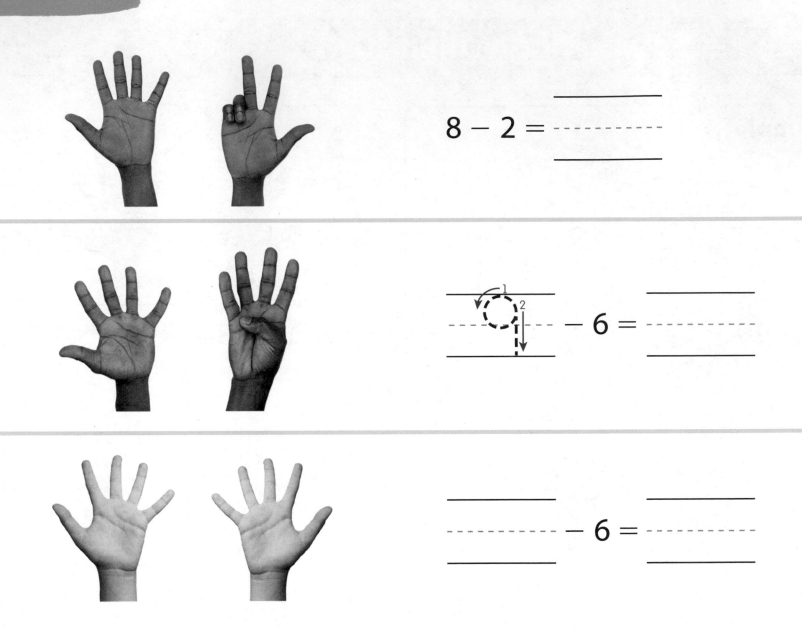

$$8 - 2 = \text{\_\_\_\_\_}$$

$$\text{\_\_\_\_} - 6 = \text{\_\_\_\_}$$

$$\text{\_\_\_\_} - 6 = \text{\_\_\_\_}$$

Ask children to compare each finger picture with the equation. Have children mark an X on fingers being taken away. Then have children complete each equation. Read each equation aloud together.

Apply It

Math Toolkit

• counters

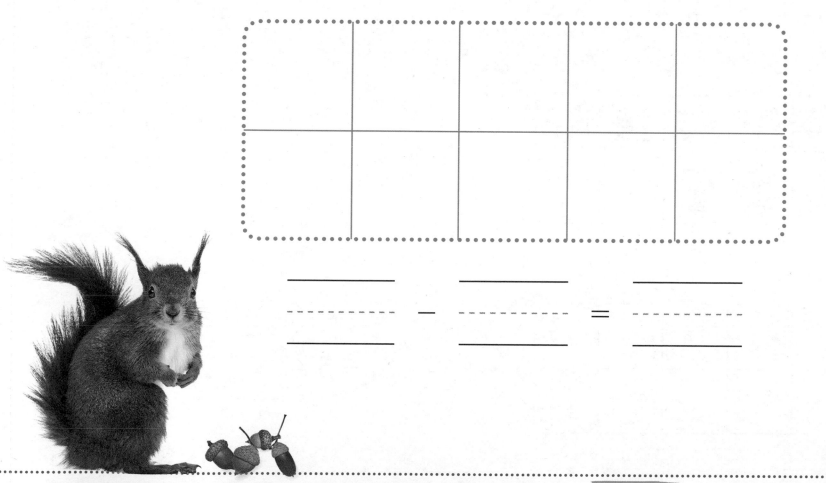

Have children model subtraction with counters on a 10-frame. Give children 10 counters each to model the subtraction story on the 10-frame. Say: *Sarah picks 9 flowers. She gives 5 away. How many flowers are left?* Draw on the 10-frame and write the equation.

Discuss It What did the 10-frame show before you took counters away? What does it show after you have taken counters away?

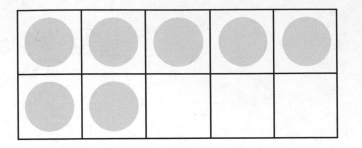

$$7 - 2 = ? \qquad \begin{array}{c} 5 \\ 7 \\ 9 \end{array}$$

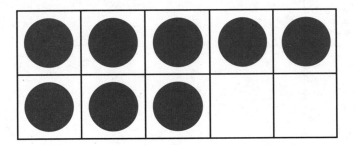

$$8 - 3 = \underline{\hspace{2cm}}$$

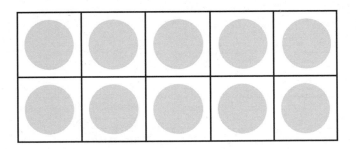

$$10 - 5 = \underline{\hspace{2cm}}$$

Encourage children to use the pictures of the counters to help them solve each problem. Have children mark an X on the number of counters being taken away and complete the equation. Have children share how they used the model with the class.

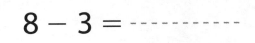 How are all the problems the same? How are they different?

464 **Lesson 23** Subtract Within 10

Dear Family,

This week your child is learning to solve addition and subtraction word problems to 10.

This lesson involves writing equations to represent and solve word problems. Your child will use counters, cubes, drawings, and pictures to find solutions to the problems. Story problems about numbers or objects connect math to the real world. Your child will see the relationship between two parts of a whole number within different real-world contexts.

Your child will be able to draw how many are in each part of an addition story, such as: *Brody finds 4 acorns. He then finds 3 more. How many acorns has Brody found in all?* Your child can draw the two groups and circle the total.

Your child will then write an equation to match: $4 + 3 = 7$.

Your child will also be able to draw how many will be taken away in a subtraction story, such as: *Luz has 6 crackers. She eats 3 of them. How many crackers does Luz have left?* Your child can draw the 6 crackers and then mark with an X the crackers that were eaten.

Your child will then write an equation to match: $6 - 3 = 3$.

Invite your child to share what he or she knows about solving addition and subtraction stories by doing the following activity together.

Activity | Addition and Subtraction Stories

Do this activity with your child to solve addition and subtraction word problems.

Materials 10 small objects, such as craft sticks, cotton balls, or buttons

- Place 10 objects on the table or floor.

- Tell an addition story, such as: *5 ducks are in a pond. 4 more join them. How many ducks are in the pond now?*

- Have your child use the objects to represent the story by gathering a group of 5 objects and a group of 4 objects.

- Have your child solve the problem and then say the equation: 5 + ___ = ___.

- Tell a subtraction story, such as: *8 bananas are in the bowl. 3 get used in a smoothie. How many bananas are left?*

- Have your child use the objects to model the problem, taking objects away to solve the problem.

- Have your child say the equation: 8 − ___ = ___.

- Repeat with other addition and subtraction stories.

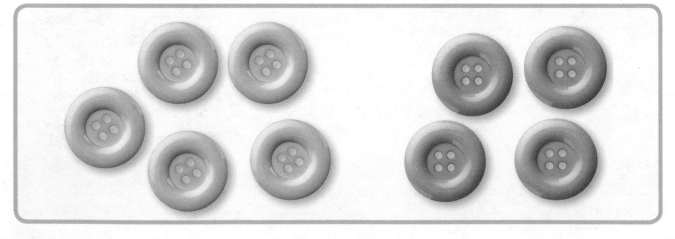

Explore Addition and Subtraction Word Problems to 10

Try It

Learning Target

- Solve addition and subtraction word problems, and add and subtract within 10.

SMP 1, 2, 3, 4, 5, 6, 7

Math Toolkit

- connecting cubes
- counters

____ + ____ = ____   ____ + ____ = ____

Have children use cubes to model an addition equation. Give children 9 cubes. Have them put the cubes into two groups. Then have children write an equation to match. Next, have children split the 9 cubes into two different groups and write an equation to match.

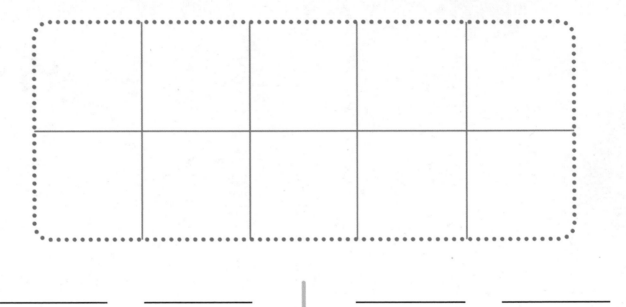

Have children use counters to model a subtraction problem. Give children 8 counters and have them place the counters on the 10-frame. Ask children to remove some of the counters and then count how many they removed and how many are left. Children then write an equation to match. Have children repeat the activity, this time taking away a different number of counters.

Prepare for Addition and Subtraction Word Problems to 10

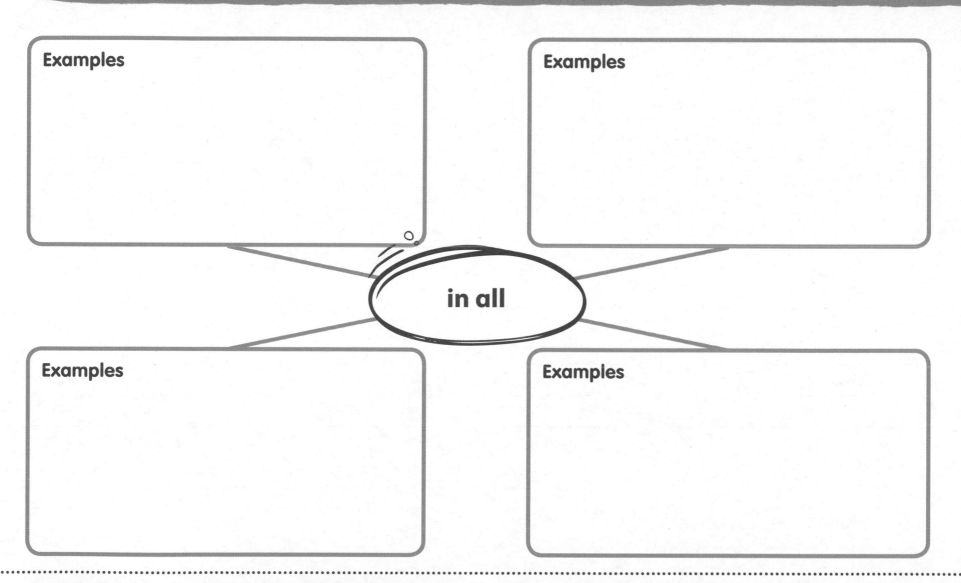

Examples

Examples

in all

Examples

Examples

Have children show the meaning of the term *in all*. Have children fill in each of the boxes to show the meaning of the term *in all*. Tell children that they can use words, numbers, and pictures. Encourage them to show as many ideas as they can.

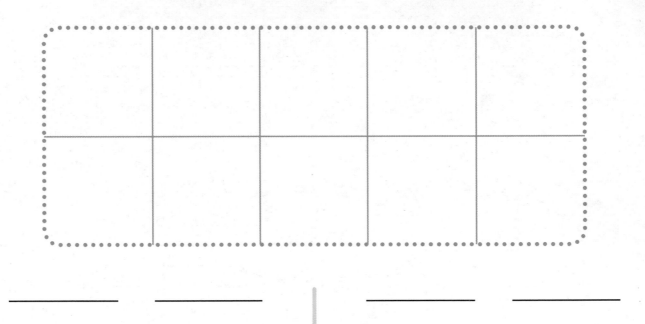

_____ _____ _____   _____ _____ _____

- - - - - - - - - — - - - - - - - - - = - - - - - - - - - | - - - - - - - - - — - - - - - - - - - = - - - - - - - - -

_____ _____ _____   _____ _____ _____

Have children use objects to model a subtraction problem. Give children 7 small objects and have them place the objects on the 10-frame. Ask children to remove 2 of the objects and then count how many they removed and how many are left. Children then write an equation to match. Have children repeat the activity, this time taking away 3 objects.

470   Lesson 24 Addition and Subtraction Word Problems to 10

Develop Solving Addition and Subtraction Word Problems to 10

Encourage children to solve problems using the picture. Say: *Kai buys 3 pink flowers and 4 yellow flowers. How many flowers does Kai buy in all?* Have children circle the flowers Kai buys to solve. Tell a subtraction story. Have children mark objects with an X to solve.

Discuss It How many red peppers would be left if 7 were sold? How did you solve the problem?

Connect It

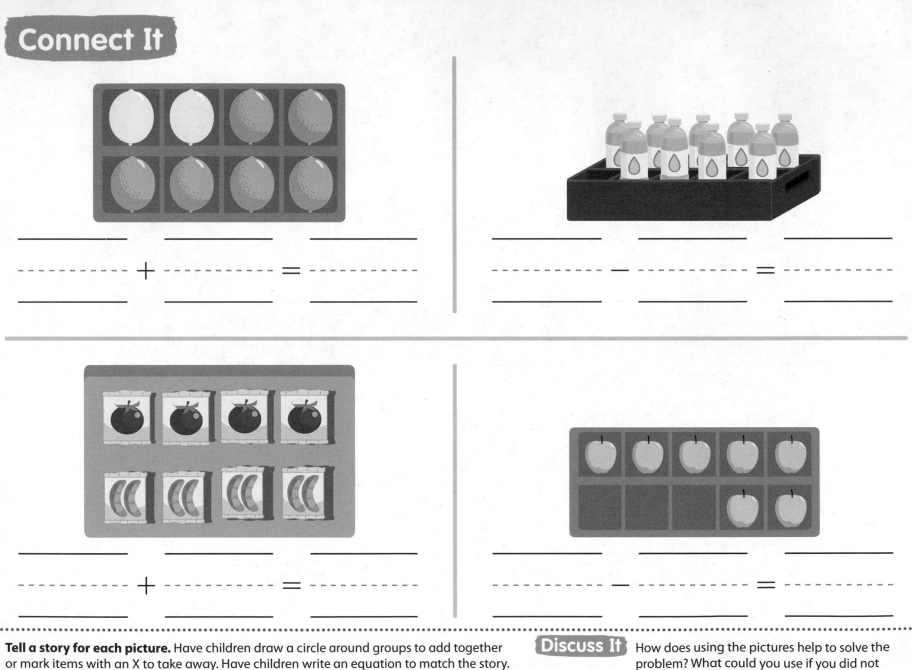

_____ + _____ = _____

_____ − _____ = _____

_____ + _____ = _____

_____ − _____ = _____

Tell a story for each picture. Have children draw a circle around groups to add together or mark items with an X to take away. Have children write an equation to match the story.

Discuss It　How does using the pictures help to solve the problem? What could you use if you did not have pictures?

Practice Solving Addition and Subtraction Word Problems to 10

Tell addition and subtraction stories using the picture. For instance, say: *Jordie buys 6 red peppers and 3 orange peppers. How many peppers does Jordie* *buy in all?* Have children color in the pictures to match the stories. Then have them circle groups or mark items with an X to solve the problems.

_____   _____   _____

- - - - - + - - - - - = - - - - -

_____   _____   _____

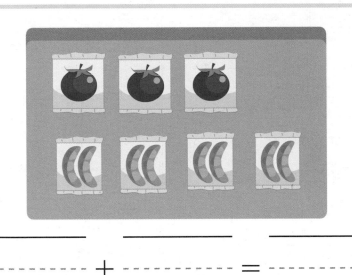

_____   _____   _____

- - - - - + - - - - - = - - - - -

_____   _____   _____

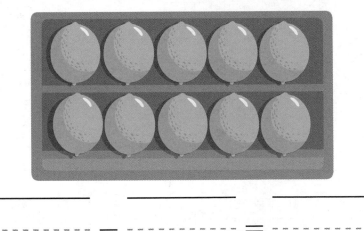

_____   _____   _____

- - - - - - - - - - = - - - - -

_____   _____   _____

Tell a story for each picture. Have children draw a circle around groups to add together or mark items with an X to take away. Have children write an equation to match the story.

474   **Lesson 24** Addition and Subtraction Word Problems to 10

Develop Solving Addition and Subtraction Word Problems to 10

Try It

Math Toolkit
• two-color counters

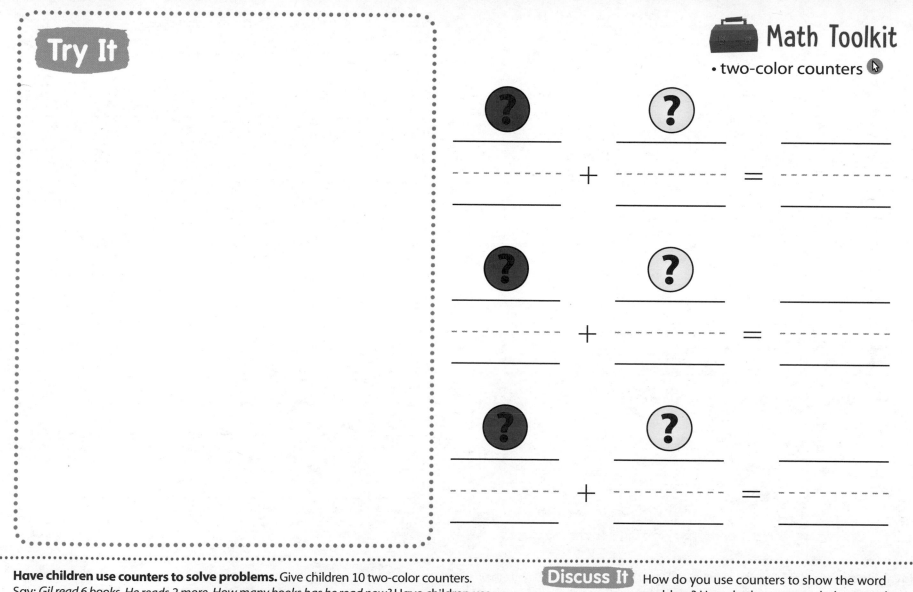

Have children use counters to solve problems. Give children 10 two-color counters. Say: *Gil read 6 books. He reads 2 more. How many books has he read now?* Have children use counters to solve and then write an equation to match. Repeat with other word problems.

Discuss It How do you use counters to show the word problem? How do the counters help you solve the problem?

Connect It

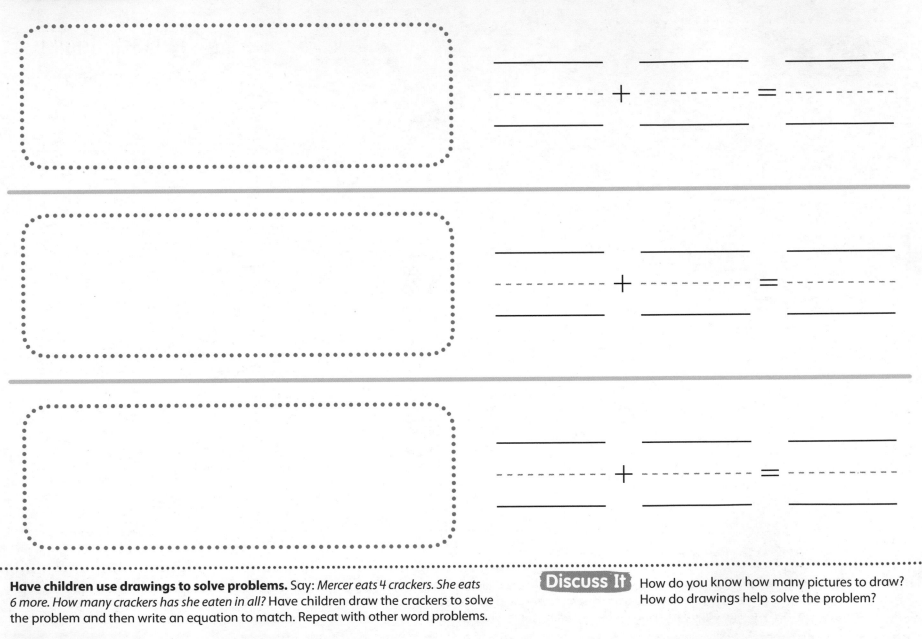

_____ + _____ = _____

_____ + _____ = _____

_____ + _____ = _____

Have children use drawings to solve problems. Say: _Mercer eats 4 crackers. She eats 6 more. How many crackers has she eaten in all?_ Have children draw the crackers to solve the problem and then write an equation to match. Repeat with other word problems.

Discuss It How do you know how many pictures to draw? How do drawings help solve the problem?

Practice Solving Addition and Subtraction Word Problems to 10

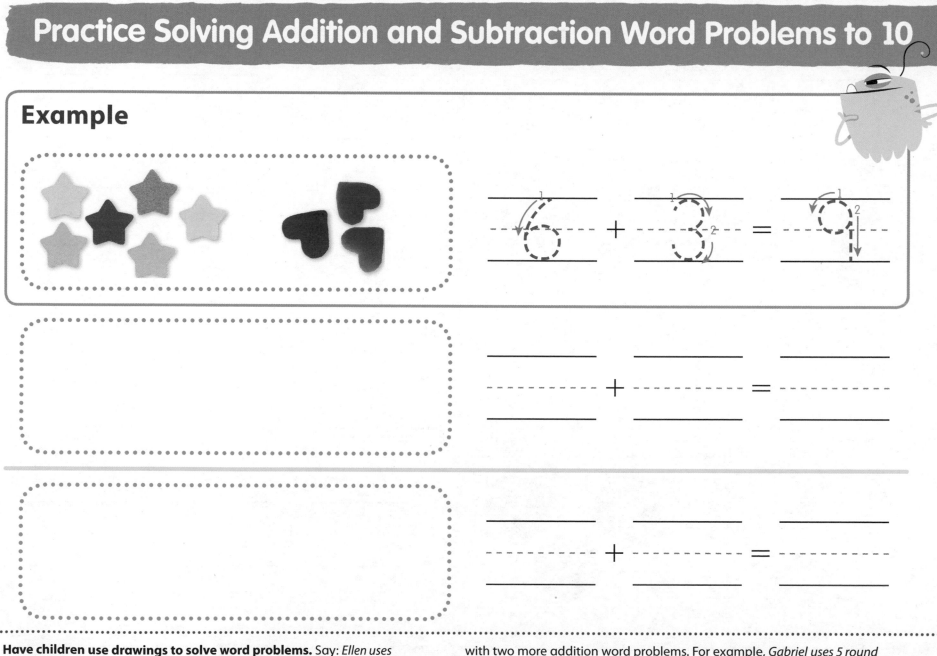

Example

Have children use drawings to solve word problems. Say: *Ellen uses 6 star beads and 3 heart beads to make her necklace. How many beads does she use in all?* Have children use drawings and write an equation to match. Repeat with two more addition word problems. For example, *Gabriel uses 5 round beads and 2 square beads. How many beads does he use in all?*

_____ + _____ = _____

_____ + _____ = _____

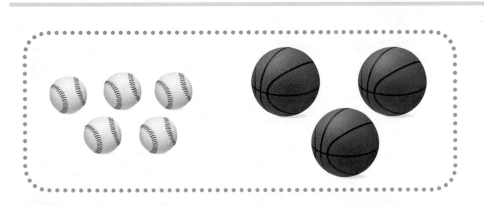

_____ + _____ = _____

Have children use drawings to solve word problems. Tell two addition word problems. Have children use drawings to represent the problem, solve it, and then write the matching equation. For example, _Niall found 4 buttons. He then found 4 more. How many buttons does he have in all?_ For the last problem, have children use the pictures to tell their own addition story and then write the matching equation.

Refine Solving Addition and Subtraction Word Problems to 10

Apply It

Math Toolkit

• connecting cubes

_____ _____ _____

- - - - - - - - - − - - - - - - - - - = - - - - - - - - -

_____ _____ _____

_____ _____ _____

- - - - - - - - - − - - - - - - - - - = - - - - - - - - -

_____ _____ _____

_____ _____ _____

- - - - - - - - - − - - - - - - - - - = - - - - - - - - -

_____ _____ _____

Have children use cubes to solve problems. Give children 10 cubes. Say: *Deon has 6 blocks. He gives 3 to Ryan. How many blocks does Deon have now?* Have children use cubes to solve and then write an equation to match. Repeat with other word problems.

Discuss It If Deon had started with 7 blocks, how many would he have after giving 3 to Ryan?

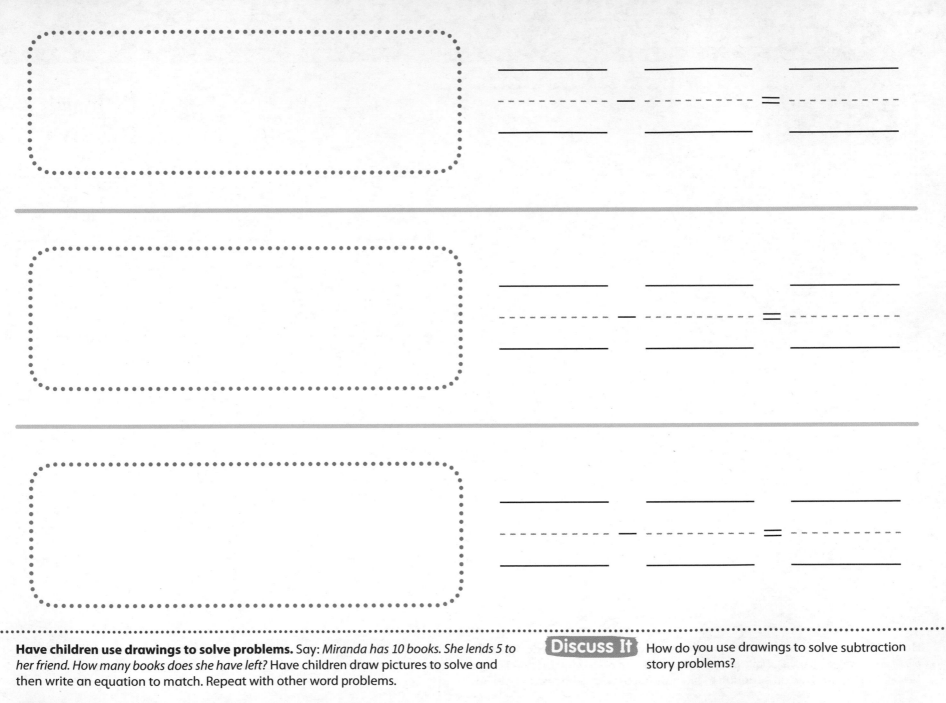

Have children use drawings to solve problems. Say: *Miranda has 10 books. She lends 5 to her friend. How many books does she have left?* Have children draw pictures to solve and then write an equation to match. Repeat with other word problems.

Discuss It How do you use drawings to solve subtraction story problems?

Practice Solving Addition and Subtraction Word Problems to 10

Example

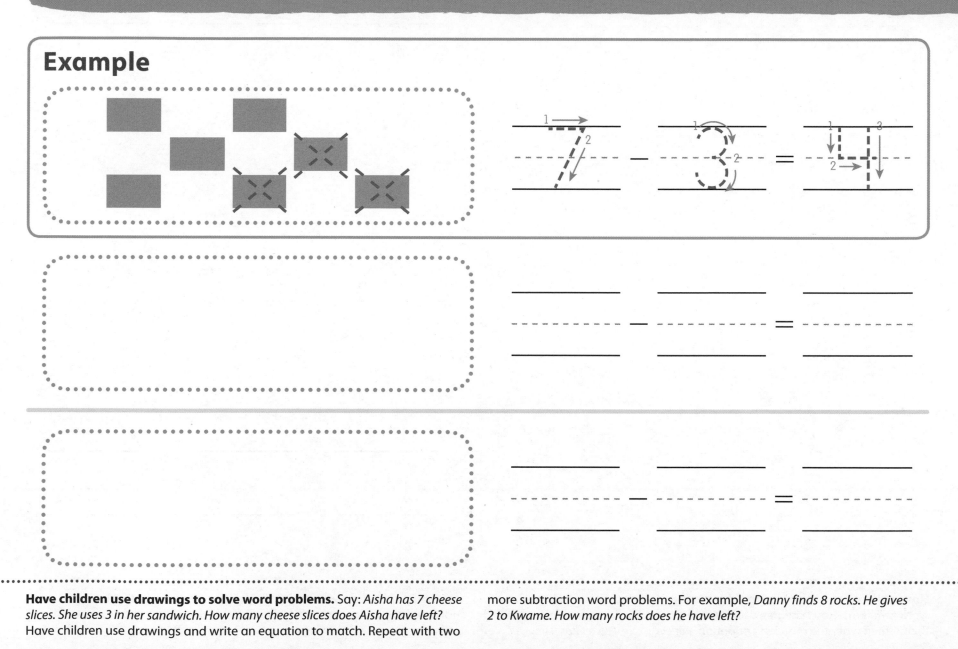

Have children use drawings to solve word problems. Say: *Aisha has 7 cheese slices. She uses 3 in her sandwich. How many cheese slices does Aisha have left?* Have children use drawings and write an equation to match. Repeat with two more subtraction word problems. For example, *Danny finds 8 rocks. He gives 2 to Kwame. How many rocks does he have left?*

_____ _____ _____

----------- — ----------- = -----------

_____ _____ _____

_____ _____ _____

----------- — ----------- = -----------

_____ _____ _____

_____ _____ _____

----------- — ----------- = -----------

_____ _____ _____

Have children use drawings to solve word problems. Tell two subtraction word problems. Have children use drawings to represent the problem, solve it, and then write the matching equation. For example, *Dexter has 9 flowers.* *He gives 2 to his teacher. How many flowers does he have left?* For the last problem, have children use the pictures to tell their own subtraction story and then write the matching equation.

Apply It

Math Toolkit
- counters
- connecting cubes

$$\underline{\hspace{3cm}} + \underline{\hspace{3cm}} = \underline{\hspace{3cm}}$$

$$\underline{\hspace{3cm}} - \underline{\hspace{3cm}} = \underline{\hspace{3cm}}$$

$$\underline{\hspace{3cm}} + \underline{\hspace{3cm}} = \underline{\hspace{3cm}}$$

Have children use counters or cubes to solve word problems. Give children 10 cubes or 10 counters. Tell an addition word problem. Have children use cubes or counters to solve the problem and then write the equation. Repeat with a subtraction, then an addition problem.

Discuss It Tell a classmate an addition problem and have him or her use cubes or counters to help solve it.

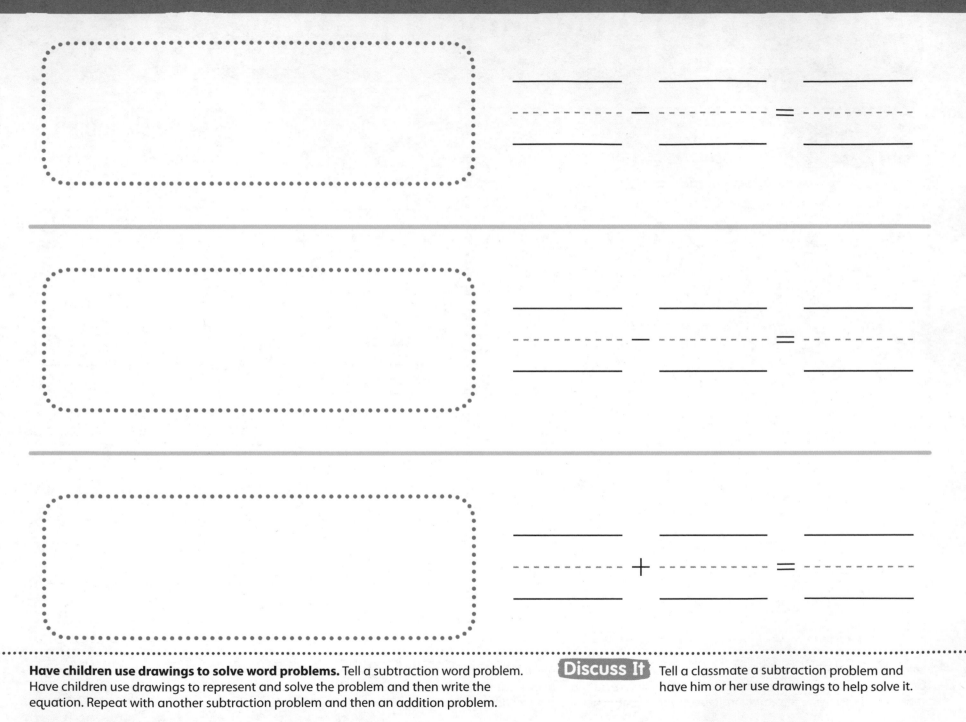

Have children use drawings to solve word problems. Tell a subtraction word problem. Have children use drawings to represent and solve the problem and then write the equation. Repeat with another subtraction problem and then an addition problem.

Discuss It Tell a classmate a subtraction problem and have him or her use drawings to help solve it.

Word Problems with Both Addends Unknown

Dear Family,

This week your child is learning to solve addition problems with two unknown numbers.

This lesson involves writing equations to represent and solve word problems involving two unknown numbers. Story problems about numbers or objects connect math to the real world. Your child will use counters, cubes, drawings, and pictures to find possible solutions to these problems. As he or she does this, your child will see the relationship between two parts of a whole number within different real-world contexts.

Your child will be able to choose how many will be in each part of an addition story, such as: *There are 7 tiles. Some are blue, and the rest are white. How many of each color can there be?* Your child may choose to color 5 of the 7 tiles blue so 2 tiles are white.

Your child will then write an equation to match: 7 = 5 + 2.

Your child will also be able to find multiple ways to solve a problem, such as: *There are 6 birds. Some are ducks, and some are pigeons. How many of each bird can there be?* Your child may choose 4 ducks and 2 pigeons, or 3 ducks and 3 pigeons, or any other pair of numbers that equal 6.

Your child will then write equations to match: 6 = 4 + 2 or 6 = 3 + 3.

Invite your child to share what he or she knows about finding unknown numbers in word problems by doing the following activity together.

Activity Solving Word Problems with Both Addends Unknown

Do this activity with your child to solve word problems with both addends unknown.

Materials 10 small objects, such as craft sticks, cotton balls, buttons, or crackers

• Place all or some of the 10 objects on the table or floor.

• Tell an addition story, such as: *There are 9 balls. Some are red, and the rest are blue. How many of each color are there?*

• Have your child move the objects into two groups to represent a group of red balls and a group of blue balls.

• Have your child say the equation: 9 = ___ + ___.

• Have your child find a different pair of numbers to represent the red and blue balls and say the matching equation.

• Tell another addition story, such as: *There are 10 crackers. How can Dario and Audi share the crackers?*

• Have your child use the objects to model the problem to show how many crackers each person could have.

• Have your child say the equation: 10 = ___ + ___.

• Have your child find another pair of numbers to represent the crackers and say the matching equation.

Explore Word Problems with Both Addends Unknown

Try It

Math Toolkit

• connecting cubes

Learning Target

• Decompose numbers less than or equal to 10 into pairs in more than one way, and record each decomposition by a drawing or equation.

SMP 1, 2, 3, 4, 5, 6, 7

Have children use connecting cubes to find missing numbers in a story problem where both addends are unknown. Say: *Mateo has 6 apples. He has two plates. How many apples can he put on each plate?*

Have children model the problem, placing cubes on the "plate" workmats. Have the class identify and discuss all the possible arrangements. Ask: *What if Mateo puts all the apples on one plate?*

Connect It

Have children represent a problem with connecting cubes.
Say: *Now Mateo has 9 apples. He has two plates. How many apples can he put on each plate?* Have children model the problem, using connecting cubes on the workmat. Ask children to share their strategies and discuss the multiple ways the problem can be solved. Encourage children to show 9 and 0 as one of the arrangements.

488   **Lesson 25** Word Problems with Both Addends Unknown

Prepare for Solving Word Problems with Both Addends Unknown

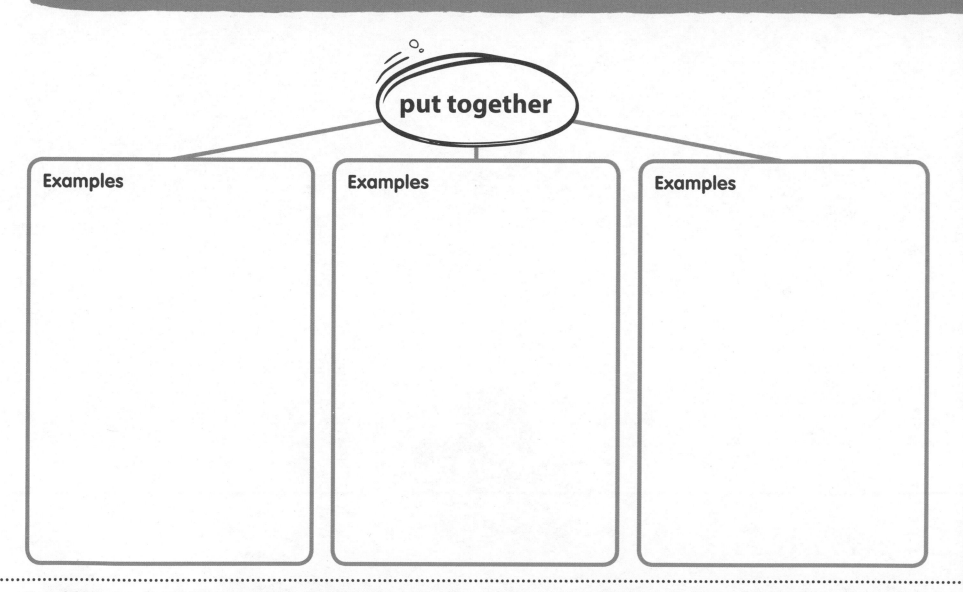

Have children show the meaning of the term *put together*. Have children fill in each of the boxes to show the meaning of the term *put together*. Tell children that they can use words, numbers, and pictures. Encourage them to show as many ideas as they can.

Have children represent a problem with small objects. Say: *Destiny has 8 grapes. She has two plates. How many grapes can she put on each plate?* Have children model the problem, using small objects on the workmat.

Ask children to share their strategies and discuss the multiple ways the problem can be solved. Encourage children to show 8 and 0 as one of the arrangements.

Develop Solving Word Problems with Both Addends Unknown

Encourage children to tell addition stories about the groups of objects. Pose problems, such as: *Cara planted 10 flowers. She will pick some. How many can be in her hand, and how many can be in the ground?* Have children circle groups of objects that show the problem.

Discuss It Suppose some of the cats go to sleep. Explain how many cats could be asleep and how many could be awake.

Lesson 25 Word Problems with Both Addends Unknown **491**

Connect It

_____ and _____

_____ and _____

_____ and _____

Tell a story about each set of pictures, such as: _There are 6 cats. Some are outside. The rest are inside._ Have children circle the two groups and then write the numbers to match.

Discuss It Did you circle the same number of objects as your partner?

Practice Solving Word Problems with Both Addends Unknown

Tell addition stories using the picture. For instance, say: *There are 4 cats. Some are orange. The rest are brown. How many cats are orange, and how many are brown?* Have children color the picture to match the problem. Say: *There* were 5 apples on the ground. Damon picked some up. How many were picked up and how many are still on the ground?* Have children color apples that were picked up.

—————   —————
- - - - -   **and**   - - - - -
—————   —————

—————   —————
- - - - -   **and**   - - - - -
—————   —————

—————   —————
- - - - -   **and**   - - - - -
—————   —————

Have children tell a story about each set of pictures. Have children circle the two groups and then write the numbers to match.

Develop Solving Word Problems with Both Addends Unknown

Try It

Math Toolkit
• two-color counters
• crayons

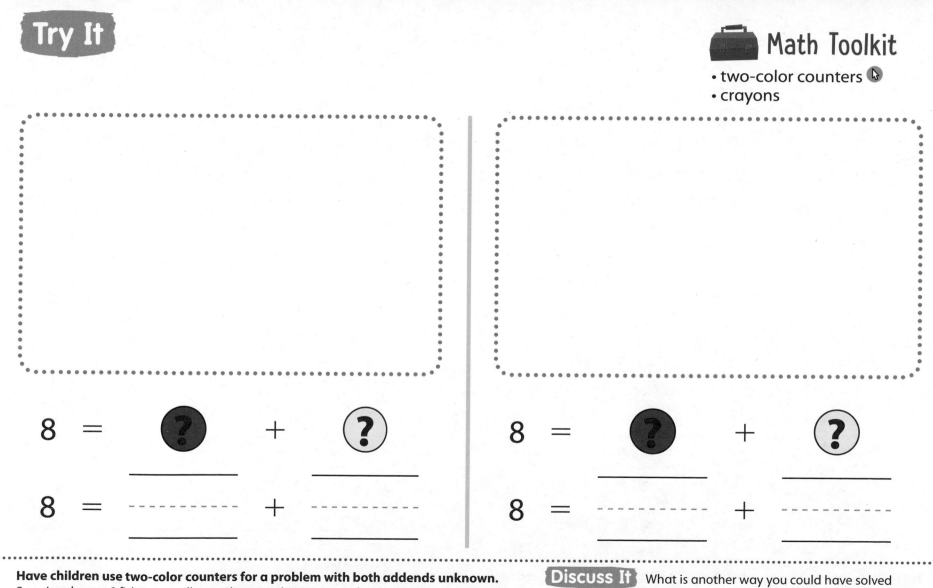

$$8 = \bigcirc{?} + \bigcirc{?}$$

_____ + _____

$$8 = \text{-----} + \text{-----}$$

_____ + _____

$$8 = \bigcirc{?} + \bigcirc{?}$$

_____ + _____

$$8 = \text{-----} + \text{-----}$$

_____ + _____

Have children use two-color counters for a problem with both addends unknown.
Say: _Jen chooses 8 fish, some yellow and some red. How many of each color can she choose?_
Have them show the problem two different ways with counters and write the equations.

Discuss It What is another way you could have solved this problem?

Connect It

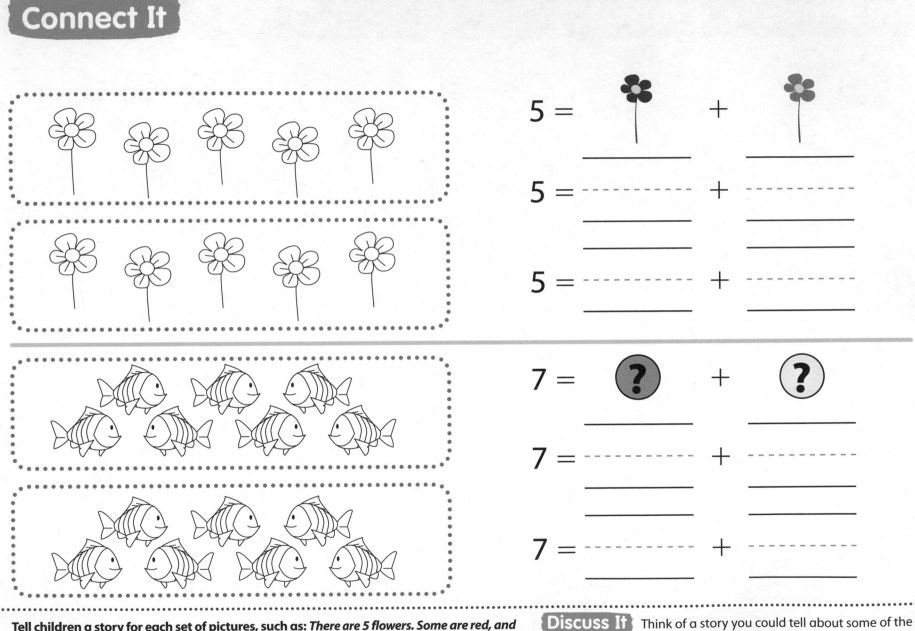

$5 =$ _____ $+$ _____

$5 =$ _____ $+$ _____

$5 =$ _____ $+$ _____

$7 =$ _____ $+$ _____

$7 =$ _____ $+$ _____

$7 =$ _____ $+$ _____

Tell children a story for each set of pictures, such as: *There are 5 flowers. Some are red, and the rest are blue.* For each set, ask children to find two different ways to color a number of objects one color and the rest the other color. Have children complete the equations to match.

Discuss It Think of a story you could tell about some of the fish hiding.

496 Lesson 25 Word Problems with Both Addends Unknown

Practice Solving Word Problems with Both Addends Unknown

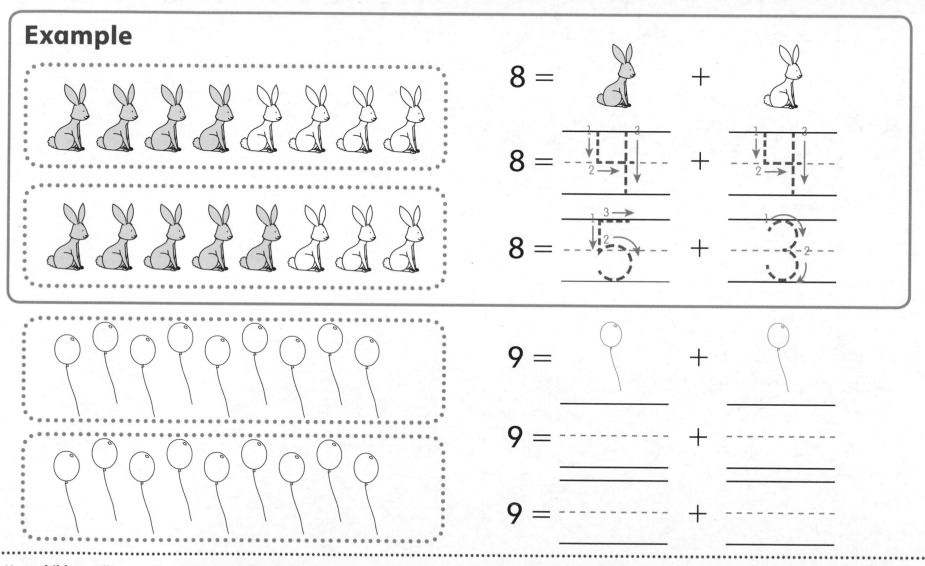

Example

$8 =$ +

$8 =$ +

$8 =$ +

$9 =$ +

$9 =$ +

$9 =$ +

Have children tell a story for each set of pictures. For example: *Misha saw 8 rabbits. Some were gray, and the rest were brown. How many of each color rabbit could there be?* Have children color each set a different way to match the story and then complete each equation.

$6 =$ $+$

_____   _____

$6 =$ - - - - - - - - $+$ - - - - - - - -

_____   _____

$6 =$ - - - - - - - - $+$ - - - - - - - -

_____   _____

_____ $=$ _____ $+$ _____

- - - - - - - - $=$ - - - - - - - - $+$ - - - - - - - -

_____   _____   _____

_____ $=$ _____ $+$ _____

- - - - - - - - $=$ - - - - - - - - $+$ - - - - - - - -

_____   _____   _____

Have children tell a story for each set of pictures. For example: _Sebastian saw 6 butterflies. Some were yellow, and the rest were blue. How many of each_ _color butterfly could there be?_ Have children color each set a different way to match the story and then complete each equation.

Refine Solving Word Problems with Both Addends Unknown

Apply It

🧰 **Math Toolkit**
• connecting cubes

$7 =$ [?] $+$ [?]

_____ _____

$7 =$ - - - - - $+$ - - - - -

_____ _____

$7 =$ [?] $+$ [?]

_____ _____

$7 =$ - - - - - $+$ - - - - -

_____ _____

Have children model a story with both parts unknown. Give children 7 connecting cubes. Say: *Deja made 7 cards. She sends some to her friends. How many cards does Deja send, and how many does she keep?* Have children use cubes to model and then write the equations.

Discuss It What other way could you solve this problem?

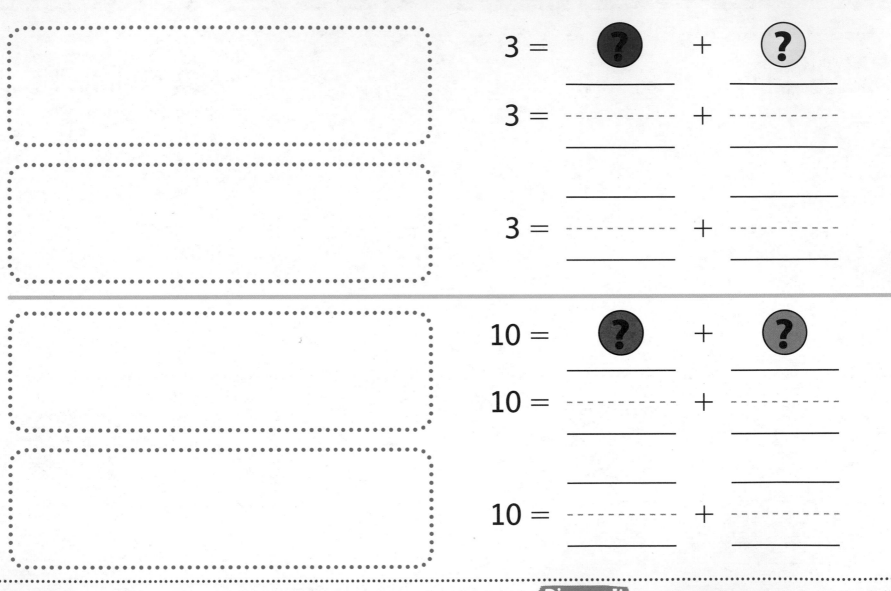

$3 =$? $+$? ___ ___

$3 =$ - - - $+$ - - - ___ ___

$3 =$ - - - $+$ - - - ___ ___

$10 =$? $+$? ___ ___

$10 =$ - - - $+$ - - - ___ ___

$10 =$ - - - $+$ - - - ___ ___

Have children use drawings to write equations for stories. Tell children a story for each problem, such as: *There are 3 balloons. Some are red and the rest are yellow. How many of each color could there be?* Have children use drawings to solve the problem two different ways.

Discuss It Sam buys 7 balloons. Some are purple, and the rest are red. How can Sam find out how many are red?

Practice Solving Word Problems with Both Addends Unknown

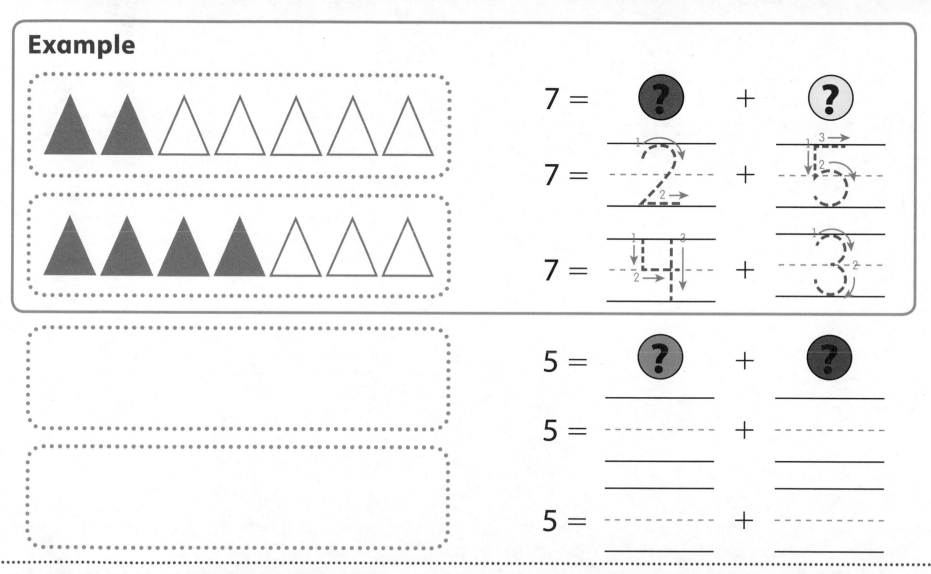

Example

$7 =$? + ?

$7 = 2 + 5$

$7 = 1 + 3$

$5 =$? + ?

$5 = $ _____ + _____

$5 = $ _____ + _____

Have children use drawings to solve problems with both addends unknown. Have children tell a story for each problem, such as: *Adra has 7 tortilla chips. Some are blue, and the rest are yellow. How many of each color of tortilla chip could she have?* Ask children to use drawings to show two different ways to solve. Have them complete the equations to match.

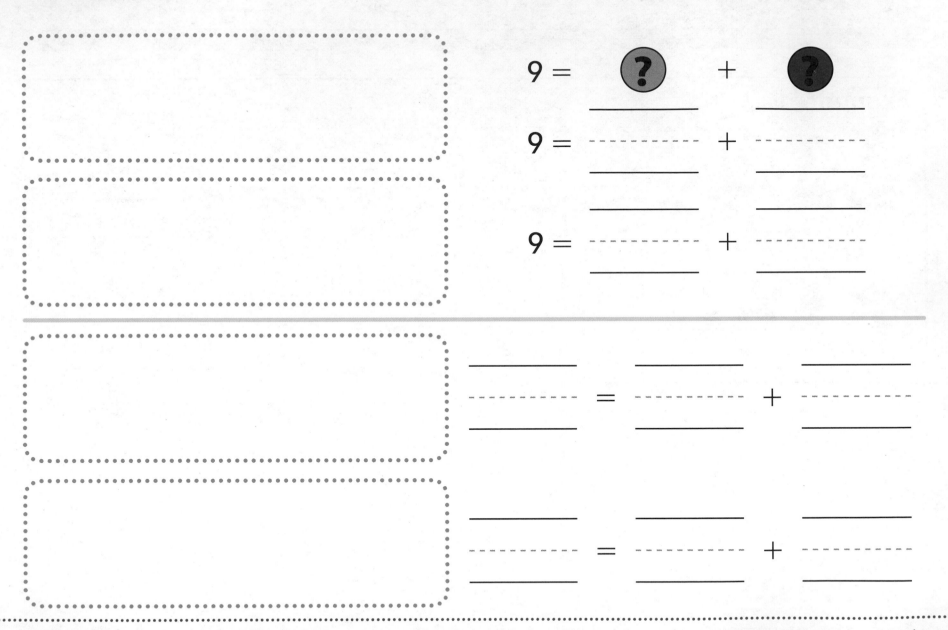

$9 =$ (?) $+$ (?)

_____   _____

$9 =$ - - - - - $+$ - - - - -

_____   _____

$9 =$ - - - - - $+$ - - - - -

_____   _____

_____   _____   _____

- - - - - $=$ - - - - - $+$ - - - - -

_____   _____   _____

_____   _____   _____

- - - - - $=$ - - - - - $+$ - - - - -

_____   _____   _____

For the first problem, have children write equations for a story with both addends unknown. Have children tell a story, such as: *Ethan has 9 apples. Some are green, and the rest are red. How many of each color apple could there be?*

For the second problem, have children choose a total, tell another story, and find two ways to solve. Ask children to use drawings to show two different ways to solve each problem and write equations to match.

502   **Lesson 25** Word Problems with Both Addends Unknown

Apply It

🧰 **Math Toolkit**
• two-color counters

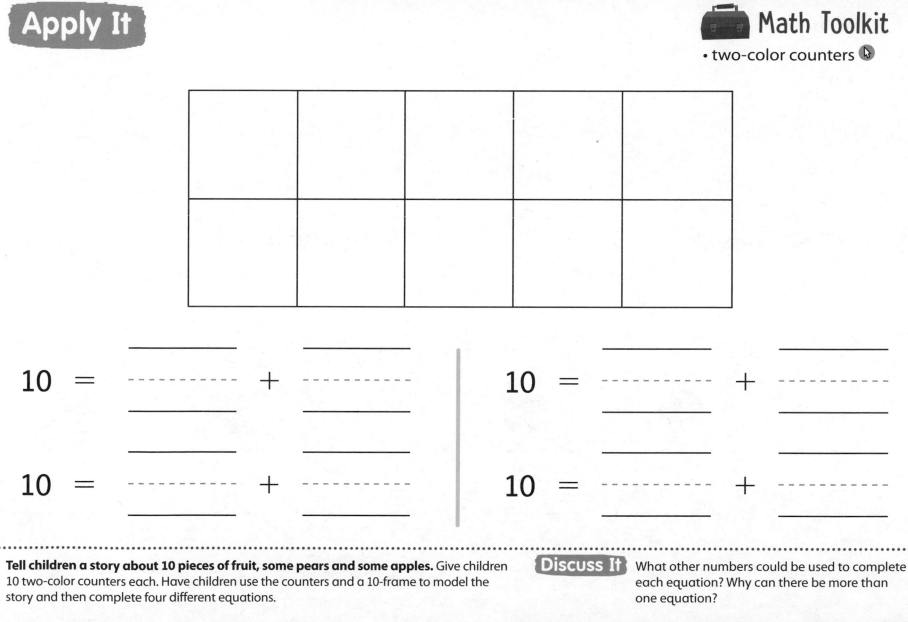

10 = _____ + _____

10 = _____ + _____

10 = _____ + _____

10 = _____ + _____

Tell children a story about 10 pieces of fruit, some pears and some apples. Give children 10 two-color counters each. Have children use the counters and a 10-frame to model the story and then complete four different equations.

Discuss It What other numbers could be used to complete each equation? Why can there be more than one equation?

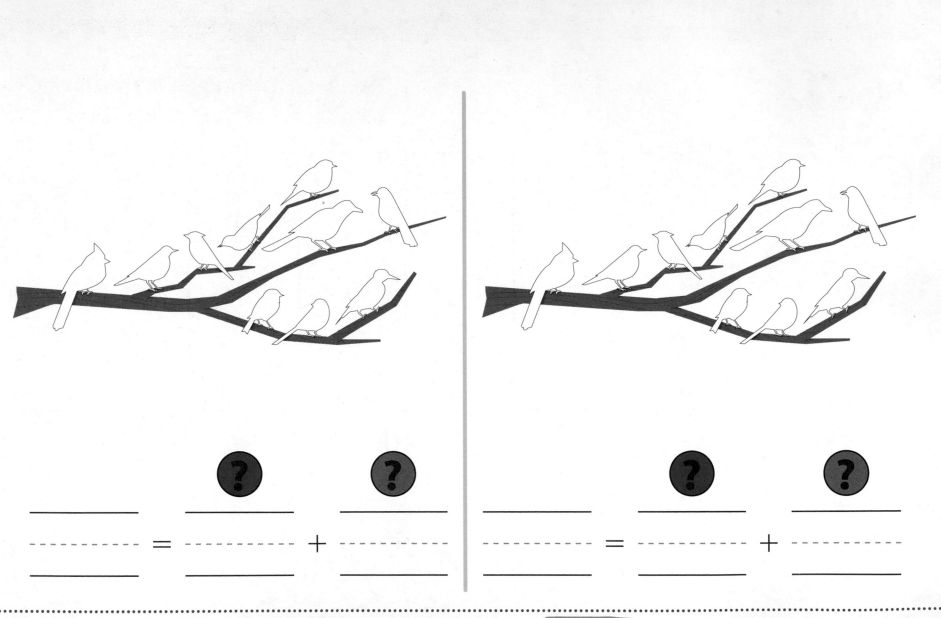

Tell children a story about the birds. Have children color each set of birds a different way to show a story and complete each equation to match.

Discuss It What do you notice about the number of blue birds as the number of red birds changes? Why is this?

Show What You Learned

Have children draw to show what they learned about adding and subtracting. Prompt children to reflect on their learning by posing questions such as: *What was the hardest math you learned? Why? What could you use more practice with? What math could you use in your everyday life?*

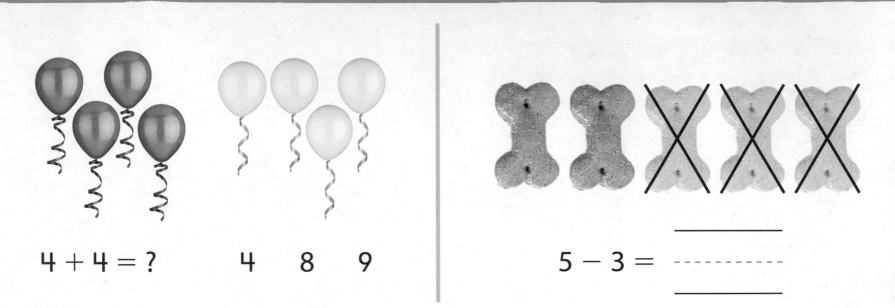

$$4 + 4 = ?$$

4   8   9

$$5 - 3 = \underline{\hspace{2cm}}$$

$$10 = \underline{\hspace{2cm}} + \underline{\hspace{2cm}}$$

For the first problem, have children compare the picture with the equation and circle the total. For the second problem, say: *Fido has 5 treats. He eats 3 treats. How many treats does Fido have left?* Have children complete the equation. For the bottom problem, have children draw more squares to show 10. Then have them complete the equation.

| 3 | 4 − 2 | 2 + 1 | 2 + 2 | 4 − 1 | 5 − 2 |

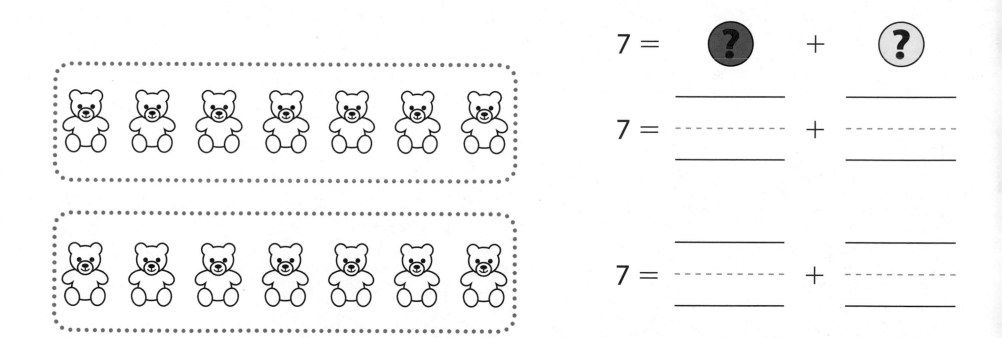

$$7 = \enspace \boxed{?} \enspace + \enspace \boxed{?}$$

$$7 = \underline{\hspace{2cm}} + \underline{\hspace{2cm}}$$

$$7 = \underline{\hspace{2cm}} + \underline{\hspace{2cm}}$$

For the top problem, have children color all the facts that equal the number on the left and mark an X on those that do not. For the bottom problem, say: *Leo has 7 bear counters. Some are blue, and the rest are yellow.*

How many could there be of each color? For each set, have children circle two groups. Then have children complete each equation to match.

$2 + 2 =$ _____

$10 - 9 =$ _____

Have children solve problems and complete equations. For the top problem, say: *Two dogs are at the park. Two more dogs join them. How many dogs are there in all?* Then have children write the total to complete the equation. For the bottom problem, have children cross out the number of fingers being taken away. Have them count and write the number of fingers left to complete the equation.

Show What You Know

Have children draw to show what they know about numbers 11–100. Tell children that after they have completed the unit, they will draw to show what they learned.

Build Your Vocabulary

My Math Words

My Academic Words

☐ explore   ☐ participate

_____

_ _

We like to _____ when we go for walks.

_____

_ _

We take turns and we all _____ in class.

Have children gather more than 10 counters. Ask them to count and place 10 of the counters in the first box and the rest in the second box. Ask children to tell how many groups of tens and how many ones they have. Review *My Academic Words* and complete the activity with children.

Understand Teen Numbers

Dear Family,

This week your child is exploring teen numbers.

Teen numbers are the numbers 11 to 19. As your child explores groups of 11 to 19 objects, he or she will learn to recognize that teen numbers are made up of a ten and some more. For example, 16 can be thought of as 10 and 6 more.

This understanding helps make the connection between teen numbers and the amounts they represent, which is important for future work with greater numbers in our place-value system.

In class, your child may model teen numbers with connecting cubes and/or 10-frames. When modeling with connecting cubes, teen numbers can be shown as a group of 10 connected cubes and some extra single cubes. When modeling with 10-frames, teen numbers can be shown by filling one 10-frame with counters and then placing the extra counters on a second 10-frame to show 10 and more.

16

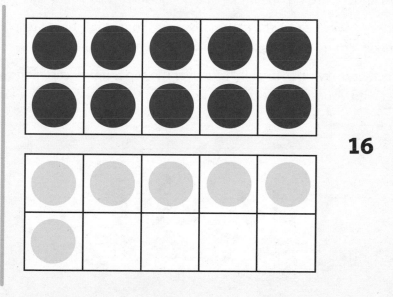

16

Invite your child to share what he or she knows about teen numbers by doing the following activity together.

Activity Exploring Teen Numbers

Do this activity with your child to understand teen numbers.

Materials 9 index cards or small pieces of paper

Make teen number cards for this activity by writing the numbers 11 to 19 on index cards or small pieces of paper. (You may want to keep these cards to reuse.) Place the cards facedown in a pile.

Tell your child that you will work together to show teen numbers with the fingers on your hands and your child's hands.

• Say: *Let us show 14. I will start by using my fingers to count 10.*

• After you count and display 10 fingers, have your child continue counting with his or her own fingers, raising one finger at a time until he or she reaches 14.

• Ask: *To make 14, we need 10 and how many more?* Your child should respond that you need 4 more to make 14.

Repeat the activity, having your child turn over the top number card and working together to show the teen number with your fingers. Continue until all the number cards have been used.

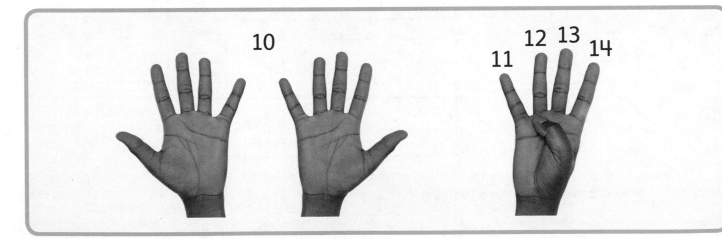

Explore Teen Numbers

Try It

Learning Target

- Compose and decompose numbers from 11 to 19 into ten ones and some further ones, and record each composition or decomposition by a drawing or equation; understand that these numbers are composed of ten ones and one, two, three, four, five, six, seven, eight, or nine ones.

SMP 1, 2, 3, 4, 5, 6, 7

🧰 Math Toolkit
- counters 🖱

Have children show teen numbers using fingers. As a class, rote count to 20, having children point to each number as they count. Pose the question: *Can I show 11 with my fingers? Why not?* Prompt children to recognize that two people can show 11 fingers. Have children work in pairs. Pose the question: *How many extra fingers do we need to make 12?* Say: *To make 12, we need all 10 fingers and 2 extra fingers.* Repeat for other teen numbers.

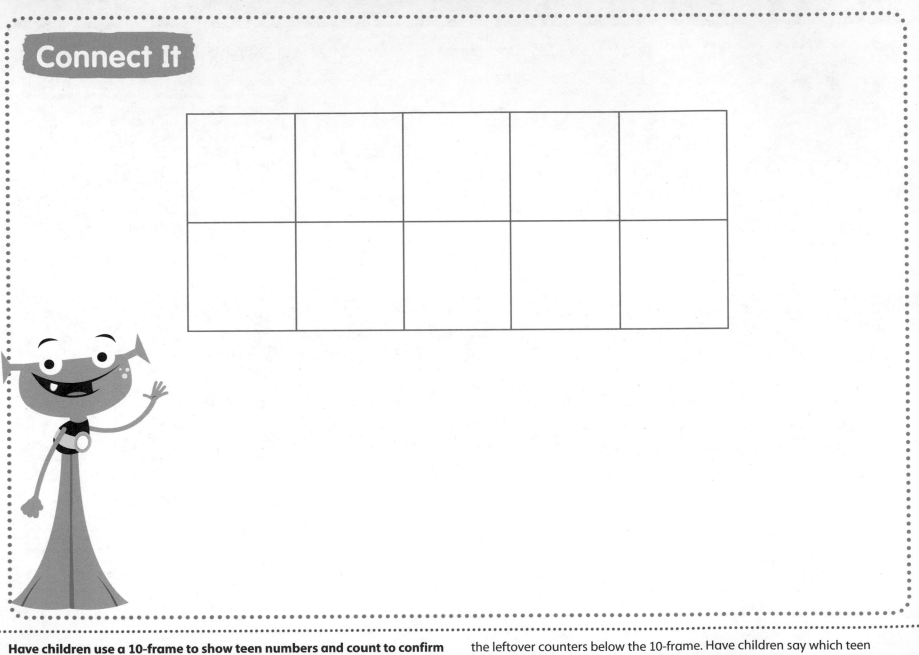

Connect It

Have children use a 10-frame to show teen numbers and count to confirm there are 10 and some more ones. Provide pairs of children with between 11 and 19 counters. Have children fill the 10-frame with counters and place the leftover counters below the 10-frame. Have children say which teen number they think they have made. Ask: *How did you decide?* Then have children count to verify.

514   Lesson 26 Understand Teen Numbers

Prepare for Teen Numbers

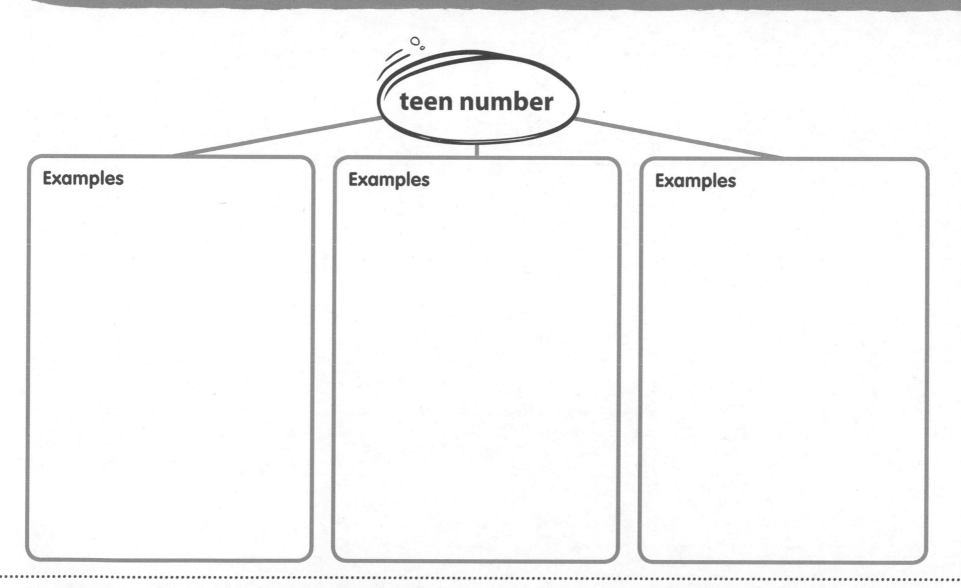

teen number

Examples

Examples

Examples

Have children show the meaning of the term *teen number*. Have children fill in each of the boxes to show the meaning of the term *teen number*. Tell children that they can use words, numbers, and pictures. Encourage them to show as many ideas as they can.

Have children use a 10-frame to show a teen number and count to confirm there are 10 and some more ones. Provide children with 13 small objects. Have children fill the 10-frame with objects and place the leftover objects below the 10-frame. Have children say which teen number they think they have made. Ask: *How did you decide?* Then have children count to verify.

Develop Understanding of Teen Numbers

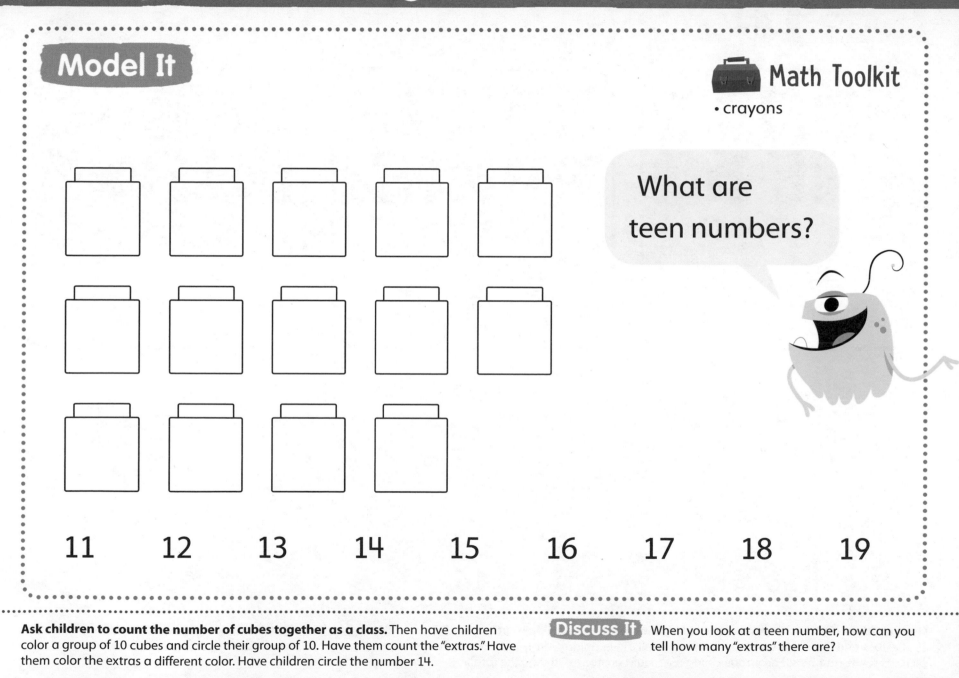

Model It

Math Toolkit
• crayons

What are teen numbers?

11   12   13   14   15   16   17   18   19

Ask children to count the number of cubes together as a class. Then have children color a group of 10 cubes and circle their group of 10. Have them count the "extras." Have them color the extras a different color. Have children circle the number 14.

Discuss It When you look at a teen number, how can you tell how many "extras" there are?

Connect It

18

15

16

Have children match groups of cubes to teen numbers. Have children circle the group of 10 cubes and then count to find how many in all. Have children draw lines to match the pictures to the numbers. Encourage children to count on from 10 to find the total.

Discuss It How does finding the group of 10 help find which teen number to match to?

Think About Teen Numbers

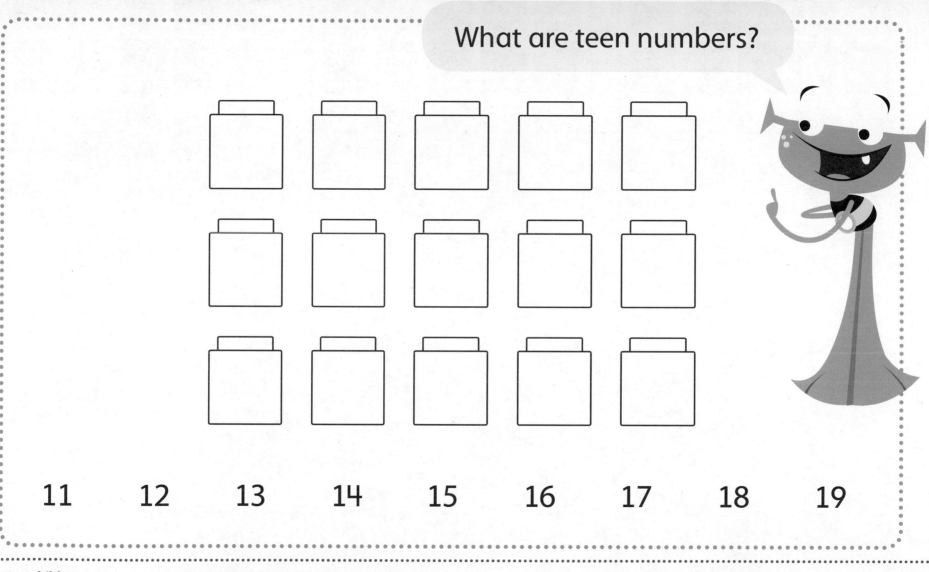

What are teen numbers?

11   12   13   14   15   16   17   18   19

Have children color a group of 10 cubes red. Then have children color the "extras" a different color. Have children circle the total number of colored cubes.

14   17   13

Have children match groups of cubes to teen numbers. Have children circle the group of 10 cubes and then count to find how many in all. Have children draw lines to match the pictures to the numbers. Encourage children to count on from 10 to find the total.

Develop Understanding of Teen Numbers

🧰 **Math Toolkit**
• connecting cubes

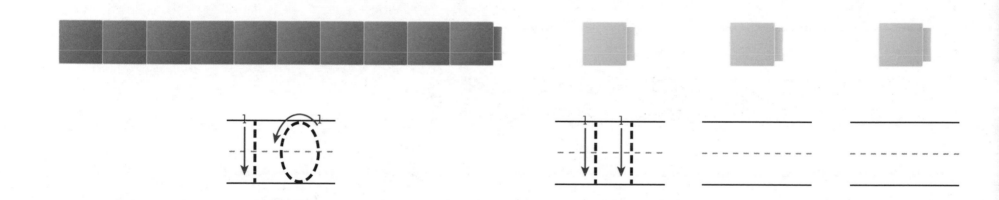

Have children count on from 10 to find a teen number. Have children count how many are in the cube train and then write the number. Ask children to point to the next cube and count one more than 10. Continue counting the cubes and then write the numbers.

Discuss It How do you know what number to count after 10 cubes? Do you need to count 10 cubes each time?

Lesson 26 Understand Teen Numbers **521**

Connect It

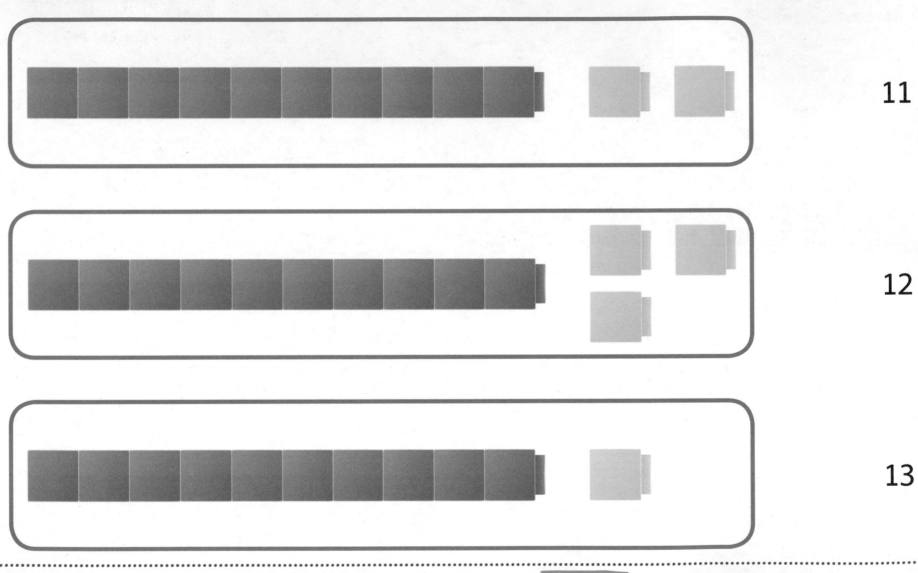

11

12

13

Have children match teen numbers to cubes that show the same number. Have children describe the cubes in each group as 10 and some number of extras. Then have children draw lines to match the pictures to the numbers.

Discuss It How can you check your answers to make sure the picture matches the number you chose?

Practice Teen Numbers

Example

14

15

16

Have children match groups of cubes to teen numbers. Have children describe the cubes in each group as 10 and some number of extras. For example, to describe the cubes in the top box, children might say: *There are* *10 cubes and 4 extras*. Then have children draw lines to match the pictures to the numbers.

18

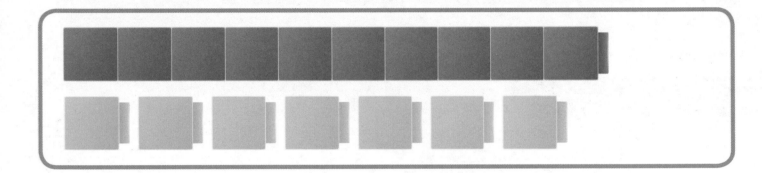

17

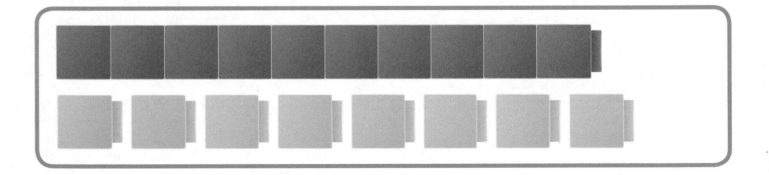

19

Have children match groups of cubes to teen numbers. Have children describe the cubes in each group as 10 and some number of extras. Then have children draw lines to match the pictures to the numbers.

Refine Ideas About Teen Numbers

Apply It

Math Toolkit
• connecting cubes

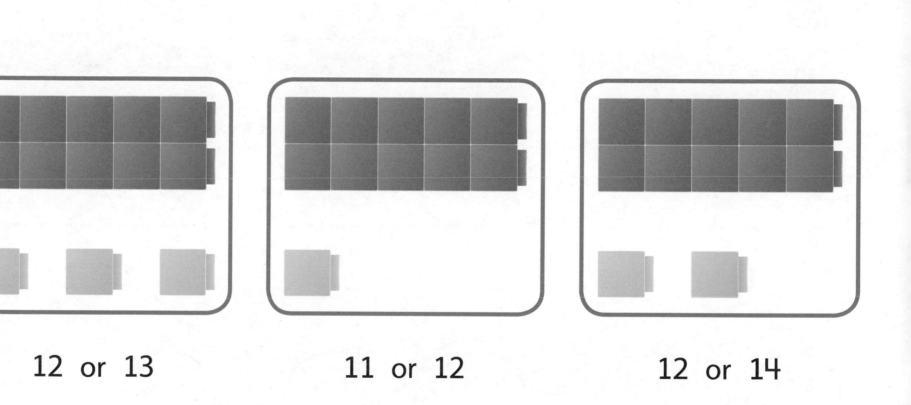

12 or 13   11 or 12   12 or 14

Have children use cubes to model each group of cubes shown at the top of the page. Then have them circle the number modeled by each group.

Discuss It How does having a group of 10 make it easier to find which number the model shows?

Connect It

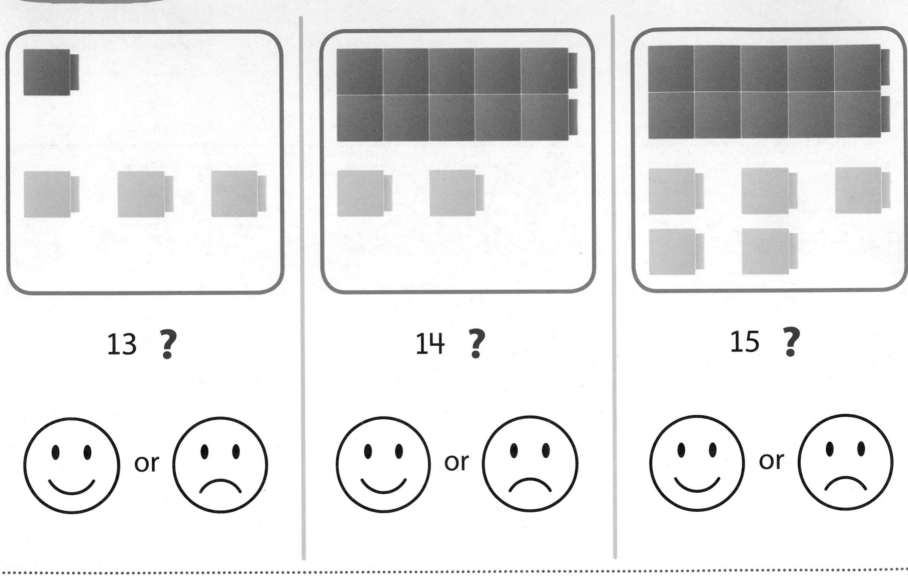

13 **?**

14 **?**

15 **?**

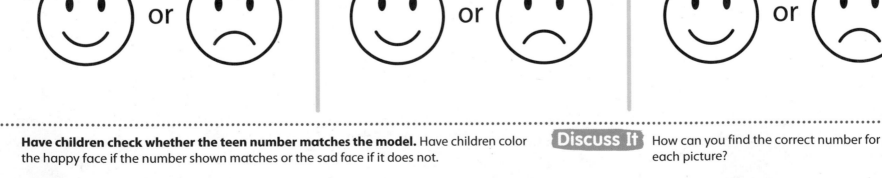

Have children check whether the teen number matches the model. Have children color the happy face if the number shown matches or the sad face if it does not.

Discuss It How can you find the correct number for each picture?

Count Teen Numbers

Dear Family,

This week your child is building counting skills with teen numbers and the number 20.

LESSON 27

The lesson provides practice counting groups of 11 to 20 objects using a variety of strategies for keeping track of what has been counted. For example, your child may point to or move each object as it is counted or mark each object in a picture as it is counted.

There will also continue to be a focus on understanding teen numbers as 10 and some more. For example, you can count pictures of objects by circling a group of 10 objects first and then counting the "extras" beyond 10 to find how many more there are.

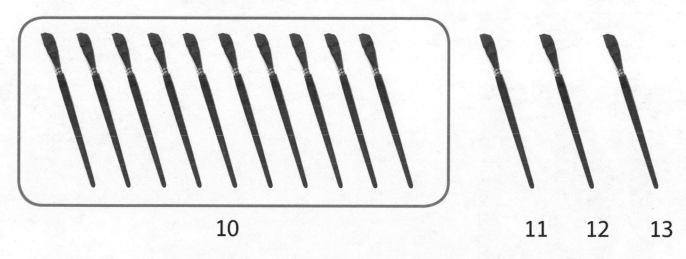

10   11   12   13

Organizing teen numbers this way when counting them will help your child prepare for work with numbers beyond 20, which can be represented as groups of tens and ones.

This lesson also includes practice with writing teen numbers and the number 20.

Invite your child to share what he or she knows about teen numbers and the number 20 by doing the following activity together.

Activity Counting and Writing Teen Numbers

Do this activity with your child to count teen numbers.

Materials shallow plastic container or shallow metal baking pan, $\frac{1}{2}$ to 1 cup of salt or sugar, colored paper (optional)

Your child will use his or her finger to practice writing the numbers 11 to 20 in a layer of salt or sugar.

- Pour $\frac{1}{2}$ to 1 cup of salt or sugar into a shallow plastic container or shallow metal pan. Spread out the salt or sugar into a fairly thin layer.

- Have your child use his or her finger to practice writing the numbers 11 to 20 in the salt or sugar. (Note: If you are working on a white table, you may wish to place a sheet of colored paper under the container so that the numbers are easier to see.)

- Show your child how to wipe a hand across the salt or sugar each time he or she is ready to write a new number.

In addition to doing the above activity, practice counting 11 to 20 objects with your child whenever you can. For example, encourage your child to count eggs in a carton, raisins on a plate, or crayons in a box.

Try It

15

🧰 **Math Toolkit**

- counters

Have children build and count a group of 15 objects and read the corresponding number. Say: *We need to make 3 relay teams. 5 children are on each team. How many children do we need?* Arrange 3 groups of 5 children in a 3 × 5 array. Together, count each child. Then have children count the squares. Ask children to circle 2 groups of 5 and say how many are in the circled group. Ask children to count the number of squares again, starting from 10.

Connect It

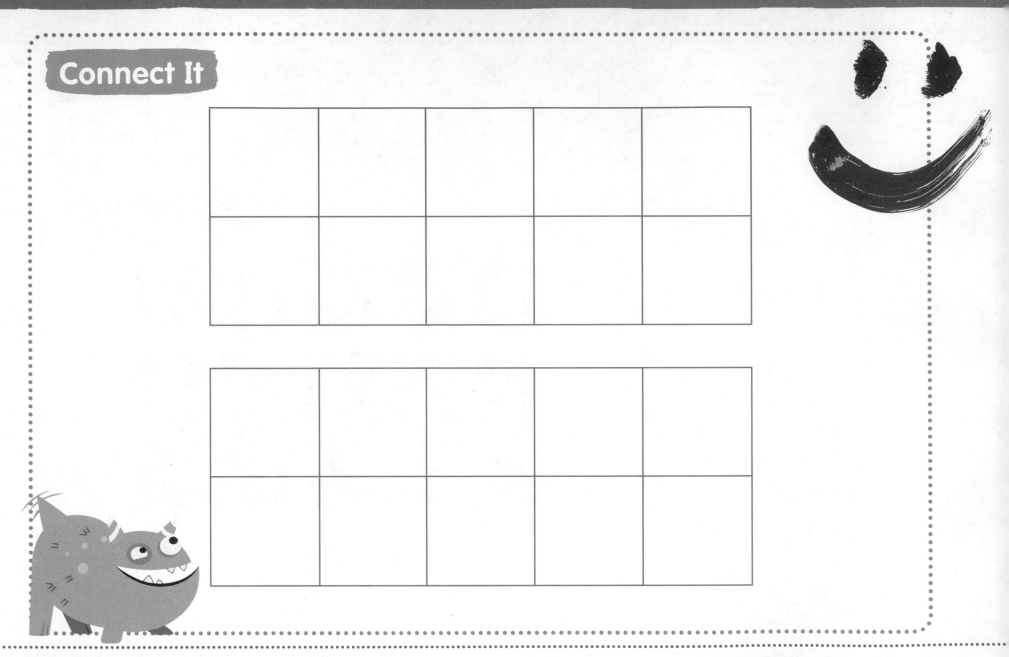

Have children build and count groups of objects from 11 to 20. Have children place 10 counters on the top 10-frame. Prompt children to recognize this as a group of 10. Have children place 1 counter on the bottom 10-frame.

Ask: *How many?* Display the number card for 11. Children continue adding 1 counter at a time to the bottom 10-frame and counting until there are 20 counters. Display the corresponding number card each time.

Prepare for Counting Teen Numbers

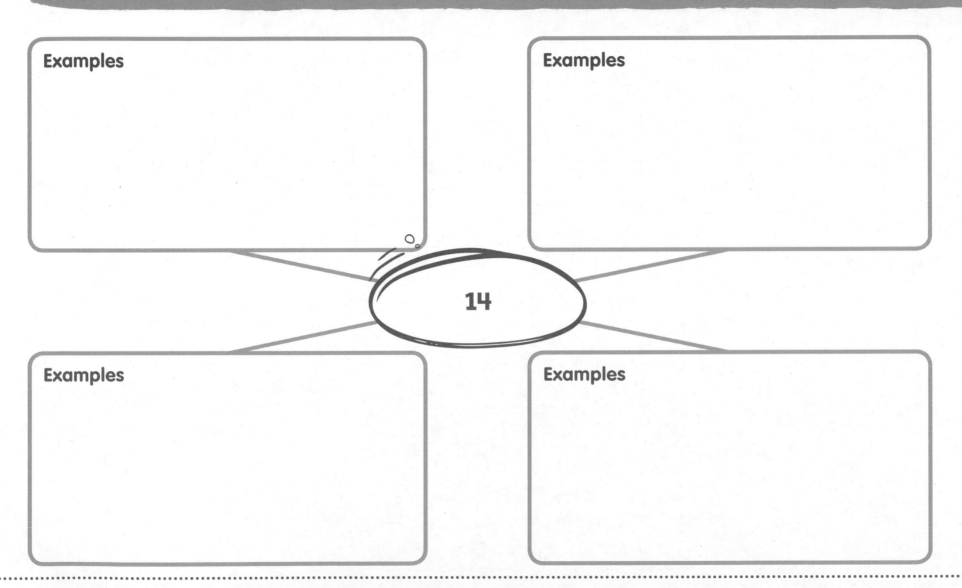

Examples

Examples

14

Examples

Examples

Have children show the meaning of 14. Have children fill in each of the boxes to show the meaning of 14. Tell children that they can use words, numbers, and pictures. Encourage them to show as many ideas as they can.

Have children build and count a group of 16 objects. Have children place 10 small objects on the top 10-frame. Prompt children to recognize this as a group of 10. Have children place 6 small objects on the bottom 10-frame. Ask: *How many?*

Develop Counting Teen Numbers

Ask children to describe the quantities they see in the picture. Together count the 10 blue paint jars and then find how many jars on the top shelf, how many tall jars, and how many jars without a label. Have children find and circle a group of 18.

Discuss It How can you keep track of which things you have counted?

Connect It

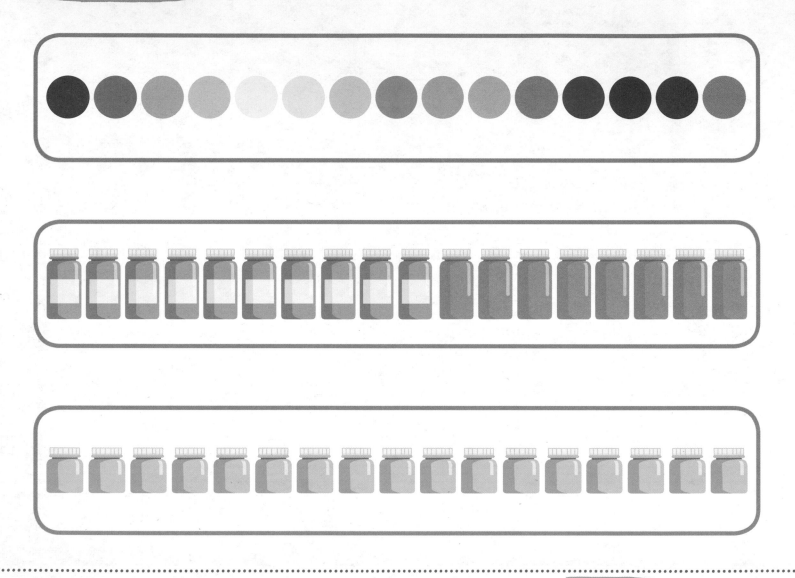

17

15

18

Have children match groups of objects to teen numbers that tell how many are in that group. Have children count the number of objects in each group. Then have children draw lines to match the pictures to the numbers.

Discuss It How do you know you have the correct total for a group of objects? How could you check?

Practice Counting Teen Numbers

Have children color a group of 15 paint jars, using green for 10 of them and orange for the extras. Tell children to color a group of 12 watercolors in the tray, using green for 10 of them and purple for 2 of them. Have children color the rest of the picture.

13

11

14

Have children match groups of objects to teen numbers that tell how many are in that group. Have children count the number of objects in each group. Then have children draw lines to match the pictures to the numbers.

536   **Lesson 27**   Count Teen Numbers

Develop Counting Teen Numbers

Try It

Math Toolkit
• counters

Have children make and write teen numbers. Give each child 20 counters. Show a dot card from 11 to 20. Have children show the number using counters on the 10-frames, filling the top frame first, and then write the number. Repeat with other numbers from 11 to 20.

Discuss It What do you notice about the top 10-frame each time?

Connect It

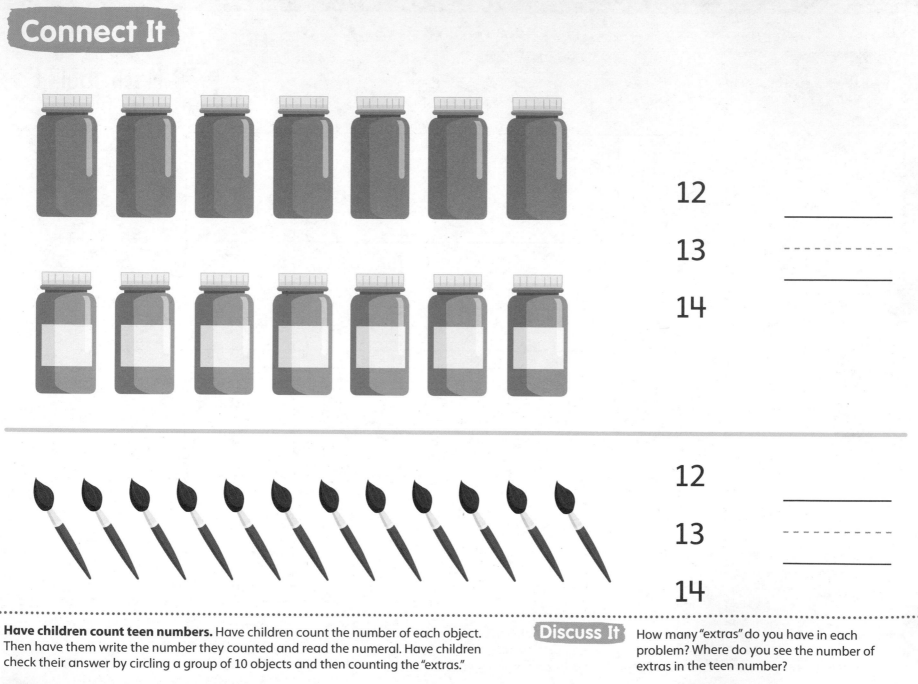

12

13

14

12

13

14

Have children count teen numbers. Have children count the number of each object. Then have them write the number they counted and read the numeral. Have children check their answer by circling a group of 10 objects and then counting the "extras."

Discuss It How many "extras" do you have in each problem? Where do you see the number of extras in the teen number?

Practice Counting Teen Numbers

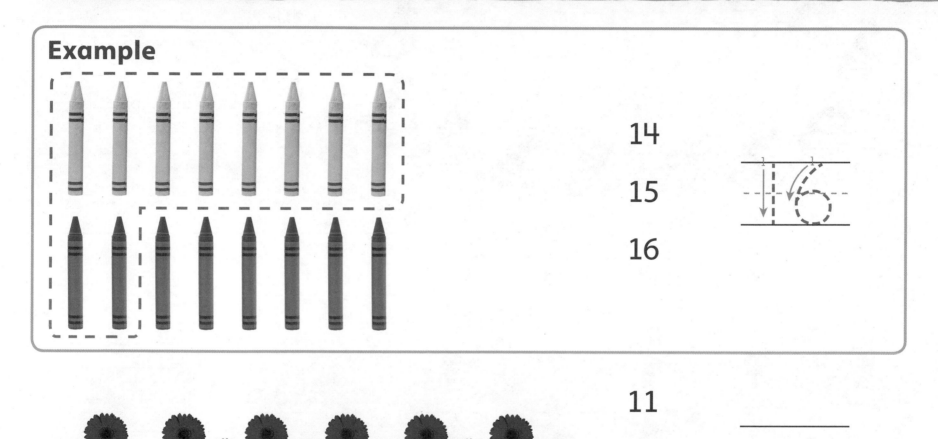

Example

14

15

16

11

12

13

Have children count teen numbers. Have children count the objects in each problem. Then have them write the number counted. Have children check their answer by circling a group of 10 objects and then counting the "extras."

14

15

16

_____

- - - - - - -

_____

18

19

20

_____

- - - - - - -

_____

Have children count teen numbers. Have children count the objects in each problem. Then have them write the number counted. Have children check their answer by circling a group of 10 objects and then counting the "extras."

Apply It

🧰 **Math Toolkit**
• counters

Have children find 1 more than a teen number. Give each child a set of 20 counters. Hold up a number card from 11 to 19. Have children show 1 more than the number using counters on the 10-frames and then write the new number. Repeat with other numbers from 11 to 19.

Discuss It How else could you find 1 more than a teen number?

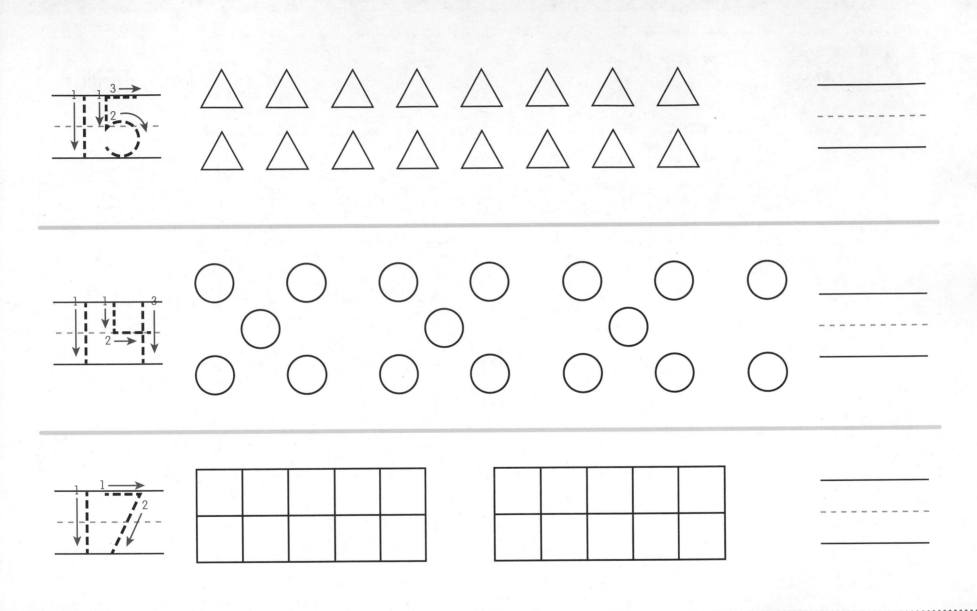

Have children trace each teen number and then count out that number of objects and find 1 more. Remind children to lightly mark each object as they count to keep track and then color them. Then have children write the number that is 1 more and color 1 more.

Discuss It Work with a partner. Did you and your partner color the same shapes in each picture? Does it matter which shapes you color?

Practice Counting Teen Numbers

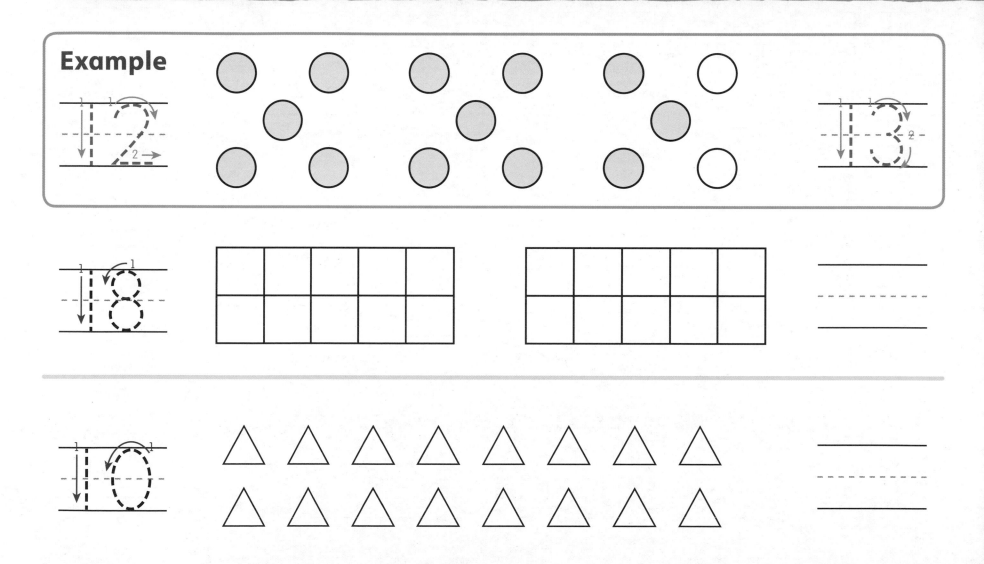

Have children trace each teen number and then count out that number of objects and find 1 more. Remind children to lightly mark each object as they count to keep track and then color them. Then have children write the number that is 1 more and color 1 more.

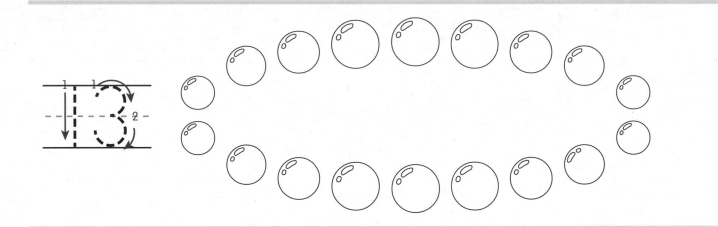

Have children trace each teen number and then count out that number of objects and find 1 more. Remind children to lightly mark each object as they count to keep track and then color them. Then have children write the number that is 1 more and color 1 more.

Refine Counting Teen Numbers

Apply It

🧰 Math Toolkit
• counters 🖱

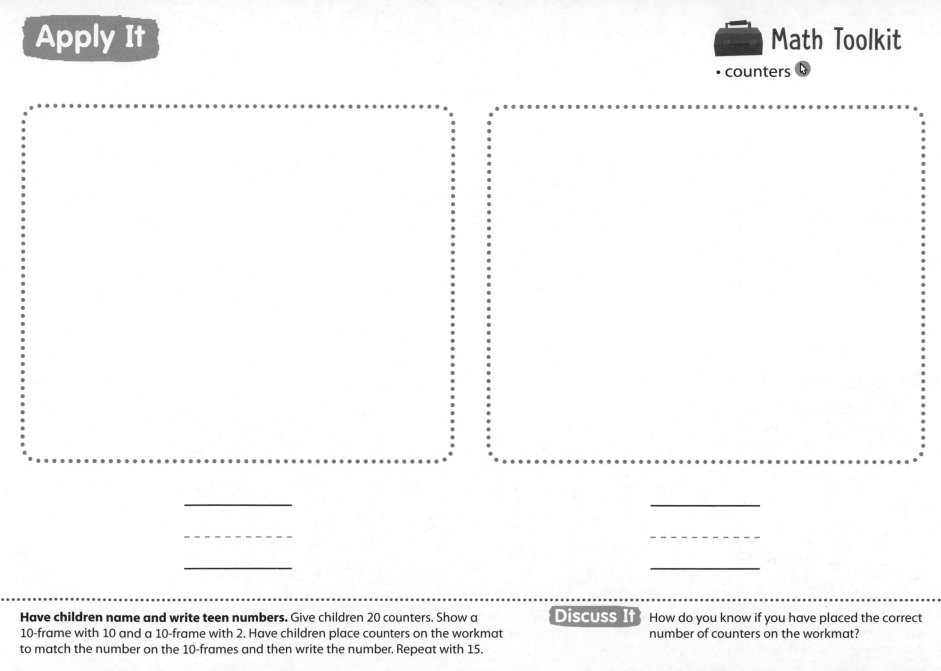

Have children name and write teen numbers. Give children 20 counters. Show a 10-frame with 10 and a 10-frame with 2. Have children place counters on the workmat to match the number on the 10-frames and then write the number. Repeat with 15.

Discuss It How do you know if you have placed the correct number of counters on the workmat?

13 13 _____ _____

Draw 13.

Have children trace and write 13 and then draw 13 objects. Tell children to trace and write the number 13. Have children draw 13 objects. You may want to suggest objects that are easy for children to draw, such as circles or happy faces.

Discuss It How did you know when to stop drawing? How would your picture be different if you were asked to draw 14?

546 Lesson 27 Count Teen Numbers

©Curriculum Associates, LLC   Copying is not permitted.

Make Teen Numbers

Dear Family,

This week your child is learning to make teen numbers by combining a group of 10 and some more.

The lesson uses pictures, 10-frames, number bonds, and equations to show the numbers 11 to 19 as a group of 10 and some extras. For example, the teen number 16 can be shown on 10-frames by placing 10 counters on one frame and 6 counters on the other.

10-Frames

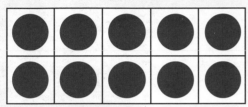 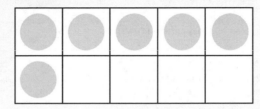

The group of 10 and group of 6 that make 16 can also be represented on a number bond. A **number bond** is a model showing the parts that make up a number. Using number bonds will help your child think about how to build and break apart numbers, which will be important for future work with addition and subtraction. The number bond below shows that 10 and 6 are parts of 16. An **equation** shows this using numbers and symbols.

Number Bond

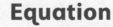

Equation

$$16 = 10 + 6$$

Invite your child to share what he or she knows about making teen numbers by doing the following activity together.

Activity Making Teen Numbers

Do this activity with your child to make teen numbers.

Materials 9 index cards or small pieces of paper, 19 small objects (such as cereal pieces or pasta shapes), full-sized paper, pencil

Make teen number cards by writing the numbers 11 to 19 on index cards or small pieces of paper, or use the cards from the Lesson 25 activity. Place the cards facedown in a pile.

Draw a large number bond that covers a full sheet of paper. Have your child complete each of the following steps to practice showing teen numbers as 10 and some more.

• Turn over a teen number card. Count out that number of objects and place them in the top box of the number bond.

• Move 10 of the objects from the top box of the number bond into the bottom left box of the number bond.

• Move the rest of the objects from the top box into the bottom right box.

• Place the number card in the top box of the number bond.

• Encourage your child to describe the number bond in terms of 10 and some more. For example, *10 and 4 more make 14*.

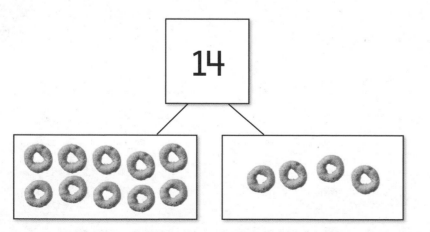

Explore Making Teen Numbers

Try It

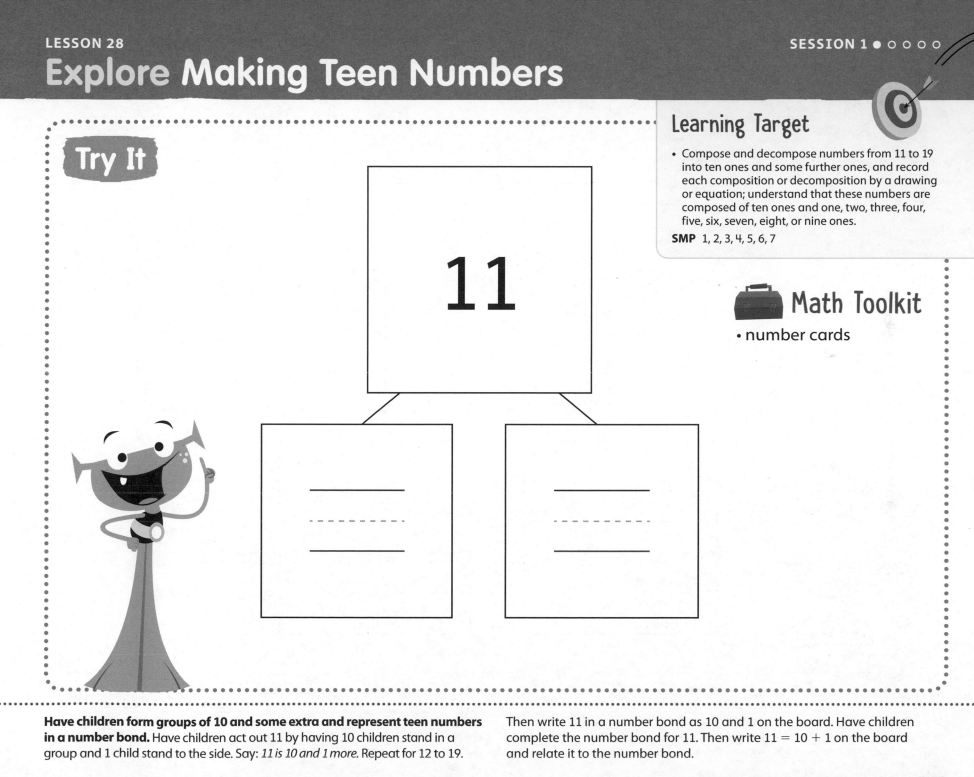

Learning Target

- Compose and decompose numbers from 11 to 19 into ten ones and some further ones, and record each composition or decomposition by a drawing or equation; understand that these numbers are composed of ten ones and one, two, three, four, five, six, seven, eight, or nine ones.

SMP 1, 2, 3, 4, 5, 6, 7

Math Toolkit

- number cards

Have children form groups of 10 and some extra and represent teen numbers in a number bond. Have children act out 11 by having 10 children stand in a group and 1 child stand to the side. Say: *11 is 10 and 1 more.* Repeat for 12 to 19.

Then write 11 in a number bond as 10 and 1 on the board. Have children complete the number bond for 11. Then write $11 = 10 + 1$ on the board and relate it to the number bond.

Connect It

Have children represent teen numbers 12 to 19 in a number bond. Write the number bond for 12 as 10 and 2 on the board. Have children use number cards to show 12 as 10 and 2 in the number bond. Together, say: *12 is 10 and 2 more.* Write 12 = 10 + 2 on the board next to the number bond. Prompt children to see how the number bond and equation are related. Repeat for the numbers 13 to 19.

Name: _____

Prepare for Making Teen Numbers

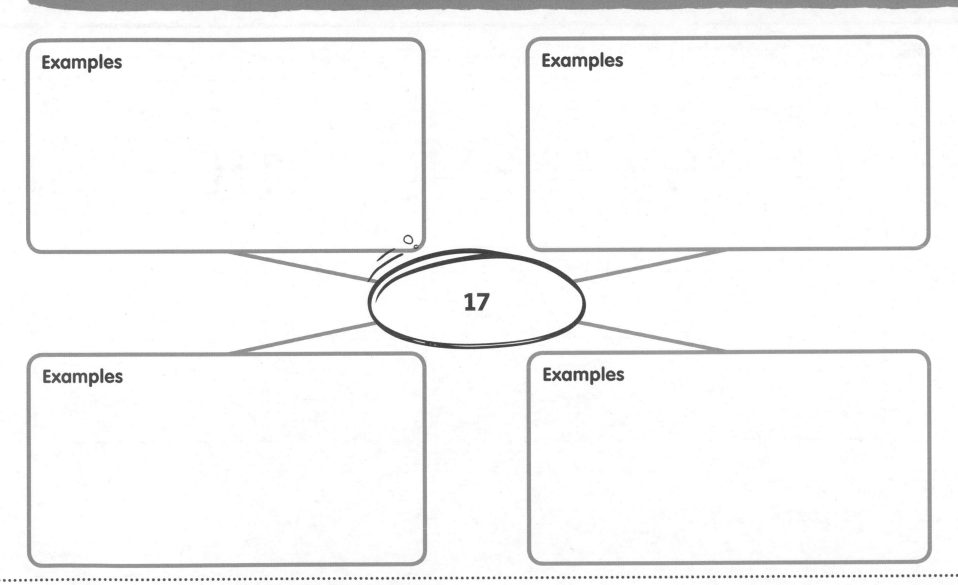

Examples

Examples

17

Examples

Examples

Have children show the meaning of 17. Have children fill in each of the boxes to show the meaning of 17. Tell children that they can use words, numbers, and pictures. Encourage them to show as many ideas as they can.

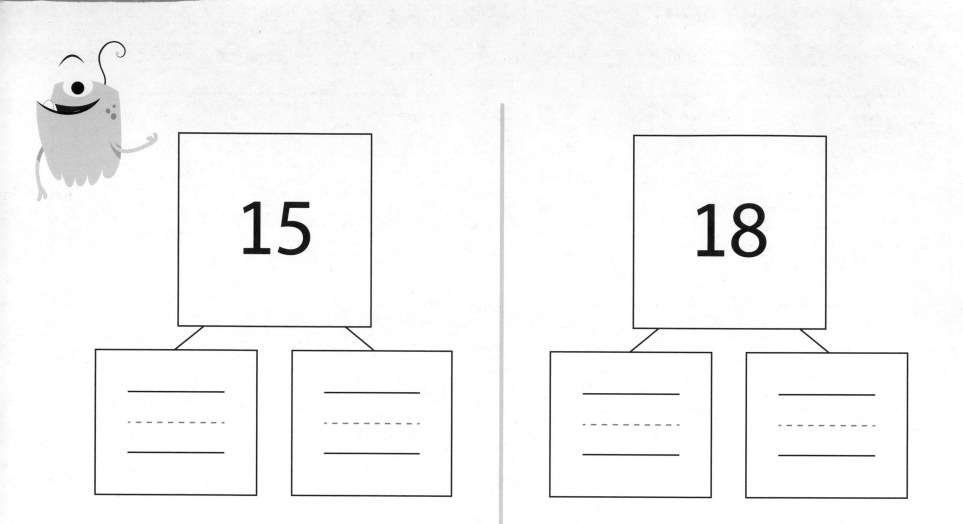

Have children represent the teen numbers 15 and 18 in number bonds.
Have children show 15 as 10 and some extras in the first number bond.
Together, say: *15 is 10 and 5 more*. Repeat for the number 18.

552   Lesson 28 Make Teen Numbers

Develop Making Teen Numbers

Encourage children to count the number of brown bears, bears with hats, and bears with bows. Identify the number in each group as 10 with some extras. Have children draw a brown bear in the bottom right and tell how many brown bears there are now.

Discuss It How can you know there are more than 10 brown bears before you count them?

Connect It

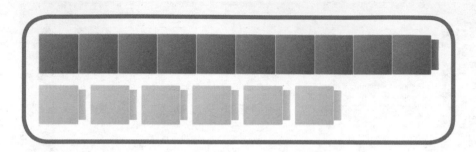

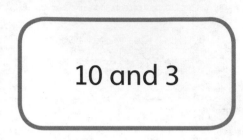

10 and 3

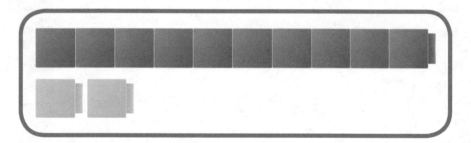

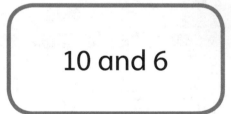

10 and 6

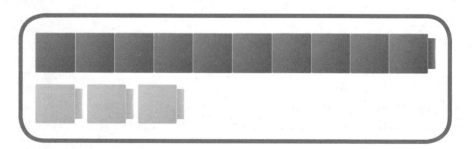

10 and 2

Have children draw lines to match each group of cubes to the number pair that describes the group. Then have children describe the cubes as 10 and some extras and say the teen number. For example, children might say: *10 cubes and 6 extras make 16.*

Discuss It What is the same about the three groups of cubes? What is different?

Practice Making Teen Numbers

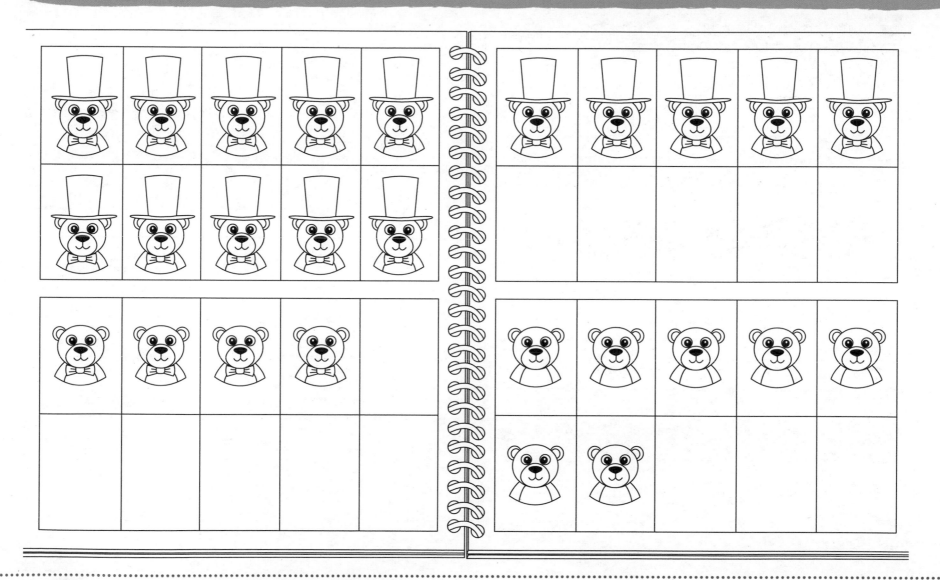

Have children color the bears in the top left 10-frame brown. Then have children color a second group of bears brown to make a total of 15 brown bears. Have children color the rest of the bears with different colors.

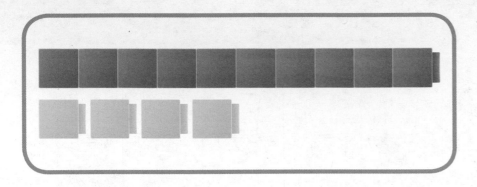

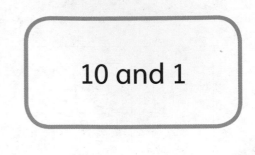

10 and 1

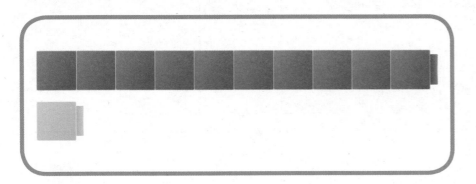

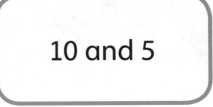

10 and 5

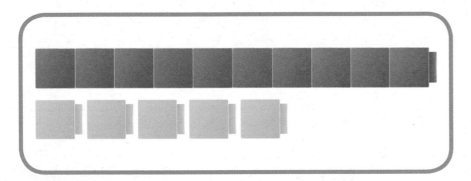

10 and 4

Have children draw lines to match each group of cubes to the number pair that describes the group. Then have children describe the cubes as 10 and some extras and say the teen number. For example, children might say: *10 cubes and 4 extras make 14.*

Develop Making Teen Numbers

Try It

Math Toolkit
• counters

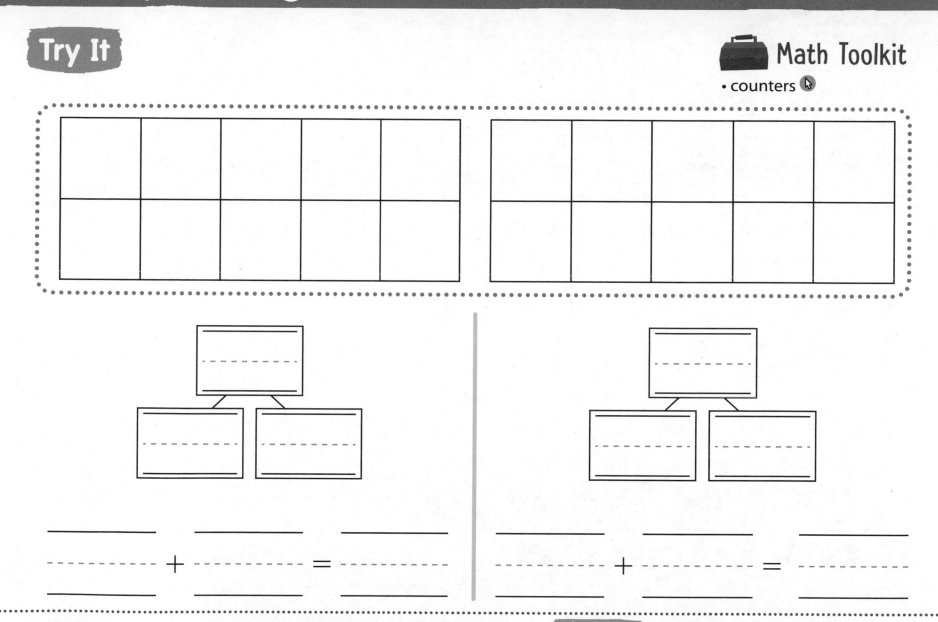

Show children two 10-frame cards to make a teen number. Have children show the number with counters on the 10-frames and then write that number in a number bond and in an equation. Repeat but have children write the equation before the number bond.

Discuss It How do you know which numbers to write in the number bond? How do you know which numbers to write in the equation?

Connect It

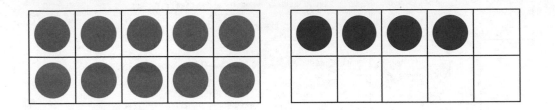

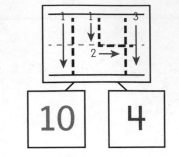

10   4

10   5

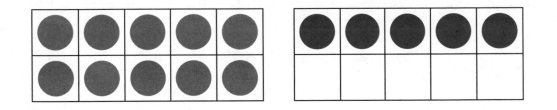

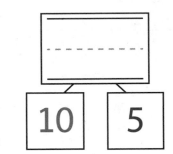

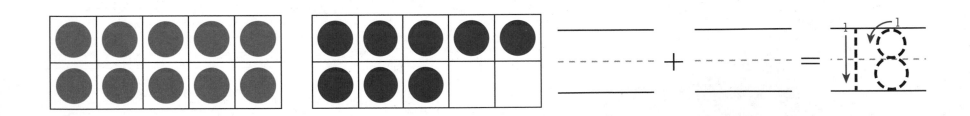

_____ + _____ = 18

Have children show teen numbers. Have children write the total number of counters at the top of the number bond. Have children complete the equation in the last problem.

Discuss It What are some things that are the same in every problem? Why do you think those things are the same?

Name: _____

Practice Making Teen Numbers

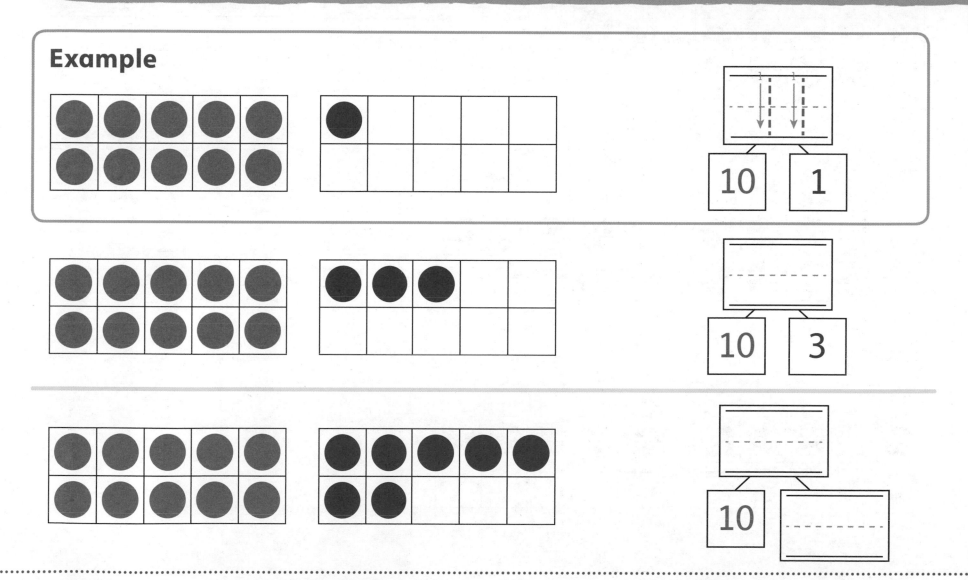

Example

Have children use 10-frames and number bonds to show teen numbers.
Have children look at the number of blue and red counters and write the total number of counters at the top of the number bond. In the last problem, have them complete the number bond. Have children describe the number as 10 and some extras. For example, to describe 11, children might say: *11 is 10 and 1 extra.*

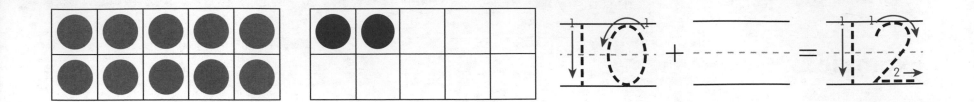

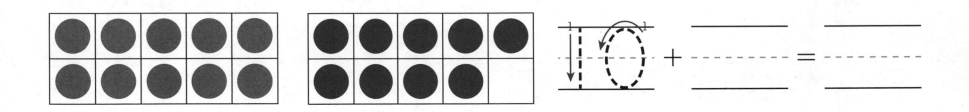

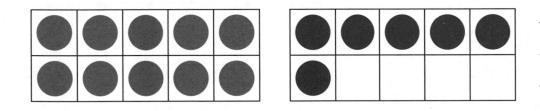

Have children use 10-frames and equations to show teen numbers. Have children write the number of counters in each frame and the total number of counters in the equations. Then have children express the number as 10 and some extras.

Refine Making Teen Numbers

Apply It

Math Toolkit

• counters

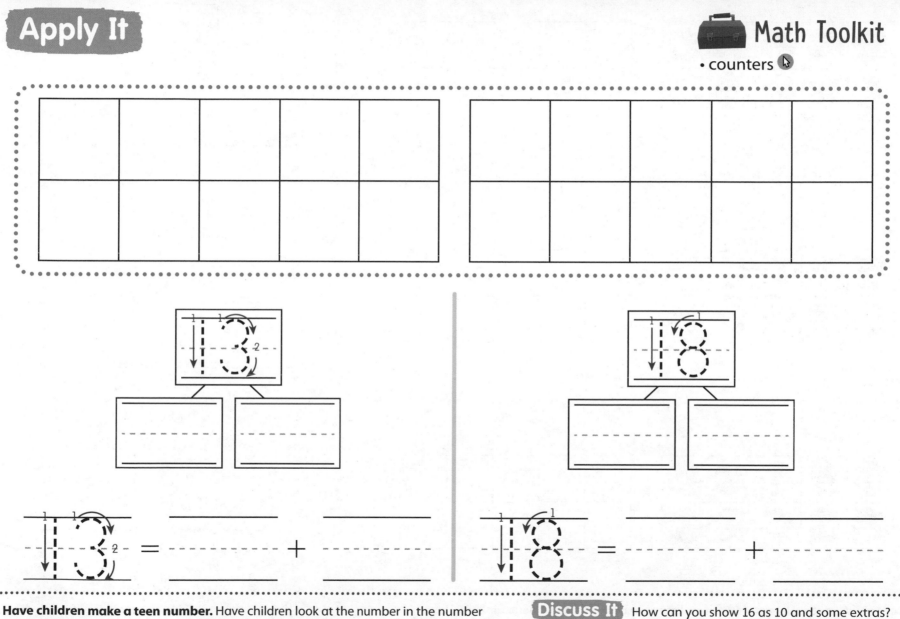

Have children make a teen number. Have children look at the number in the number bond and equation and make it on the 10-frames using counters. Then have children complete the number bond and equation. Repeat.

Discuss It How can you show 16 as 10 and some extras?

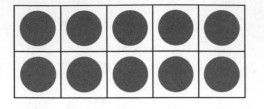

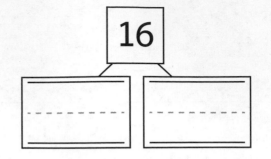

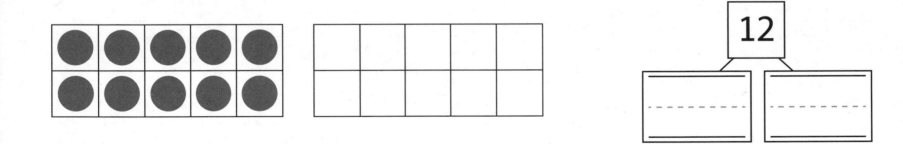

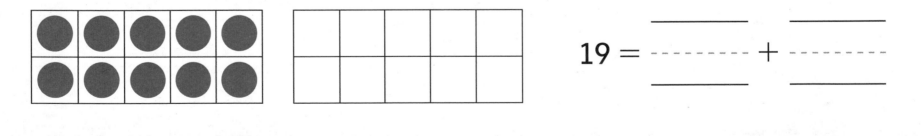

Have children complete 10-frames and number bonds to show teen numbers. Have children draw the counters needed to match the number in the number bond, then write the parts to complete the number bond. Have them complete the equation in the last problem.

Discuss It How did you decide how many counters to draw to finish each picture?

Practice Making Teen Numbers

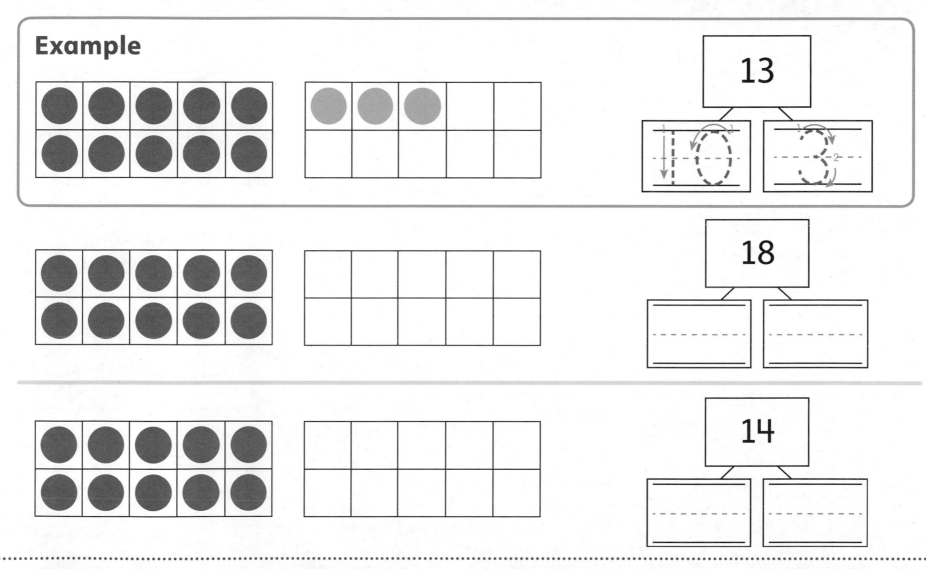

Example

13

18

14

Have children complete 10-frames and number bonds to show teen numbers. Have children draw the counters needed to match the number in the number bond. Then have children write the parts to complete the number bond.

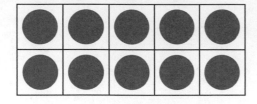   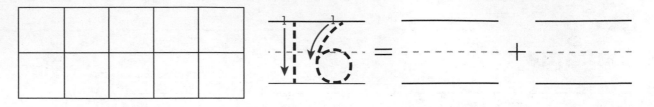

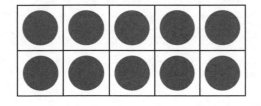   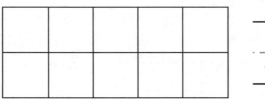   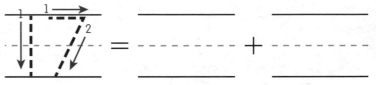

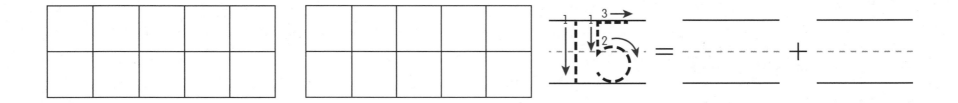

Apply It

🧰 **Math Toolkit**
• counters

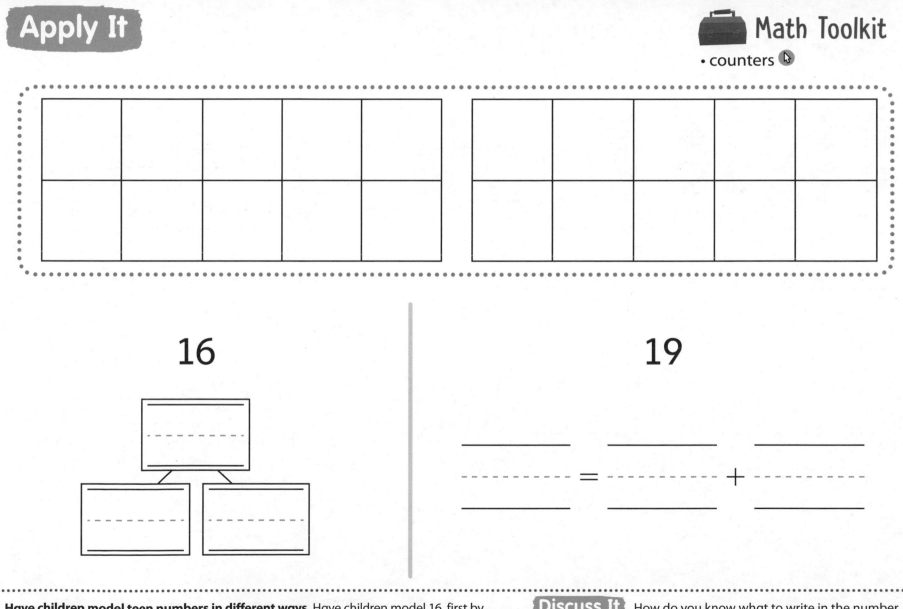

16

19

Have children model teen numbers in different ways. Have children model 16, first by placing counters on the 10-frames and then by completing a number bond. Next, have children model 19 using 10-frames and an equation.

Discuss It How do you know what to write in the number bond and in the equation?

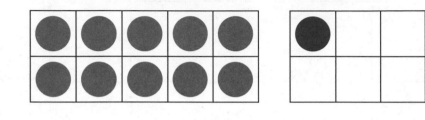

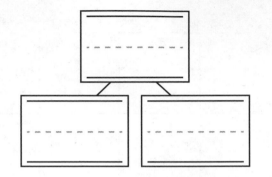

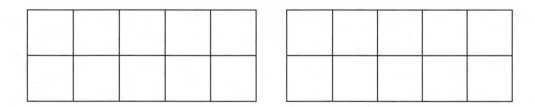

$$10 + 7 = \underline{}$$

Have children complete 10-frames, a number bond, and an equation to model teen numbers. In the first problem, have children use the 10-frames to complete the number bond. In the second problem, have them draw counters to match the equation, then write the total.

Discuss It Which problem was easier for you? Why?

Count to 100 by Tens

Dear Family,

This week your child is learning to count to 100 by tens.

Counting by tens involves reciting the multiples of 10 (10, 20, 30, 40, etc.) to 100. Learning to count by tens will help prepare your child for counting by ones across these numbers. For example, being able to recite *10, 20, 30* will help your child later count *19, 20, 21* and *29, 30, 31*.

Counting objects organized into groups of 10 helps to emphasize that each multiple of 10 is 10 more than the previous multiple of 10.

10   20   30   40   50

Each pot has 10 flowers.
You can count by tens to find
there are 50 flowers in all.

Your child will also practice counting by tens without objects or pictures.

Invite your child to share what he or she knows about counting to 100 by tens by doing the following activity together.

Counting to 100 by Tens

Do this activity with your child to count to 100 by tens.

Practice counting by tens with your child whenever you can: 10, 20, 30, 40, 50, 60, 70, 80, 90, 100! To help your child learn the sequence and to make practicing more fun, you can add motions as you count, such as clapping, marching, or tapping your toes as you say each number. You may want to have you and your child take turns choosing a motion to do.

If your child needs an extra challenge, count by tens in a four-number sequence and clap instead of saying one of the numbers. Then your child says the number that is missing. For example, say: *30, 40, [clap], 60.* Your child should say that 50 is the missing number.

"10, 20, 30, 40, 50, 60, 70, 80, 90, 100"

Explore Counting to 100 by Tens

Try It

Learning Targets

- Count to 100 by ones and by tens.
- Count forward beginning from a given number within the known sequence.

SMP 1, 2, 3, 4, 5, 6, 8

Math Toolkit

- connecting cubes

Have children build a 100-cube train from 10-cube trains. Place a piece of tape the length of 100 cubes on the floor. Ask: *How many cubes do you think will fit on this line? How could you count them?* Have each child build a 10-cube train.

Invite 10 children to place their trains on the tape. As each train is added, count the cubes by tens. Repeat with different children placing their trains.

Connect It

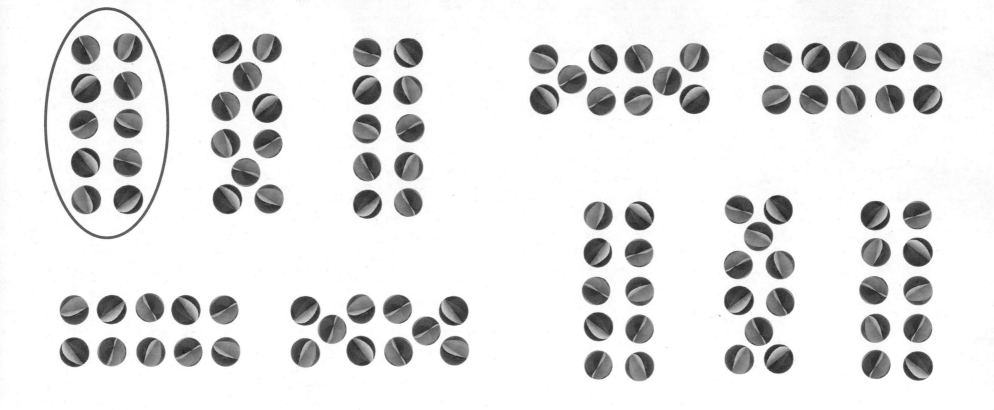

Have children use fingers to show groups of ten and then count to 100 by tens. Have 1 child show a group of 10 fingers to the class. Invite 9 more children to do the same. As a class, count the fingers by tens. Then count the circled marbles and identify them as a group of ten. Have children count and circle all the groups of 10. Ask: *How many marbles do you think there are in all?* Count by tens aloud together as children point to each group.

Prepare for Counting to 100 by Tens

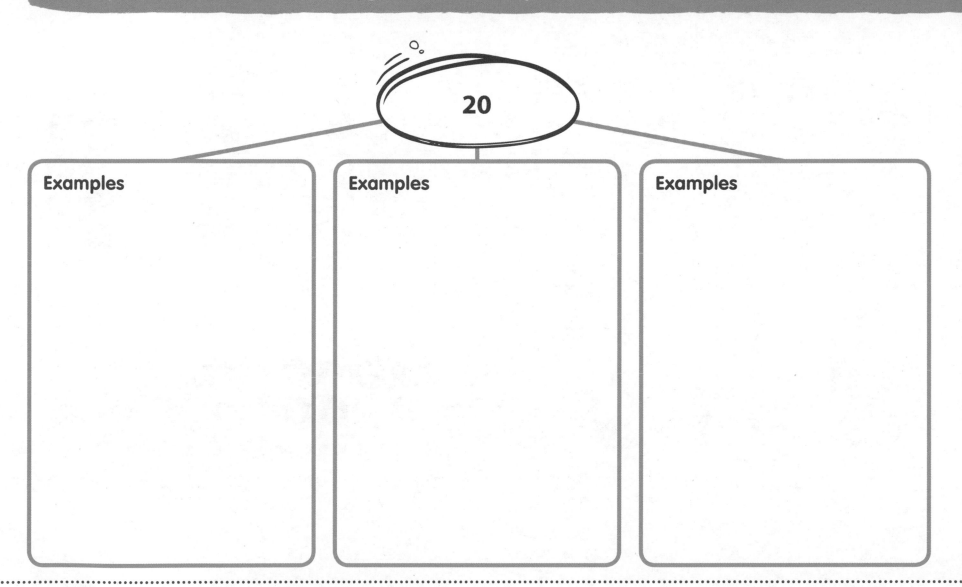

20

| Examples | Examples | Examples |

Have children show the meaning of 20. Have children fill in each of the boxes to show the meaning of 20. Tell children to use words, numbers, and pictures. Encourage them to show as many ideas as they can.

Have children count to 100 by tens. Have children count the circled beads and identify them as a group of ten. Have children count and circle all the groups of 10. Ask: *How many beads do you think there are in all?* Count by tens aloud together as children point to each group of beads.

572   Lesson 29 Count to 100 by Tens

Develop Counting to 100 by Tens

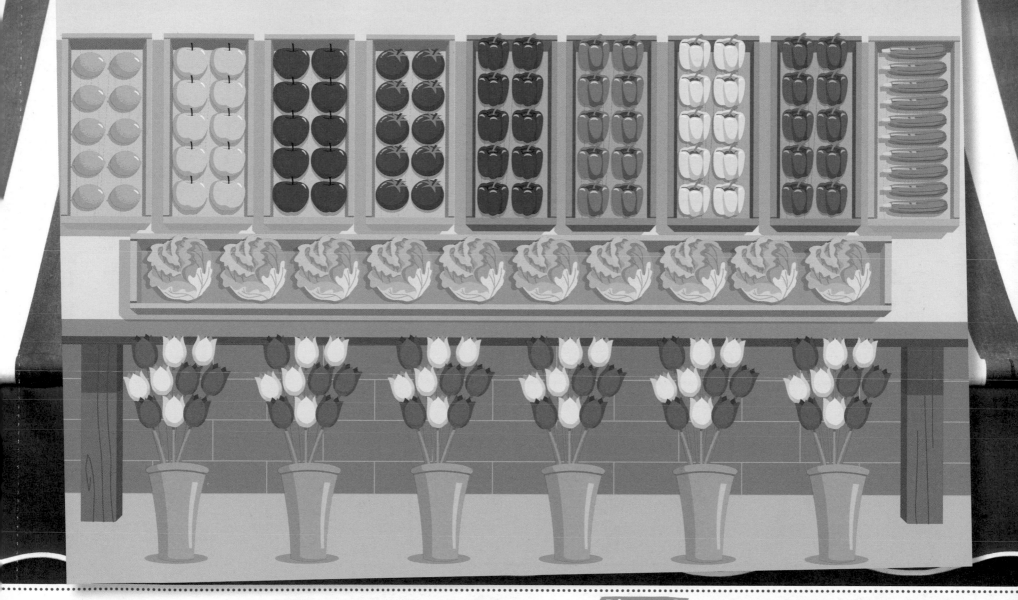

Encourage children to count different groups of objects by tens. Tell children each tray and vase of flowers has 10 objects in it. Then count the groups of objects, such as all the green food items, by tens. Have children circle 40 flowers.

Discuss It How does knowing how to count to 10 help you count by tens?

Connect It

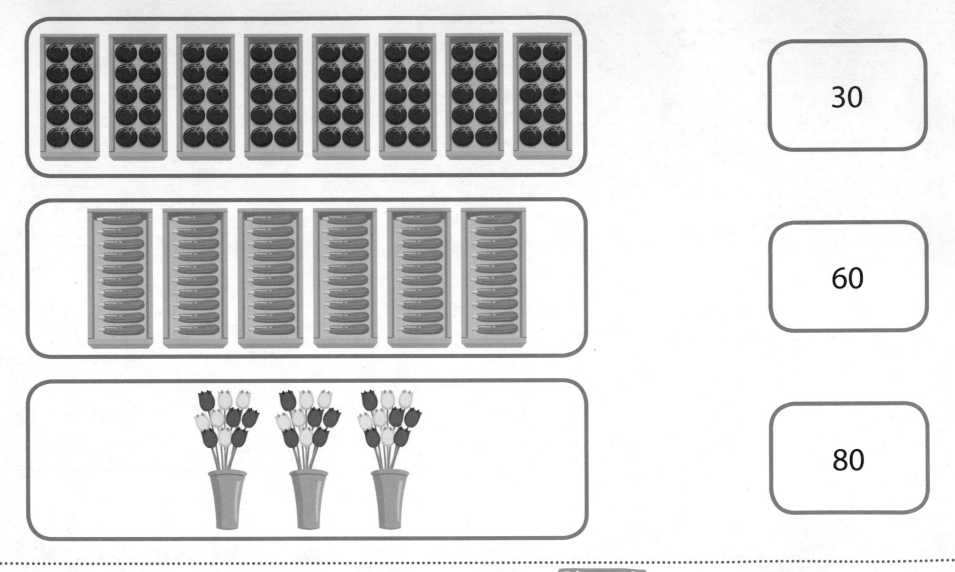

Have children draw lines to match each set of objects to the number that tells how many.
Tell children that each vase or tray has 10 objects in it. Have children count by tens to find how many objects are in each set and then draw lines to the matching totals.

Discuss It How does counting by tens help you count greater numbers?

Practice Counting to 100 by Tens

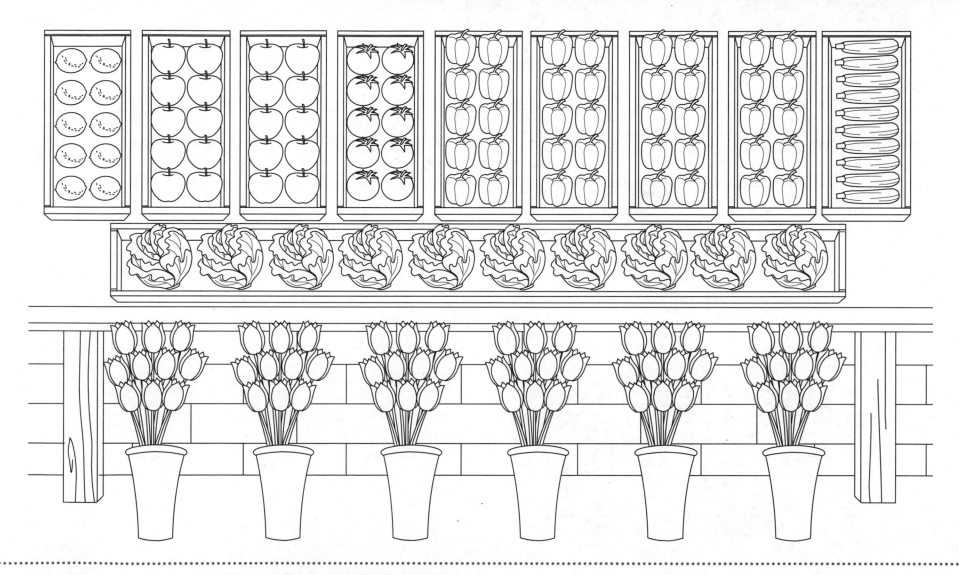

Have children color 3 groups of 10 flowers and then count by tens to find how many they colored. Have children color 7 groups of 10 fruits and/or vegetables and count them by tens. Have children color the rest of the picture.

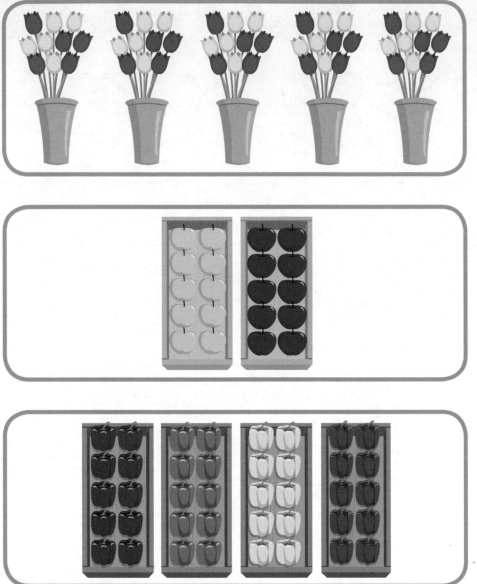

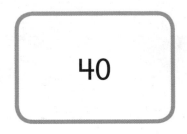

20

40

50

Have children draw lines to match each set of objects to the number that tells how many. Tell children that each vase or tray has 10 objects in it.

Have children count by tens to find how many objects are in each set and then draw lines to the matching totals.

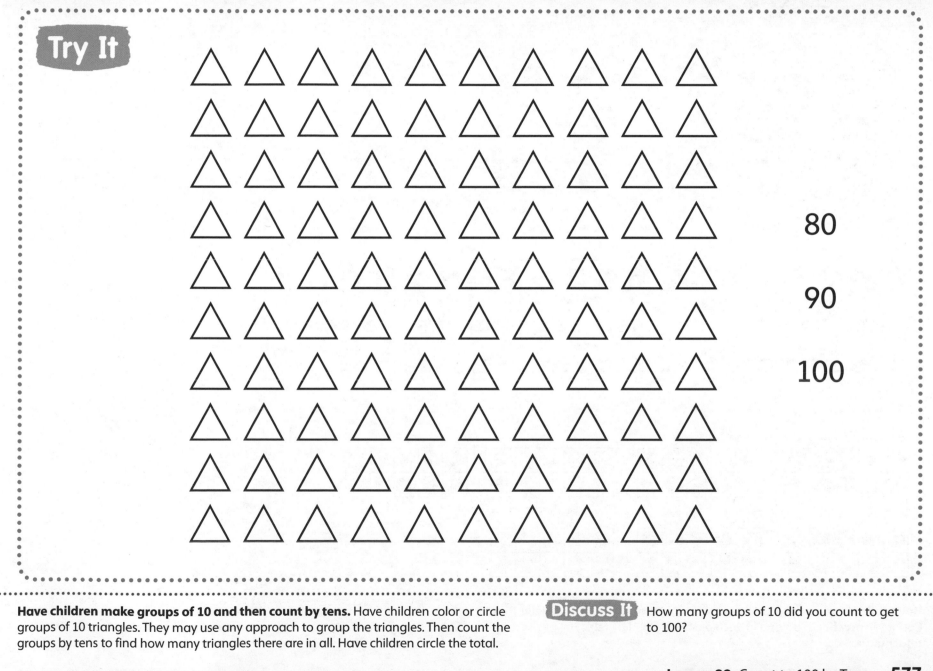

Try It

80

90

100

Have children make groups of 10 and then count by tens. Have children color or circle groups of 10 triangles. They may use any approach to group the triangles. Then count the groups by tens to find how many triangles there are in all. Have children circle the total.

Discuss It How many groups of 10 did you count to get to 100?

Connect It

50   60   70

70   80   90

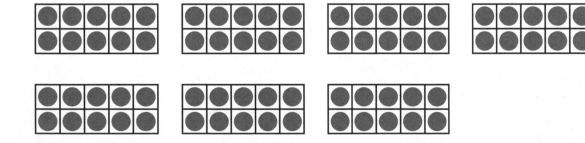

60   70   80

Have children count objects by tens. Explain that there are 10 objects in each group. Count the number of objects in each problem aloud by tens. Have children circle the total number.

Discuss It Which do you think is easier: counting each square or counting the squares by tens? Why?

Practice Counting to 100 by Tens

Example

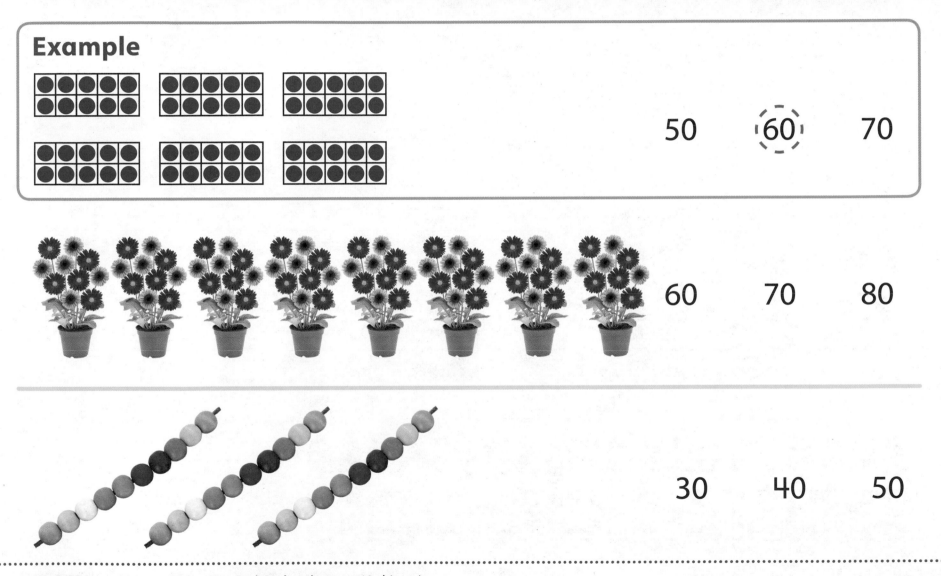

50   (60)   70

60   70   80

30   40   50

Have children count objects by tens. Explain that there are 10 objects in each group. Have children count aloud by tens to find the total number of objects in each problem. Then have children circle the total number.

80   90   100

70   60   50

10   90   100

Have children count objects by tens. Explain that there are 10 objects in each group. Have children count aloud by tens to find the total number of objects in each problem. Then have children circle the total number.

580   Lesson 29 Count to 100 by Tens

Refine Counting to 100 by Tens

Apply It

 **Math Toolkit**
• crayons

1	2	3	4	5	6	7	8	9	10
11	12	13	14	15	16	17	18	19	20
21	22	23	24	25	26	27	28	29	30
31	32	33	34	35	36	37	38	39	40
41	42	43	44	45	46	47	48	49	50
51	52	53	54	55	56	57	58	59	60
61	62	63	64	65	66	67	68	69	70
71	72	73	74	75	76	77	78	79	80
81	82	83	84	85	86	87	88	89	90
91	92	93	94	95	96	97	98	99	100

Have children name tens in a hundred chart. Point to the last column of the hundred chart. Together, count by tens, pointing to each number recited. Have children find the number 20 and color the box yellow. Have them find 50 and mark it with a purple X.

Discuss It What pattern do you notice in the numbers in the hundred chart as you count by tens?

1	2	3	4	5	6	7	8	9	☐
11	12	13	14	15	16	17	18	19	20
21	22	23	24	25	26	27	28	29	30
31	32	33	34	35	36	37	38	39	☐
41	42	43	44	45	46	47	48	49	☐
51	52	53	54	55	56	57	58	59	60
61	62	63	64	65	66	67	68	69	70
71	72	73	74	75	76	77	78	79	☐
81	82	83	84	85	86	87	88	89	90
91	92	93	94	95	96	97	98	99	☐

10   20   30

30   40   50
30   40   50

80   90   100

80   90   100

Have children circle the numbers that complete the hundred chart. Count aloud to 10 by ones to solve the first problem. Then have children focus on the last column and count together by tens to complete the page.

Discuss It Nolan is counting by tens. He has trouble remembering what number is after 20. What can you tell him to help him remember?

582   **Lesson 29** Count to 100 by Tens

Practice Counting to 100 by Tens

1	2	3	4	5	6	7	8	9	☐
11	12	13	14	15	16	17	18	19	20
21	22	23	24	25	26	27	28	29	☐
31	32	33	34	35	36	37	38	39	40
41	42	43	44	45	46	47	48	49	50
51	52	53	54	55	56	57	58	59	60
61	62	63	64	65	66	67	68	69	☐
71	72	73	74	75	76	77	78	79	80
81	82	83	84	85	86	87	88	89	☐
91	92	93	94	95	96	97	98	99	100

(10)	20	30
30	40	50

60	70	80
70	80	90

For each row on the hundred chart with a missing number, have children circle the number to the right that completes that row. Have children count aloud to 10 by ones to find which number completes the first row. Then have children focus on the last column and count together by tens, having children circle the numbers that complete the chart.

1	2	3	4	5	6	7	8	9	10
11	12	13	14	15	16	17	18	19	
21	22	23	24	25	26	27	28	29	30
31	32	33	34	35	36	37	38	39	
41	42	43	44	45	46	47	48	49	50
51	52	53	54	55	56	57	58	59	
61	62	63	64	65	66	67	68	69	70
71	72	73	74	75	76	77	78	79	80
81	82	83	84	85	86	87	88	89	
91	92	93	94	95	96	97	98	99	

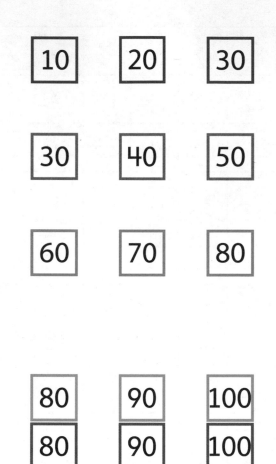

10	20	30
30	40	50
60	70	80
80	90	100
80	90	100

For each row on the hundred chart with a missing number, have children circle the number to the right that completes that row. Have children focus on the last column. Count together by tens, having children circle the numbers that complete the chart.

Refine Counting to 100 by Tens

 **Apply It**

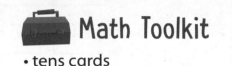 **Math Toolkit**

• tens cards

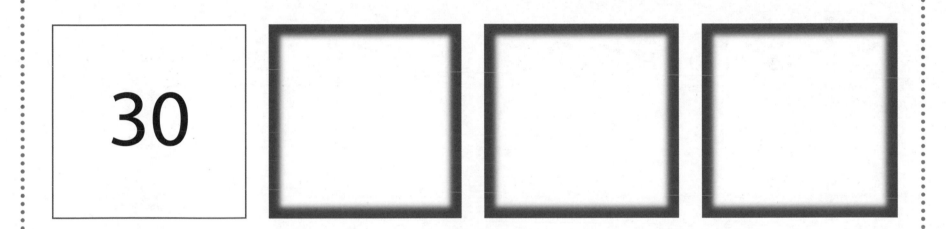

| 30 | | | |

Have children count tens numbers in sequence. Hold up a tens number card, such as 40, and have children say the number and the next three tens numbers. Repeat. Then have children name the number on the page and place and say the next three numbers.

Discuss It How do you know which tens numbers come next?

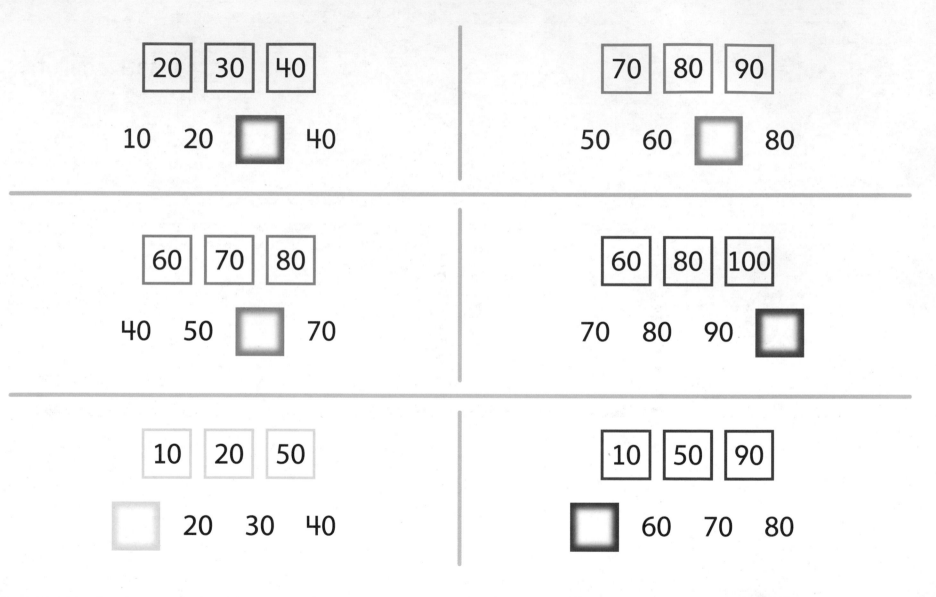

| 20 | 30 | 40 |

10   20   ☐   40

| 70 | 80 | 90 |

50   60   ☐   80

| 60 | 70 | 80 |

40   50   ☐   70

| 60 | 80 | 100 |

70   80   90   ☐

| 10 | 20 | 50 |

☐   20   30   40

| 10 | 50 | 90 |

☐   60   70   80

Have children circle the number to complete each list. The problems in the bottom row ask for the first number in the list. Allow children to struggle. Provide time for them to try strategies on their own. They may realize they can try each number to see which one "sounds right."

Discuss It   How did you decide which number to circle?

Count to 100 by Ones

Dear Family,

This week your child is learning to count to 100 by ones.

It is important to practice counting to 100 by ones, starting at 1 or any other number. The focus is on learning to say the numbers in order, rather than on counting objects or writing numbers. In class, your child may do various movement activities while counting, such as clapping or passing a ball in a group.

This lesson also involves working with a hundred chart, which is a chart that shows the numbers 1 to 100 in ten rows and ten columns. The hundred chart helps to reinforce the sequence of numbers and shows patterns in our number system.

Hundred Chart

1	2	3	4	5	6	7	8	9	10
11	12	13	14	15	16	17	18	19	20
21	22	23	24	25	26	27	28	29	30
31	32	33	34	35	36	37	38	39	40
41	42	43	44	45	46	47	48	49	50
51	52	53	54	55	56	57	58	59	60
61	62	63	64	65	66	67	68	69	70
71	72	73	74	75	76	77	78	79	80
81	82	83	84	85	86	87	88	89	90
91	92	93	94	95	96	97	98	99	100

Invite your child to share what he or she knows about counting to 100 by ones by doing the following activities together.

Activity Counting to 100 by Ones

Do these activities with your child to practice counting by ones.

Help your child practice counting from 1 to 100 whenever you can, and do the following activities together.

- Ask your child to predict how far you can walk by taking 100 steps. For example, the prediction might be that it will take 100 steps to walk from your front door to the mailbox or from the playground swings to the slide. Then walk with your child, counting each step together, to find how many steps it takes.

- Practice counting from numbers other than 1. For example, start counting at 32. After your child joins in to count with you, continue for at least 10 more numbers. For an extra challenge, say just one or two numbers and have your child continue counting on his or her own.

- Play a stop-and-start counting game. Count aloud with your child starting from different numbers. Raise your hand to show when to stop counting, and lower your hand to show when to continue counting where you left off. For an extra challenge, have your child count aloud alone as you raise and lower your hand to show when to stop and when to start counting.

Explore Counting to 100 by Ones

Try It

March

Sunday	Monday	Tuesday	Wednesday	Thursday	Friday	Saturday
1	2	3	4	5	6	7
8	9	10	11	12	13	14
15	16	17	18	19	20	21
22	23	24	25	26	27	28
29	30	31				

Have children review counting to 31 using a calendar. Say: *A calendar is a chart that shows numbers in order. We use the calendar to count the days in each month.* Have children point to the dates in order, and lead the class in saying each number aloud together.

Connect It

1	2	3	4	5	6	7	8	9	10
11	12	13	14	15	16	17	18	19	20
21	22	23	24	25	26	27	28	29	30
31	32	33	34	35	36	37	38	39	40
41	42	43	44	45	46	47	48	49	50
51	52	53	54	55	56	57	58	59	60
61	62	63	64	65	66	67	68	69	70
71	72	73	74	75	76	77	78	79	80
81	82	83	84	85	86	87	88	89	90
91	92	93	94	95	96	97	98	99	100

Children count to 100 using a hundred chart and in a circle. Introduce the hundred chart. Say: *A hundred chart is another chart that shows numbers in order.* Have children point to each number and say the number aloud as the class counts to 100 together. Repeat the counting several times. Then have children form a circle and count to 100 together while passing an object around the circle.

Prepare for Counting to 100 by Ones

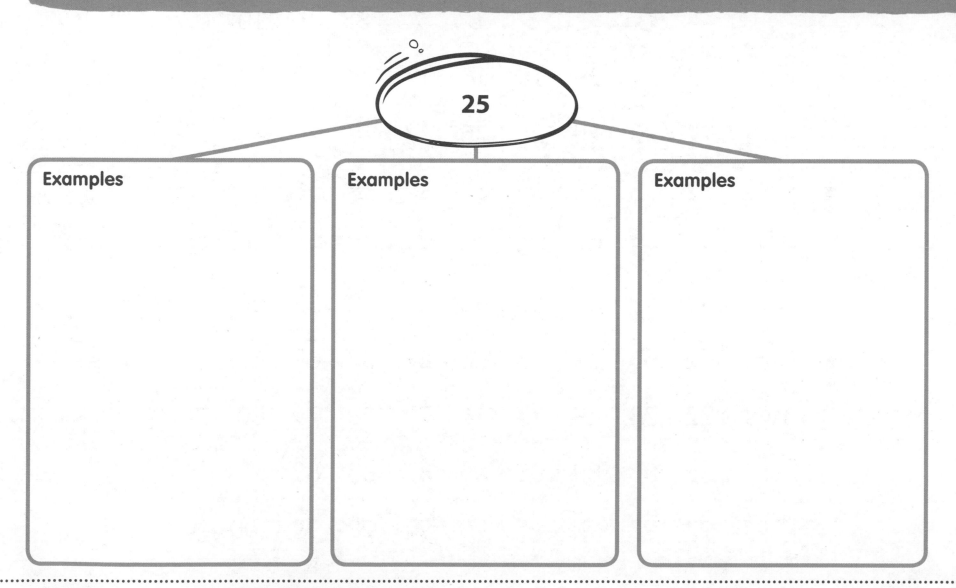

25

Examples

Examples

Examples

Have children show the meaning of 25. Have children fill in each of the boxes to show the meaning of 25. Tell children to use words, numbers, and pictures. Encourage them to show as many ideas as they can.

1	2	3	4	5	6	7	8	9	10
11	12	13	14	15	16	17	18	19	20
21	22	23	24	25	26	27	28	29	30
31	32	33	34	35	36	37	38	39	40
41	42	43	44	45	46	47	48	49	50
51	52	53	54	55	56	57	58	59	60
61	62	63	64	65	66	67	68	69	70
71	72	73	74	75	76	77	78	79	80
81	82	83	84	85	86	87	88	89	90
91	92	93	94	95	96	97	98	99	100

Have children count to 100 using a hundred chart. Say: *A hundred chart is a chart that shows numbers in order.* Have children point to each number and say the number aloud as they count to 100. Repeat the counting several times.

Develop Counting to 100 by Ones

1 2 3 4 5 6 7 8 9 10 11 12 13 14 15 16 17 18 19 20 21 22 23 24

48 49 50 51 52 53 54 55 56 57 58 59 60 61 62 63 64 65 66 67 68

47 46 45 44 43 42 41 40 39 38

84 85 86 87 88 89 90 91 92 93 94 95 96

83 82 81 80 79 78 77 76 75 74 73 72 71 70 69

100 99 98 97

37 36 35 34 33 32 31 30 29 28 27 26 25

Have children count by ones to 100 to help the bunny count its hops until it gets to the carrot. Tell children to point to the numbers to keep track. Have children circle all the numbers said when counting by tens.

Discuss It How does knowing how to count from 1 to 10 help you count to 100?

©Curriculum Associates, LLC   Copying is not permitted.

Lesson 30 Count to 100 by Ones   **593**

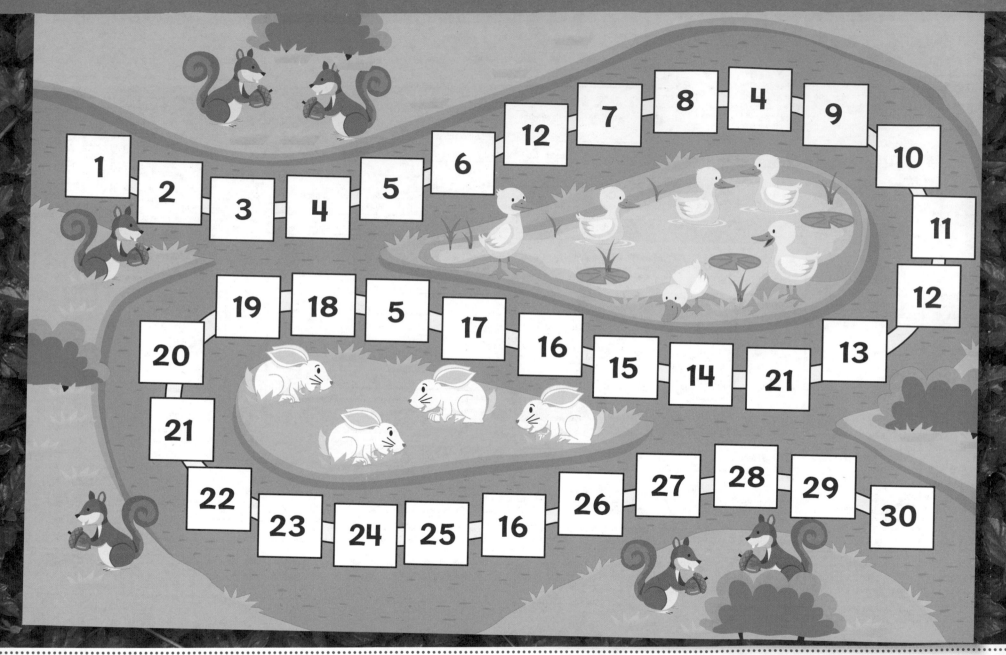

Have children count from 1 to 30. Have children point to each square as they count. When children get to a number that does not belong, have them cross it out. Then have children check by counting the numbers 1 to 30 that are left.

Discuss It How do you know which numbers do not belong? If you continued the path with 10 more squares, which numbers would you write?

©Curriculum Associates, LLC　Copying is not permitted.

Practice Counting to 100 by Ones

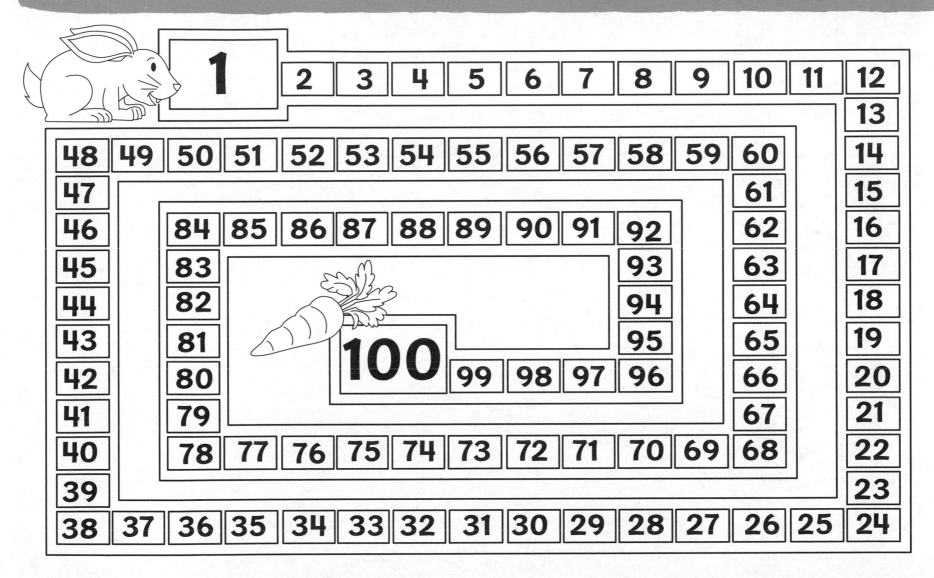

Have children use one color to color the first 10 spaces on the game board. Then have children color each group of 10 spaces a different color.

Have children move a counter along the board and count aloud by ones to 100.

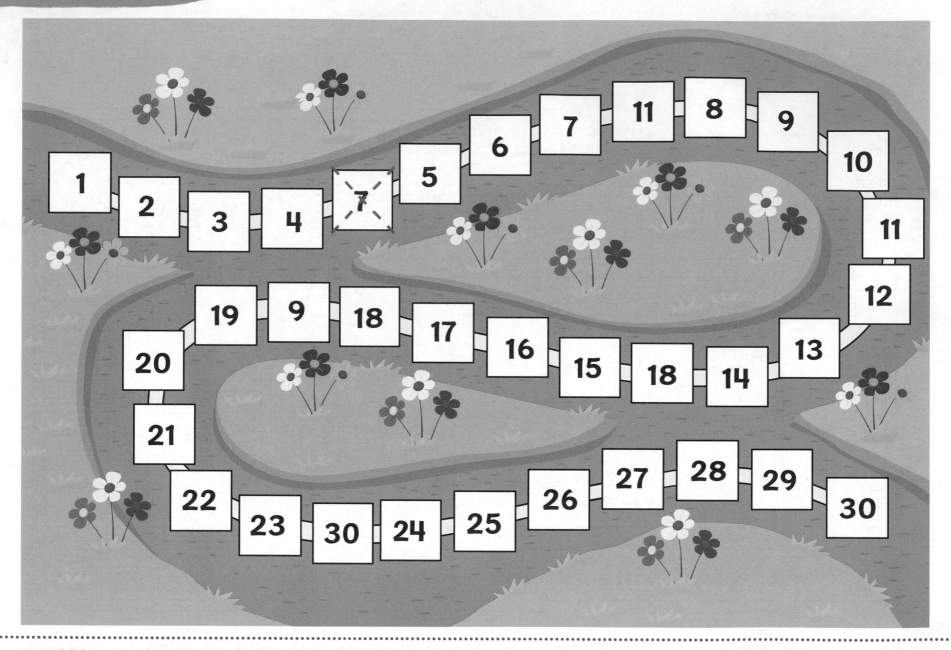

Have children count from 1 to 30, color the numbers they say, and cross out the numbers that do not belong. Then have children count from 1 to 30 again, pointing to each colored number as they say it.

Develop Counting to 100 by Ones

Try It

1	2	3	4	5	6	7	8	9	10
11	12	13	14	15	16	17	18	19	20
21	22	23	24	25	26	27	28	29	30
31	32	33	34	35	36	37	38	39	40
41	42	43	44	45	46	47	48	49	50
51	52	53	54	55	56	57	58	59	60
61	62	63	64	65	66	67	68	69	70
71	72	73	74	75	76	77	78	79	80
81	82	83	84	85	86	87	88	89	90
91	92	93	94	95	96	97	98	99	100

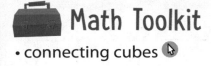

Math Toolkit

- connecting cubes

Have children find a missing number on a hundred chart. Give each pair a connecting cube. One child turns away while the other uses the cube to cover a number on the chart. The first child turns back and figures out which number is covered. Repeat.

Discuss It What helps you figure out which number has been covered?

Connect It

1	2	3	4	5	6	7	8	9	10
11	12	13	14	15	16	17	18	19	20
21	22	23	☐	25	26	27	28	29	30
31	32	33	34	35	36	37	38	39	40
41	42	43	☐	45	46	47	48	49	50
51	52	53	54	55	56	57	58	59	60
61	62	63	64	65	66	67	68	69	☐
71	72	73	74	75	76	77	78	79	80
☐	82	83	84	85	86	87	88	89	90
91	92	93	94	95	96	97	98	☐	100

24	25	26
34	44	54
60	70	90
81	90	91
90	99	100

Have children circle the numbers that complete the hundred chart. Count aloud by ones until you get to the first box with a colored border. Together, determine the missing number and which one to circle. Count on together from 24 until you reach the next box.

Discuss It What patterns can you find in the hundred chart?

Practice Counting to 100 by Ones

1	2	3	4	5	6	7	8	9	10
11	12	13	14	15	16	17	18	19	20
21	22	23	24		26	27	28	29	30
31	32	33	34	35	36	37	38	39	40
41	42		44	45	46	47	48	49	50
	52	53	54	55	56	57	58	59	60
61	62	63	64	65	66	67	68	69	70
71	72	73	74	75	76	77	78	79	
81	82	83	84	85	86		88	89	90
91	92	93	94	95	96	97	98	99	100

25   26   35

42   43   44
51   60   61

60   70   80
87   88   96

For each row on the hundred chart with a missing number, have children circle the number to the right that completes that row. Have them count aloud by ones until they get to the first box with a colored border.

Have children find the missing number to the right of the hundred chart and circle it. Have them count on until they reach the next box with a colored border, and repeat the process.

1	2	3	4	5	6	7	8	9	10
11	12	13	14	15	16	17	18	19	20
21	22	23	24	25	26	27		29	30
31	32	33	34	35	36	37	38	39	40
41	42	43	44	45	46	47	48	49	50
51		53	54	55	56	57	58	59	60
61	62	63	64	65		67	68	69	70
71	72	73	74	75	76	77	78	79	80
81	82	83	84	85	86	87	88	89	
	92	93	94	95	96	97	98	99	100

8	26	28

52	53	62
66	70	75

80	90	91
82	90	91

For each row on the hundred chart with a missing number, have children circle the number to the right that completes that row. Have children count aloud by ones until they get to the first box with a colored border.

Have children find the missing number to the right of the hundred chart and circle it. Have them count on until they reach the next box with a colored border, and repeat the process.

Refine Counting to 100 by Ones

 Apply It

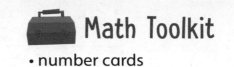 **Math Toolkit**
- number cards

Give partners 4 consecutive 2-digit cards, such as 34, 35, 36, 37. Have children put the cards on the page in order, starting with the card with a star. One child looks away while the other turns over one card. The first child figures out which number is missing. Repeat.

Discuss It How did you figure out which number had been turned over?

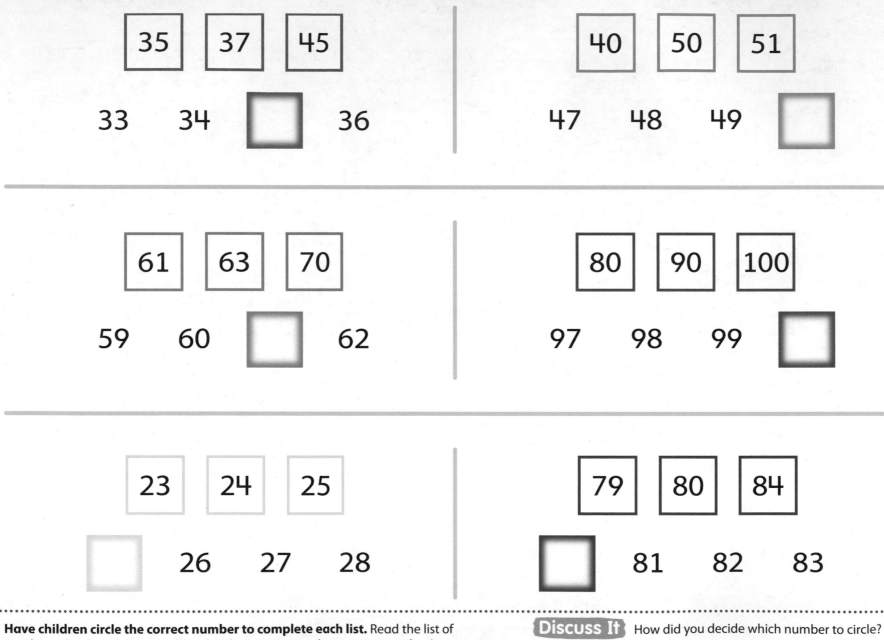

| 35 | 37 | 45 |

33   34   ☐   36

| 40 | 50 | 51 |

47   48   49   ☐

| 61 | 63 | 70 |

59   60   ☐   62

| 80 | 90 | 100 |

97   98   99   ☐

| 23 | 24 | 25 |

☐   26   27   28

| 79 | 80 | 84 |

☐   81   82   83

Have children circle the correct number to complete each list. Read the list of numbers aloud, and discuss. Allow the class time to work out a strategy for determining the correct choice.

Discuss It How did you decide which number to circle?

Practice Counting to 100 by Ones

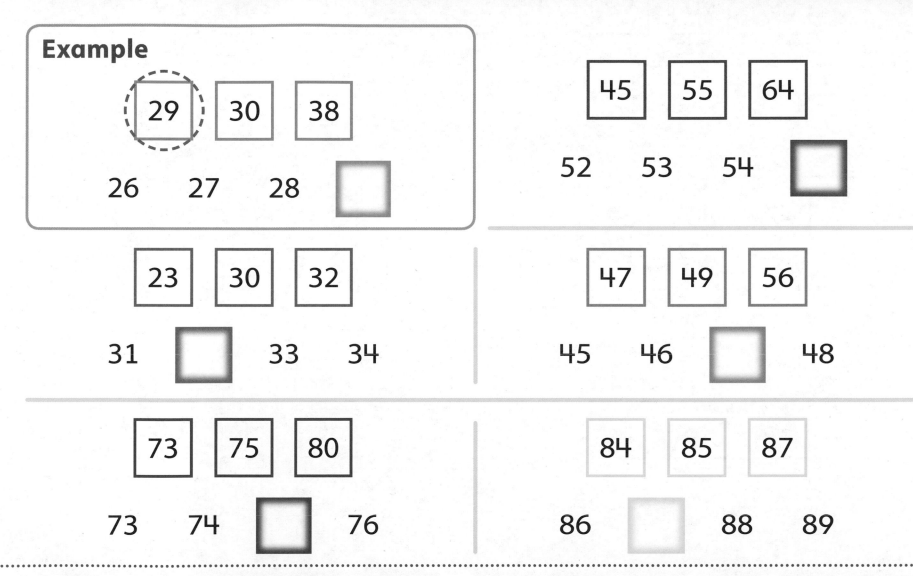

Example

29   30   38

26   27   28   ☐

---

45   55   64

52   53   54   ☐

---

23   30   32

31   ☐   33   34

---

47   49   56

45   46   ☐   48

---

73   75   80

73   74   ☐   76

---

84   85   87

86   ☐   88   89

Have children circle the correct number to complete each list. Have children read aloud the list of numbers in the bottom row of each problem, decide what the missing number is, and circle that number above. Then have children read the completed list of numbers to check their answer.

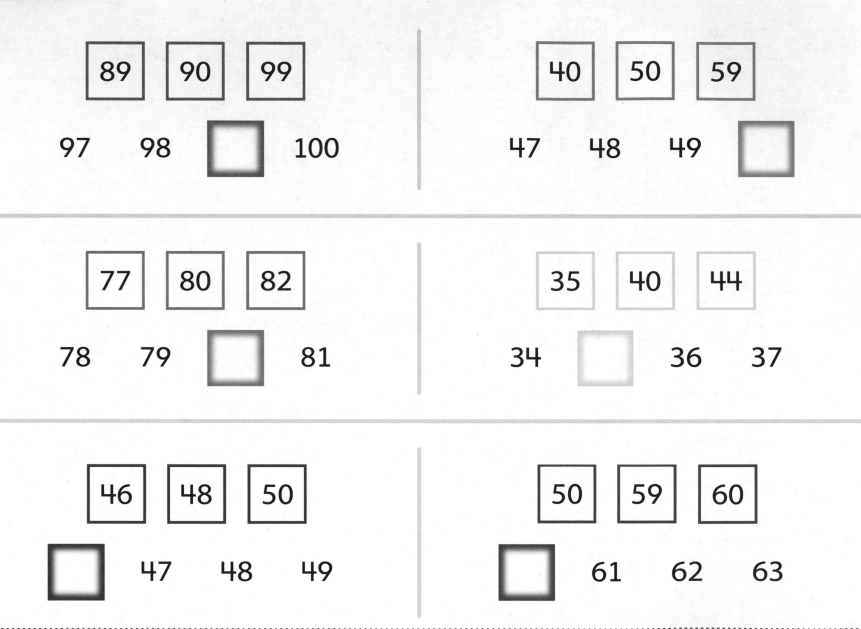

| 89 | 90 | 99 |

97   98   ☐   100

| 40 | 50 | 59 |

47   48   49   ☐

| 77 | 80 | 82 |

78   79   ☐   81

| 35 | 40 | 44 |

34   ☐   36   37

| 46 | 48 | 50 |

☐   47   48   49

| 50 | 59 | 60 |

☐   61   62   63

Have children circle the correct number to complete each list. Have children read aloud the list of numbers in the bottom row of each problem, decide what the missing number is, and circle that number above. Then have children read the completed list of numbers to check their answer.

Refine Counting to 100 by Ones

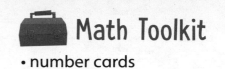 **Math Toolkit**

• number cards

Give pairs of children four 2-digit cards, three consecutive and one not, such as 42, 43, 44, 54. Have children place the card with a star on the workmat. Then have them place the numbers that come next and find the number that does not belong. Repeat.

Discuss It How did you find which number does not belong? Did your partner find that number in a different way?

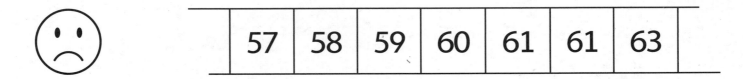

| 20 | 21 | 22 | 32 | 24 | 25 | 26 |

| 57 | 58 | 59 | 60 | 61 | 61 | 63 |

| 74 | 75 | 76 | 77 | 78 | 79 | 88 |

Have children cross out the box that shows the incorrect number on the number path.
Read each list of numbers aloud, and have children independently decide which number
does not belong. Check answers as a class, asking children to say the correct number.

Discuss It How did you decide which numbers did
not belong?

©Curriculum Associates, LLC   Copying is not permitted.

Self Reflection

Show What You Learned

Have children draw to show what they learned about numbers 11–100.
Prompt children to reflect on their learning by posing questions such as: *What do you know how to do well? What do you still need to work on? What is the most important math you learned? Why?*

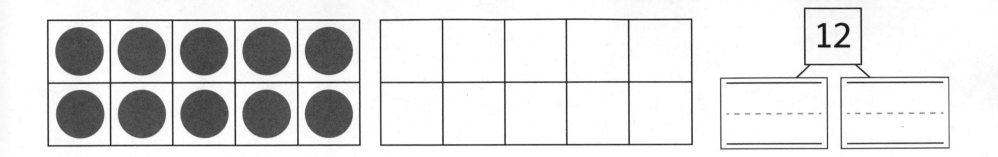

14

For the top problem, have children draw counters to match the number in the number bond, then write the number of counters in each frame to complete the number bond. For the bottom problem, have children count the number of buttons and write the number they counted.

16 or 17

   50   60   70

   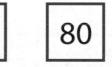 30   40   80

1	2	3	4	5	6	7	8	9	10
11	12		14	15	16	17	18	19	20
21	22	23	24	25	26	27	28	29	30
31	32	33	34	35	36	37	38	39	40
41	42	43	44	45	46		48	49	50
51	52	53	54	55	56	57	58	59	
61	62	63	64	65	66	67	68	69	70
71	72	73	74	75	76	77	78	79	80
81	82	83	84	85	86	87	88	89	90
91	92	93	94	95	96	97	98	99	100

13	14	23

38	47	56
50	60	70

Have children count by ones. Have children count aloud by ones until they get to the first box with a colored border on the hundred chart. Have children find the missing number to the right of the hundred chart and circle it.

Have them count on until they reach the next box with a colored border, and repeat the process.

Show What You Know

Have children draw to show what they know about length, height, and weight. Tell children that after they have completed the unit, they will draw to show what they learned.

Build Your Vocabulary

My Math Words

1 A ruler is shorter/longer than a crayon.

2 A sharpener is heavier/lighter than a table.

3 An eraser is longer/shorter than a pencil.

4 A book is lighter/heavier than a penny.

My Academic Words

☐ decide   ☐ describe

_____

Every morning I _____ what to eat for breakfast.

_____

We can _____ popcorn by using our five senses.

Have children cross out the incorrect Review word. Review My Academic
Words and complete the activity with children.

Compare Length and Height

Dear Family,

This week your child is learning to compare objects by length and by height.

You can compare two objects by **length** or by **height** to find which object is **longer**, **taller**, or **shorter**. Your child will compare the lengths and heights of objects in pictures as well as actual objects. When comparing the lengths or heights of actual objects, it is important to line up the objects at one end to see which object extends farther up (for height) or farther left or right (for length).

Learning to recognize and understand the attributes of length and height will help your child prepare to do other measurement activities in later grades, including using measuring tools (such as rulers and tape measures) and measuring with standard units (such as inches and centimeters).

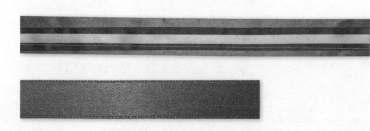

The striped ribbon is longer than the solid ribbon.

The pink flower is shorter than the red flower.

Invite your child to share what he or she knows about **comparing length** and **comparing height** by doing the following activities together.

Activity Comparing Length and Comparing Height

Do these activities with your child to compare length and height.

Materials a spoon and other household objects for comparing length

Tell your child that you are going on a length hunt together.

- Explain that you will look for three objects around your home that are longer than a spoon and three objects that are shorter than a spoon.

- As your child compares household objects with a spoon, encourage him or her to line up one end of the spoon with one end of the object whose length is being compared.

- Some examples of objects that might be longer than a spoon are a book, a table, and a shoe. Some items that might be shorter than a spoon are a key, a toy car, and a paper clip.

Take your child on a height hunt. Have your child find three objects that are taller than he or she is, such as a door, a floor lamp, or a tree. Then have your child find three objects that are shorter than he or she is, such as a chair, a toy, or a book.

In addition to doing the above activities, ask your child to compare length or height whenever you have the opportunity. For example, at the dinner table, you might ask: *Which is longer, the fork or the spoon? Which is shorter?*

Explore Comparing Length and Height

Learning Target

- Directly compare two objects with a measurable attribute in common, to see which object has "more of"/"less of" the attribute, and describe the difference.

SMP 1, 2, 3, 4, 5, 6, 8

🧰 Math Toolkit

- pencils

Have children identify attributes of shoes and make comparison statements based on length. Display two shoes of different sizes. Invite children to describe the two shoes. Model a comparison statement, such as: *The blue shoe is longer than the white shoe.* Have children make comparison statements using *shorter* and *longer*. Have children make comparison statements about the shoes shown on the page and circle the one that is longer.

Connect It

Have children compare lengths of pencils and make comparison statements. Give pairs two pencils of different lengths. Have children compare the length of each pencil with the pencil shown. Have them describe each pencil in relation to the picture of the pencil using *shorter* or *longer*.

Prepare for Comparing Length and Height

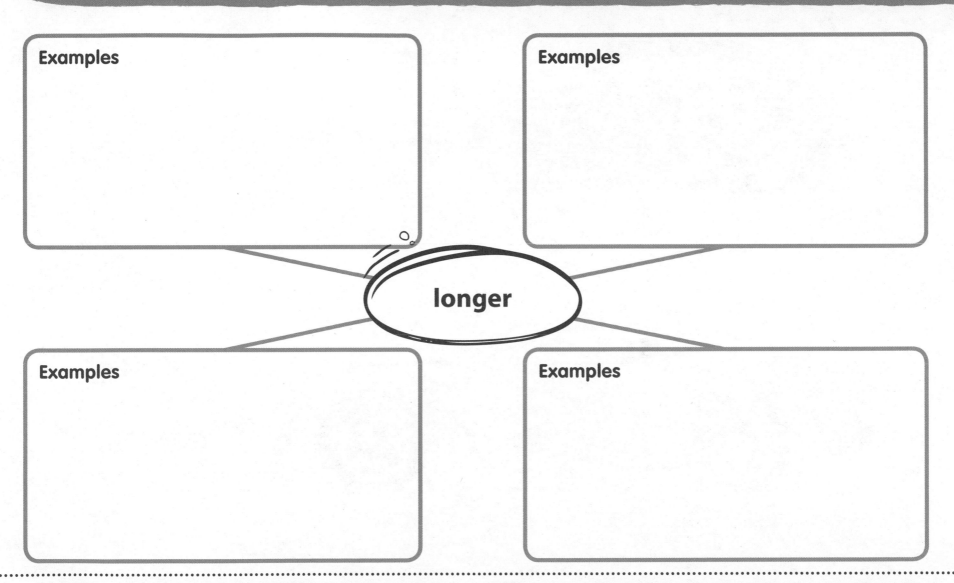

Examples

Examples

longer

Examples

Examples

Have children show the meaning of the word *longer*. Have children fill in each of the boxes to show the meaning of the word *longer*. Tell children to use words, numbers, and pictures. Encourage them to show as many ideas as they can.

Have children identify attributes of toys and make comparison statements based on length. Display two toys of different sizes. Invite children to describe the two toys. Model a comparison statement, such as: *The toy car is longer than* *the action figure.* Have children make comparison statements using *shorter* and *longer*. Have children make comparison statements about the toy cars shown and circle the one that is longer.

618   Lesson 31 Compare Length and Height

Develop Comparing Length and Height

Encourage children to compare objects based on their heights or lengths. Model statements such as: *The yellow bat is longer than the red bat.* Have children circle the taller or longer object for each comparison.

Discuss It Which is shorter, the red boat or the purple boat?

Connect It

Have children compare the heights or lengths of the objects. Have children compare the heights of the flowers, the lengths of the pencils, and the heights of the children. Have them circle the taller or longer object in each pair.

Discuss It If the flowers were the same height, which flower would be taller?

Practice Comparing Length and Height

Have children use red to color the taller tree, the taller flowers, the longer bench, and the longer bat. Ask children what word they could use to describe the other tree, flowers, bench, and bat. Then have children color the rest of the picture.

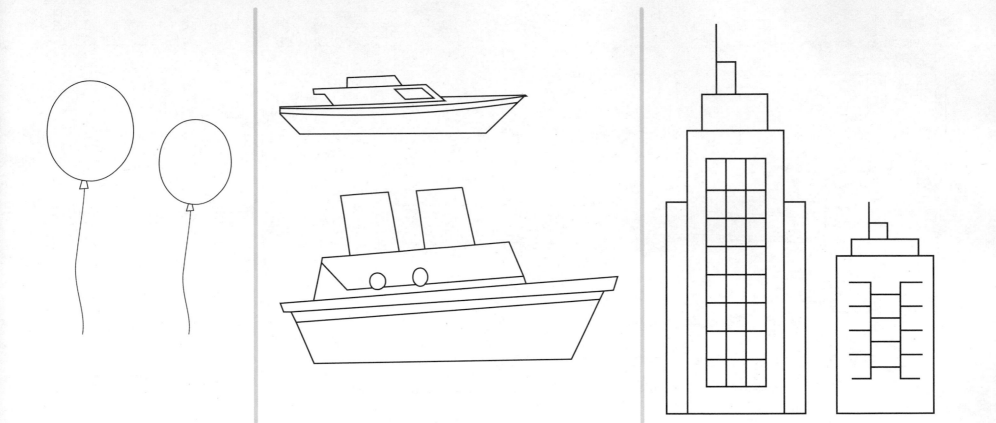

Have children compare the heights or lengths of the objects. Have children compare the heights of the balloons, the lengths of the boats, and the heights of the buildings. Have them color the shorter object in each pair.

Develop Comparing Length and Height

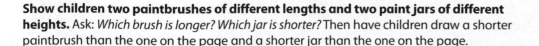

Show children two paintbrushes of different lengths and two paint jars of different heights. Ask: *Which brush is longer? Which jar is shorter?* Then have children draw a shorter paintbrush than the one on the page and a shorter jar than the one on the page.

Discuss It How do you know if an object is shorter than another object?

Connect It

Have children find which objects are taller or longer and which objects are shorter. Have children circle the shorter object in each pair. Ask children to explain why the object is shorter than the other object.

Discuss It How did you decide which bat is shorter?

Practice Comparing Length and Height

Example

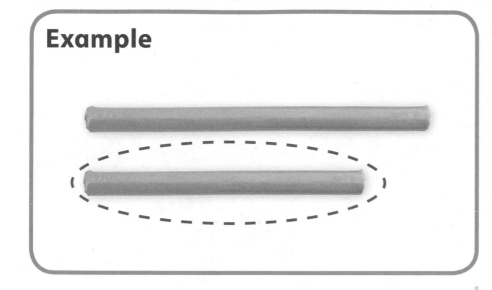

Have children find which objects are longer and which are shorter. Have children circle the shorter object in each pair. Ask children to explain how they decided which object is shorter.

Have children find which objects are taller and which are shorter. Have children circle the shorter object in each pair. Ask children to explain how they decided which object is shorter.

626 **Lesson 31** Compare Length and Height

Refine Comparing Length and Height

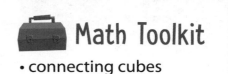
Math Toolkit
• connecting cubes

Have children work in pairs to each make a cube train and a cube tower. Have each pair compare their trains and towers and say which is longer/taller. Then have children make a train longer than the yellow cube train and a tower shorter than the blue cube tower.

Discuss It How can you find which cube train is longer?
How can you find which cube tower is taller?

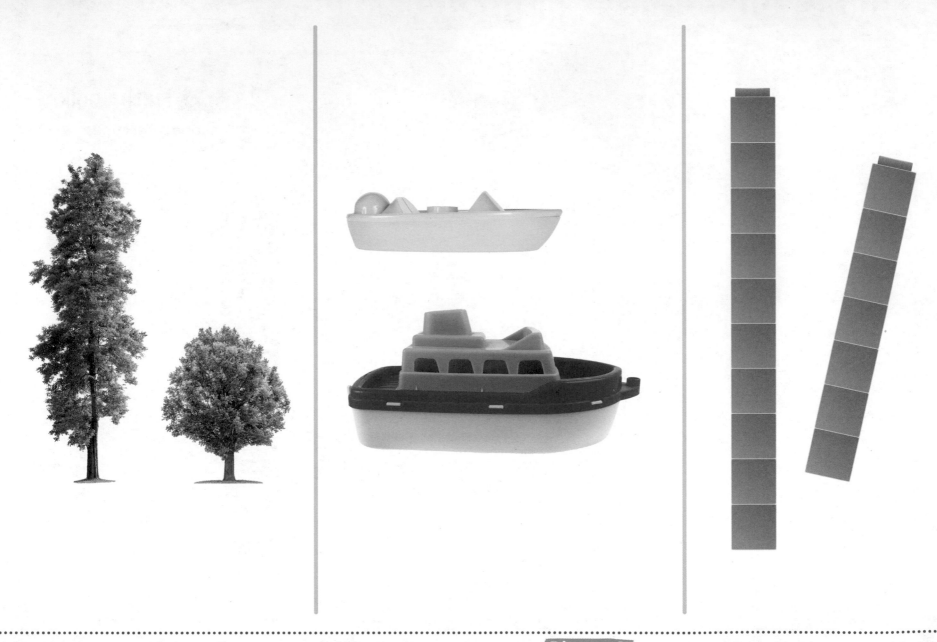

Have children find which objects are taller or longer and which objects are shorter.
Have children circle the taller or longer object in each pair. Ask children to explain how they decided which object is taller or longer.

Discuss It How could you be sure which group of cubes is longer?

Practice Comparing Length and Height

Example

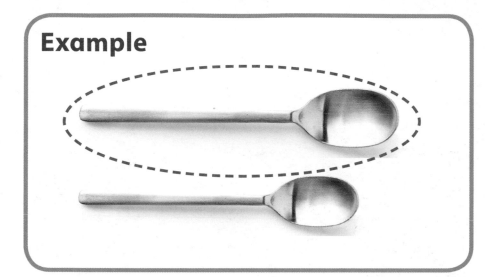

Have children find which objects are longer and which are shorter. Have children circle the longer object in each pair. Ask children to explain how they decided which object is longer.

Have children find which objects are taller and which are shorter. Have children circle the taller object in each pair. Ask children to explain how they decided which object is taller.

Apply It

🧰 Math Toolkit

• pencils

Have children compare the length of their pencil with the lengths of other objects in the classroom. Then have them choose one object they found that was shorter than their pencil and draw it on the page. Have children draw an object they found that was longer.

Discuss It Which of the two objects you drew is longer? How do you know?

Have children draw pictures to show *taller* and *shorter*. Have children draw a flower that is taller and a bat that is shorter than those shown. After completing the page, have children describe how they decided how to draw the items.

Discuss It How would you draw a flower that is not shorter than and not taller than the flower shown?

Compare Weight

Dear Family,

This week your child is learning to compare objects by weight.

Comparing two objects by **weight** involves finding which object is **heavier** or **lighter**. Your child will compare the weights of actual objects as well as the weights of objects shown in pictures. To compare weights, it may be helpful to think of a heavier object as harder to lift and a lighter object as easier to lift.

There will be some focus on recognizing that larger objects are not necessarily heavier than smaller objects. For example, even if a balloon is larger than a basketball, the balloon will be lighter than the basketball. This focus emphasizes that weight and size are different attributes. Understanding and comparing weights will help prepare your child for work with measurement units in later grades.

Invite your child to share what he or she knows about **comparing weight** by doing the following activity together.

Activity Comparing Weight

Do these activities with your child to compare weight.

Tell your child that you are going to play an imagination game involving weights of objects. Then ask several questions about which imaginary bag full of objects would be heavier or which would be lighter. For example:

- *Which do you think would be heavier, a bag full of feathers or a bag full of rocks?*

- *Which do you think would be lighter, a bag full of popcorn or a bag full of potatoes?*

- *Which do you think would be heavier, a bag full of bricks or a bag full of balloons?*

If your child needs guidance with the terms *heavier* and *lighter*, ask which bag would be easier or harder to pick up, and connect this to the ideas of heavier and lighter. After you have asked several of these questions, encourage your child to ask you a question about which of two bags would be heavier or lighter. Take turns asking each other questions, and use your imagination!

Ask your child to compare objects by weight whenever you have the chance. For example, at the dinner table, you might ask: *Which is heavier, your spoon or your cup of milk? Which is lighter?* When your child is getting ready for school, you might ask: *Which is lighter, your lunchbox or your backpack? Which is heavier?*

Explore Comparing Weight

Have children identify and describe measurable attributes of objects and then describe their weights. Display a jug of water. Ask: *How can you describe the size of this object?* Explain that *weight* is the word for how heavy or light an object is. Invite children to hold the jug of water, describe it as *heavy* or *light*, and explain why. Repeat with the other objects. Have children circle the heavy objects and mark the light objects with an X.

Connect It

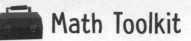 Math Toolkit

- books
- crayons
- feathers

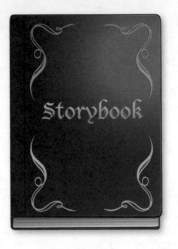

Have children compare the weights of objects and determine the heavier object. Give each pair a book, a crayon, and a feather. Have each child hold the book in one hand and the crayon in the other and say which they think is heavier. Encourage the pairs to come to a consensus and circle the heavier object. Then have the pair compare the crayon and the feather and circle the heavier object.

Prepare for Comparing Weight

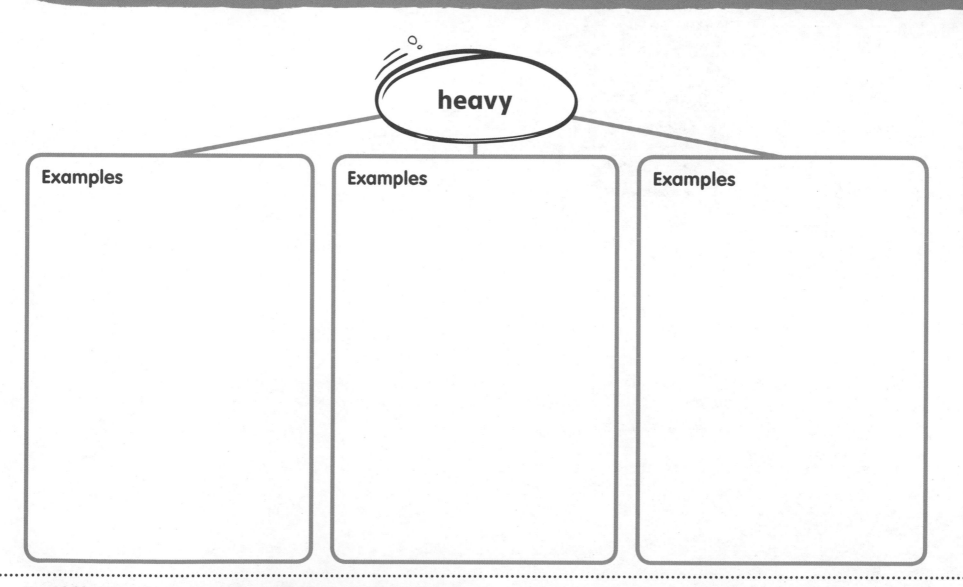

heavy

Examples

Examples

Examples

Have children show the meaning of the word *heavy*. Have children fill in each of the boxes to show the meaning of the word *heavy*. Tell children to use words, numbers, and pictures. Encourage them to show as many ideas as they can.

Have children compare the weights of objects and determine the heavier object. Give children a mug, a pencil, and a paper clip. Have children hold the mug in one hand and the pencil in the other and say which they think is heavier. Have children circle the heavier object. Then have children compare the pencil and the paper clip and circle the heavier object.

Develop Comparing Weight

cereal   potatoes
pumpkin   apple
tuna
bread   watermelon
juice box   milk
chips
soup   tissues
    cups

Have children describe objects based on weight. Encourage statements such as: *The jug of milk is heavier than the apple*. Have children cross out three objects that are lighter than the jug of milk. Ask children to think of other measurable attributes of the objects.

Discuss It How did you decide which items are lighter than the jug of milk?

Connect It

Ask children to underline the loaf of bread. Have children look for objects that are lighter than the loaf of bread and mark them with an X. Then have children look for objects that are heavier than the loaf of bread and circle them.

Discuss It   How did you decide which objects are heavier than the loaf of bread?

640   **Lesson 32** Compare Weight

Practice Comparing Weight

Have children color the can of soup red. Next, have children use purple to color two objects that are heavier than the can of soup. Then have children use yellow to color one object that is lighter than the can of soup. Have children color the rest of the picture.

Have children circle the box of cereal. Have children look for objects that are lighter than the box of cereal and color them blue. Then have children look for objects that are heavier than the box of cereal and color them red.

Develop Comparing Weight

Have children compare weight and size. Show children a basketball and a larger beach ball. *Which is bigger? Which is heavier?* Have children draw an object that is similar in size to a basketball and another that is similar in weight to a basketball.

Discuss It Is a bigger object always heavier than a smaller object? Why or why not?

Connect It

Have children find which objects are heavier. Have children circle the heavier object in each pair. On the top row, have children mark with an X the objects that are longer. On the bottom row, have children mark with an X the objects that are taller.

Discuss It   How did you decide which object is heavier? Are the taller or longer objects always heavier? Why or why not?

Practice Comparing Weight

Example

Have children find which objects are heavier. Have children circle the heavier object in each pair. Ask children to explain why they think that the object circled is heavier than the other object.

Have children find which objects are heavier. Have children circle the heavier object in each pair. Ask children to explain why they think that the object circled is heavier than the other object. Then have children mark with an X the objects in the top row that are longer and the objects in the bottom row that are taller.

Refine Comparing Weight

 **Apply It**

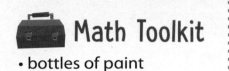 **Math Toolkit**

• bottles of paint

Have children find lighter objects. Give small groups a bottle of paint. Have them find 3 objects that are lighter than the bottle. At least one of the objects must be bigger than the bottle. Have them draw the objects and circle any that are bigger than the bottle.

Discuss It Which is lighter, 1 soccer ball or a bag of soccer balls? Is one object always lighter than a group of that same object?

Have children find which objects are lighter. Have children mark the lighter object with an X. Ask children to explain how they decided which object is lighter. Have children circle the shorter object in each pair.

Discuss It Is the shorter object always lighter? Why or why not? How do you know that one cup weighs less than a bag of cups?

Practice Comparing Weight

Example

Have children find which objects are lighter. Have children mark the lighter object in each pair with an X. Ask children to explain how they decided which object is lighter.

Have children find which objects are lighter. Have children mark the lighter object in each pair with an X. Then have children circle the object in each pair that is shorter.

 Apply It

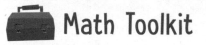 Math Toolkit

- crayons
- backpacks
- classroom items

Have children draw pictures to show one object that is heavier than an empty backpack and one object that is lighter than an empty backpack. After children draw their pictures, have them circle the heavier object in red and the lighter one in blue.

Discuss It Can you think of an object that is smaller than an empty backpack but is heavier?

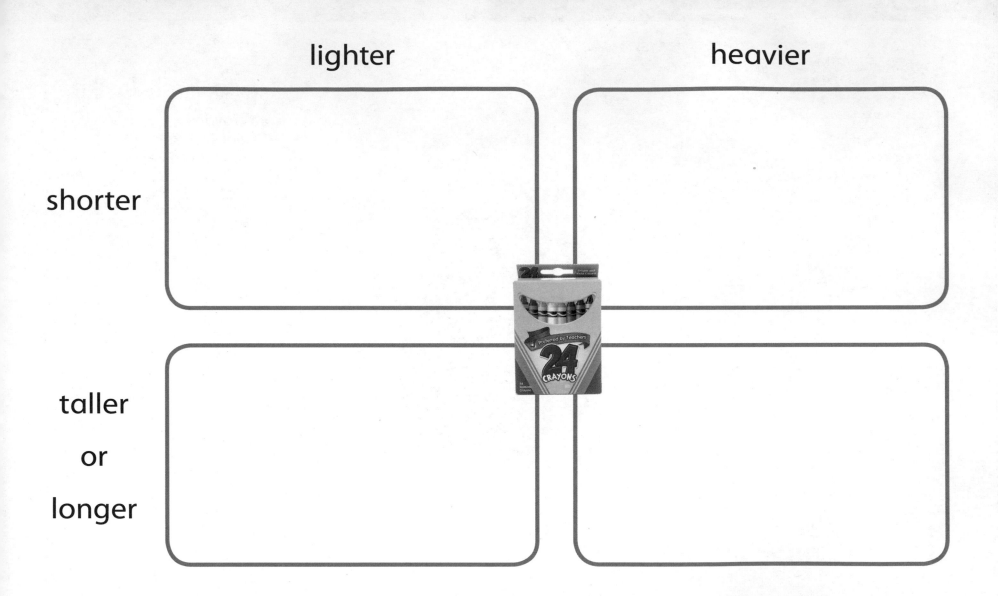

lighter   heavier

shorter

taller

or

longer

On the left, have children draw an object that is lighter and shorter than the box of crayons, then an object that is lighter and taller (or longer). On the right, have them draw an object that is heavier and shorter, then an object that is heavier and taller (or longer).

Discuss It How did you think of what object to draw in each corner?

Self Reflection

Show What You Learned

Have children draw to show what they learned about length, height, and weight. Prompt children to reflect on their learning by posing questions such as: *What did you work hardest to learn? What would you like to know more about? What is a question you still have?*

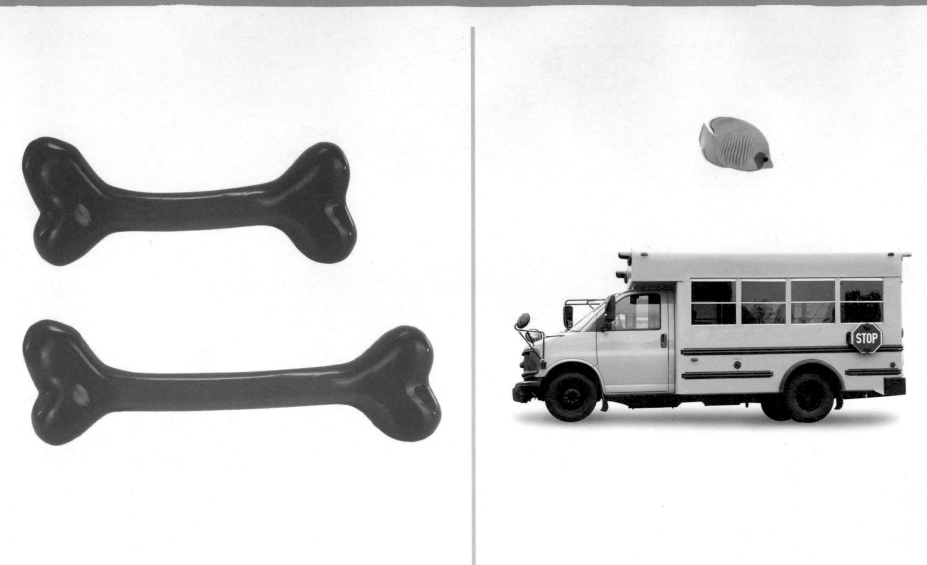

Have children compare lengths and weights of objects. For the first problem, have children circle the shorter dog toy. For the second problem, have children circle the lighter object. Ask children to describe how they chose each item.

Have children draw pictures to show *taller* and *shorter*. On the side with the black dot, have children draw an object that is taller than then tiger shown. Then, on the side with the white dot, have them draw an object that is shorter than the tiger shown. Ask children to describe how they decided to draw the items.

For the first problem, have children circle the heavier object and mark the longer object with an X. For the second problem, have children circle the heavier object and mark the shorter object with an X. Ask children to describe how they chose each item to circle or mark with an X.

♥ Count and Write to 10

● Write and Count Out

_____   _____   _____

- - - - - - - - -   - - - - - - - - -   - - - - - - - - -

_____   _____   _____

♥ **Have children count and write how many objects.** First, have children count and write the number of balloons. Next, have children count and write the number of purple handles. Then have children count and write the number of red hats.

● **Have children write and count out numbers.** First, have children write the number 2 and circle two of the same item. Then have children write the number 3 and draw a line under three of the same item. Last, have children write the number 5 and draw a rectangle around five of the same item.

▲ Compare Objects

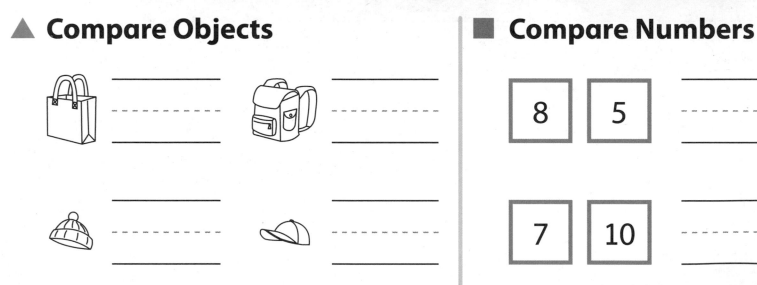

■ Compare Numbers

8	5	_____

7	10	_____

▲ **Have children compare quantities.** Have children count and write how many shopping bags and how many backpacks, then circle the number that is less. Repeat with how many red hats and how many yellow hats.

■ **Have children find which number is greater.** For each pair of numbers, ask children to write the number that is greater.

★ Find 1 More

1 More

_____ _____

_____ _____

_____ _____

_____ _____

● Find Number Pairs

6   _ _ _ _ _ _ _ and _ _ _ _ _ _ _

_____   _____

7   _ _ _ _ _ _ _ and _ _ _ _ _ _ _

★ **Have children find 1 more.** Have children count and write the number of rockets, then draw one more and write the new total. Next, repeat with the number of plants..

● **Have children tell the different numbers that make up the same kind of item.** Ask children to circle two groups that make up 6 items altogether and write how many in each group. Repeat with drawing a rectangle around groups that make 7.

✿ Make 10

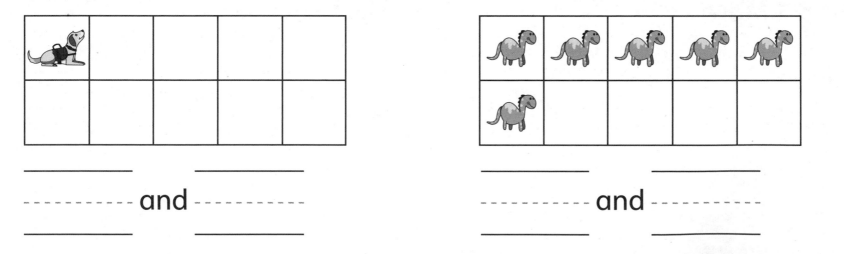

_____ _____

---------- and ----------

_____ _____

✿ **Have children make 10.** First, have children count and write the total number of dogs. Then have them write how many more would be needed to make 10 dogs.

Next, have children count and write the number of dinosaurs. Then have them write how many more would be needed to make 10 dinosaurs.

Cumulative Practice

Name: _____

♥ Add Within 5

1 🪰
3 🦋

$1 + 3 =$ _____

_____

3 🦋
2 🦗

$3 + 2 =$ _____

_____

● Add Within 10

🐝 $6 + 3 =$ _____

_____

🪲 $5 + 2 =$ _____

_____

♥ **Have children add groups of bugs.** Say: *1 fly and 3 moths. How many bugs?* Children write the total. Repeat. Say: *3 moths and 2 grasshoppers. How many bugs?*

● **Have children add more bugs to the groups shown.** Say: *6 bees next to the light. If 3 more bees come, how many bees in all?* Have children write the total. Repeat. Say: *5 beetles on the wall. If 2 more beetles come, how many beetles in all?*

▲ Make 10

5 + - - - - - - - - - - = 10

2 + - - - - - - - - - - = 10

■ Find Two Addends

8 = - - - - - - - - - + - - - - - - - - -

5 = - - - - - - - - - + - - - - - - - - -

6 = - - - - - - - - - + - - - - - - - - -

▲ **Find how many more are needed to make 10.** Say: *There are 5 beetles. How many more are needed to make 10 beetles?* Have children write the number in the equation. Repeat. Say: *There are 2 grasshoppers. How many more are needed to make 10 grasshoppers?*

■ **Tell children an addition story for each problem.** Say: *There are 8 ladybugs. Some fly away and the rest stay near the light. How many fly away and how many stay?* Have children complete the equation to show their answer. Repeat with 5 beetles and with 6 bees.

Cumulative Practice

Name: _____

★ Subtract Within 5

$4 - 2 =$ _____
_____

$5 - 1 =$ _____
_____

● Subtract Within 10

$8 - 3 =$ _____
_____

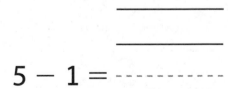
$7 - 4 =$ _____
_____

★ **Have children subtract objects.** Say: *4 pillows. Take away 2 pillows. How many pillows are left?* Children may mark an X on the pillows they are subtracting. Repeat with 5 − 1 cats.

● **Have children subtract objects.** Say: *8 cans of food. Take away 3 cans of food. How many cans of food are left?* Children may mark an X on the cans they are subtracting. Repeat for 7 − 4 toy mice.

✿ Word Problems

2 + 6 = _____

7 − 2 = _____

✦ Practice Facts to 5

4 − 1 = _____

1 + 2 = _____

5 − 3 = _____

✿ **Have children solve word problems.** Say: *There are 2 bowls. The cats get 6 more bowls. How many bowls in all?* Have children write the answer in the equation. Repeat. Say: *There are 7 toy mice. 2 toy mice get lost. How many are left?*

✦ **Have children complete each fact.** Ask children to complete each fact and write the answer in the equation.

Cumulative Practice

Name: _____

♥ Count Teen Numbers

♥ **Have children count teen numbers.** Have children count the number of red tomatoes and write the number they counted. Repeat for the orange peppers and the yellow beans.

Unit 6 Cumulative Practice   **CP9**

● Teen Numbers in a Number Bond

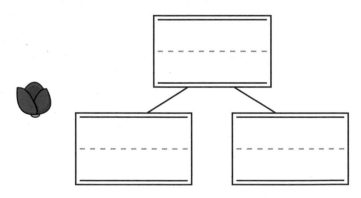

▲ Teen Numbers in Equations

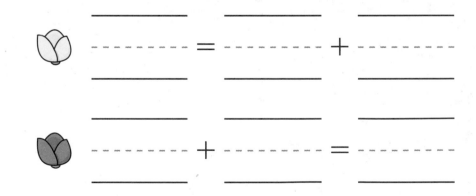

● **Complete the number bond to show how to make a teen number.** Have children count the pink flowers on the top shelf. Have them complete the number bond to show what they see.

▲ **Have children make teen numbers.** Have children count the yellow flowers on the middle shelf and complete the equation to show what they see. Repeat for the blue flowers on the bottom shelf.

Cumulative Practice

Name: _____

■ Add

3

4

$3 + 4 =$ _____

6

2

$6 + 2 =$ _____

★ Subtract

$5 - 2 =$ _____

$8 - 4 =$ _____

■ **Have children add groups of objects.** Say: *3 barrel cactuses and 4 saguaro cactuses. How many cactuses in all?* Children write the total. Repeat. Say: *6 snakes and 2 lizards. How many in all?*

★ **Have children subtract objects.** Say: *5 birds. Take away 2 birds. How many birds are left?* Have children mark an X on the birds they are subtracting. Repeat for *8 − 4 scorpions.*

● Make 10

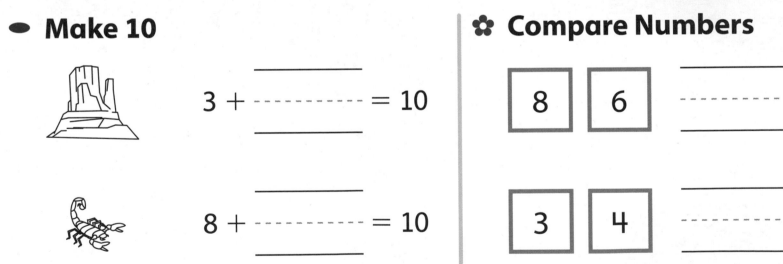

$$3 + \underline{\hspace{2cm}} = 10$$

$$8 + \underline{\hspace{2cm}} = 10$$

✿ Compare Numbers

| 8 | 6 | _____ |

| 3 | 4 | _____ |

● **Find how many more are needed to make 10.** Say: *There are 3 rocks. How many more are needed to make 10 rocks?* Have children write the number in the equation. Repeat. Say: *There are 8 scorpions. How many more are needed to make 10 scorpions?*

✿ **Have children find which number is less.** For each pair of numbers, ask children to write the number that is less.

Glossary • Glosario

Aa

above • sobre

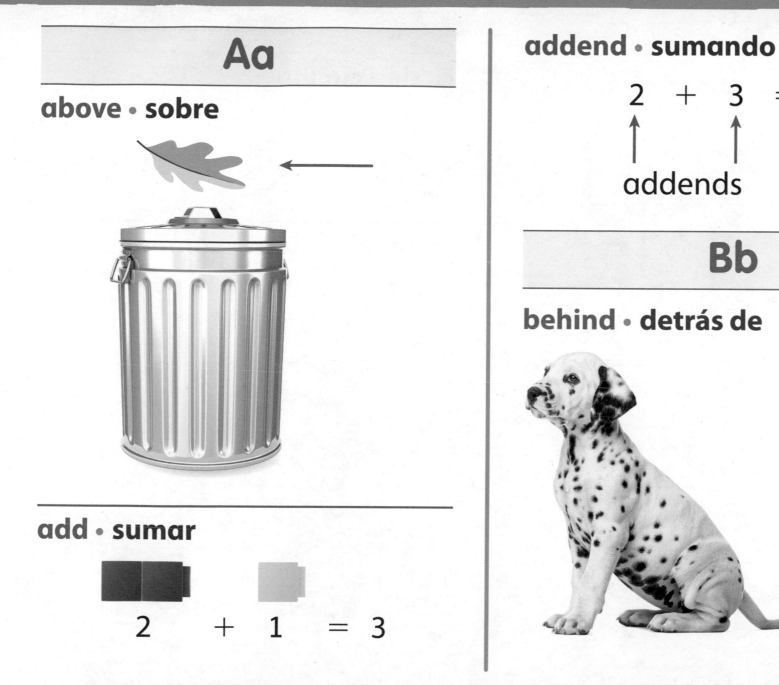

add • sumar

2   +   1   =   3

addend • sumando

2 + 3 = 5
    ↑   ↑
    addends

Bb

behind • detrás de

below • debajo de

beside • junto a

Cc

circle • círculo

compare height • comparar la altura

compare length • comparar la longitud

compare numbers • comparar números

3

5

compare weight • comparar el peso

cone • cono

corner • esquina

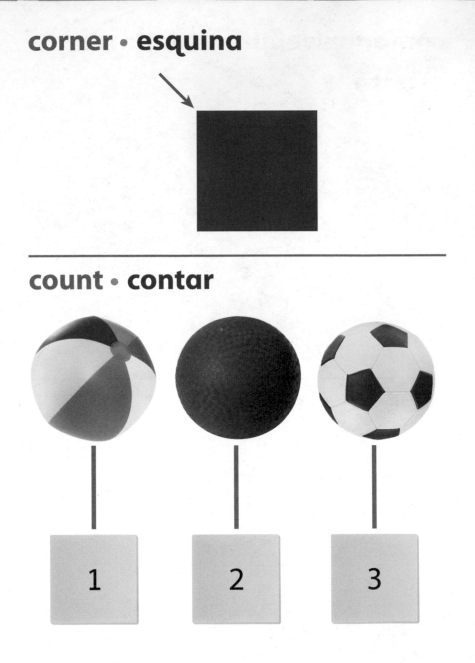

count • contar

count on • contar hacia delante

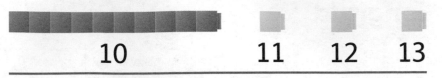

10   11   12   13

cube • cubo

cylinder • cilindro

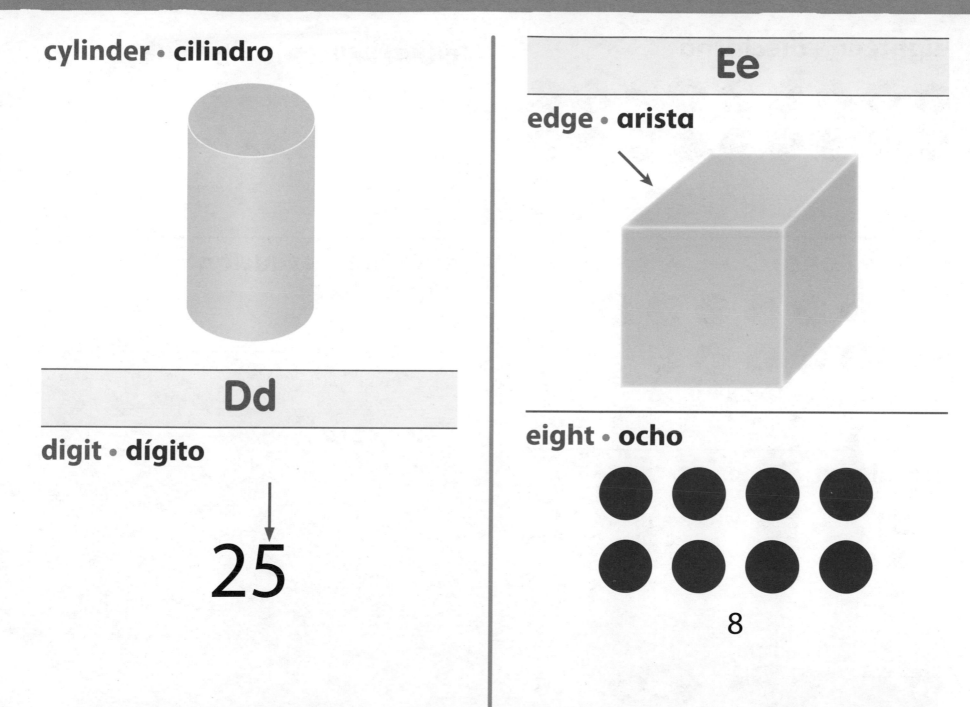

Dd

digit • dígito

25

Ee

edge • arista

eight • ocho

8

eighteen • dieciocho

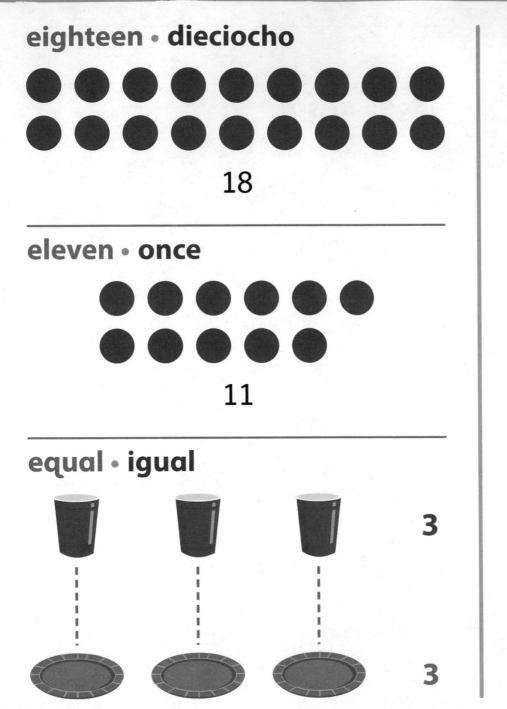

18

---

eleven • once

11

---

equal • igual

3

3

---

equal sign (=) • signo de igual (=)

2 + 3 = 5

---

equation • ecuación

6 − 2 = 4

Ff

face • cara

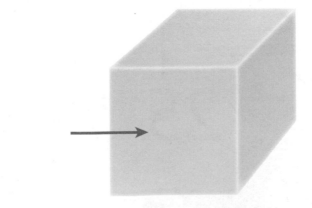

---

fewer, fewer than • menos, menos que

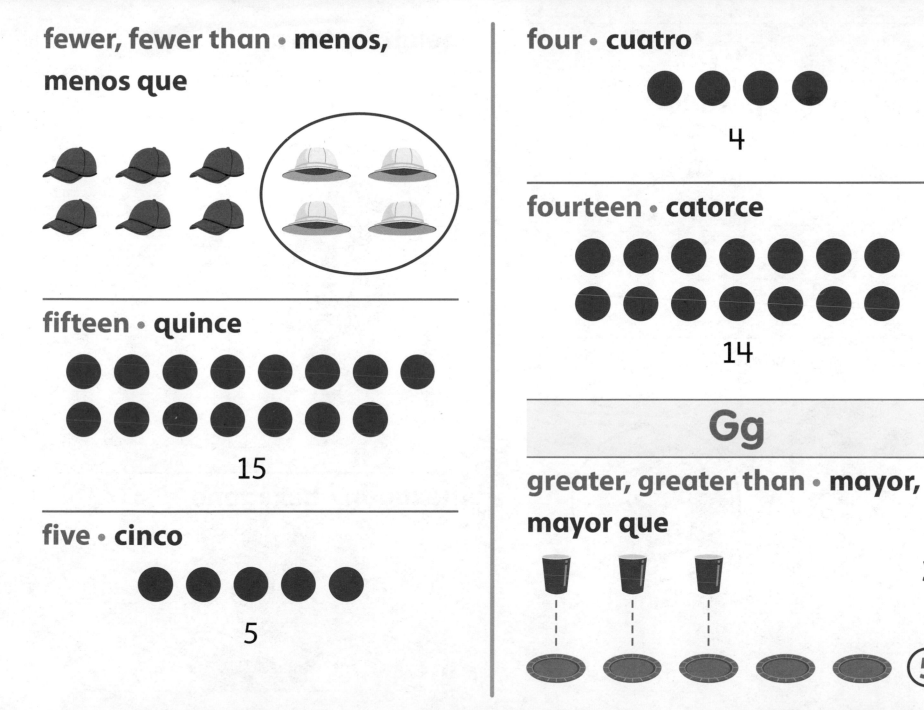

fifteen • quince

15

five • cinco

5

four • cuatro

4

fourteen • catorce

14

Gg

greater, greater than • mayor, mayor que

3

5

Hh

heavier • más pesado

heavy • pesado

height • altura

hexagon • hexágono

Ii

in front of • delante de

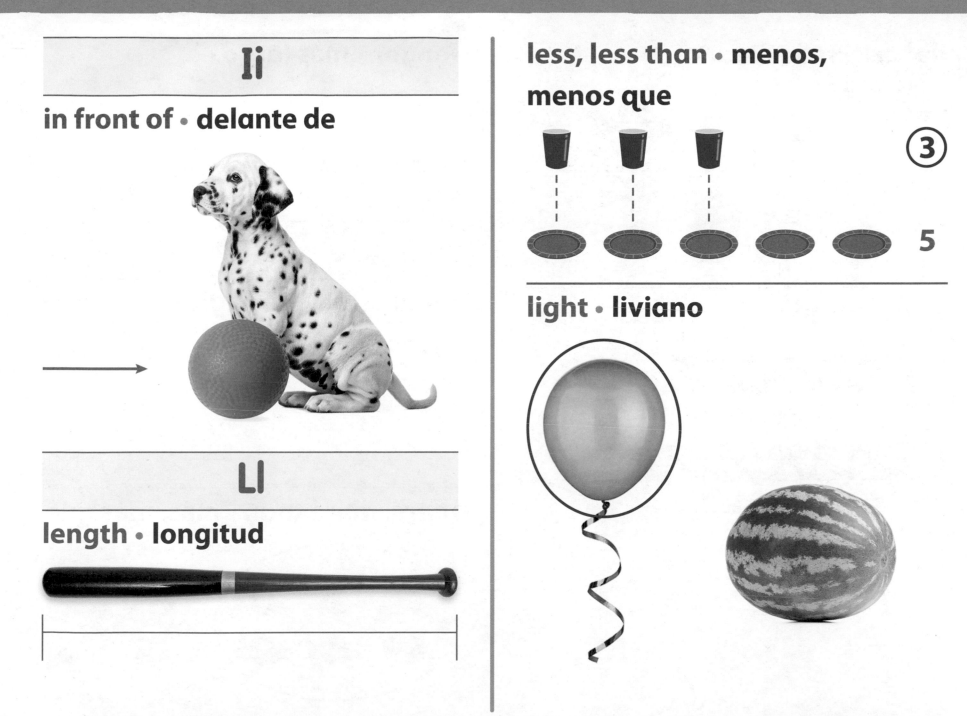

Ll

length • longitud

less, less than • menos, menos que

③

5

light • liviano

lighter • más liviano

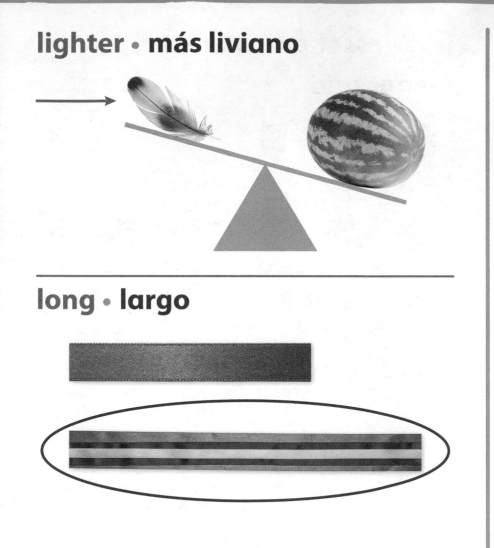

long • largo

longer • más largo

Mm

minus sign (−) • signo menos (−)

$$5 \quad - \quad 3 \quad = \quad 2$$

more, more than • más, más que

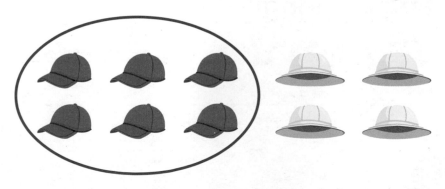

Nn

next to • al lado de

nine • nueve

9

nineteen • diecinueve

19

number • número

5

number bond • enlace numérico

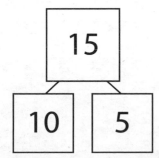

15

10   5

Oo

one • uno

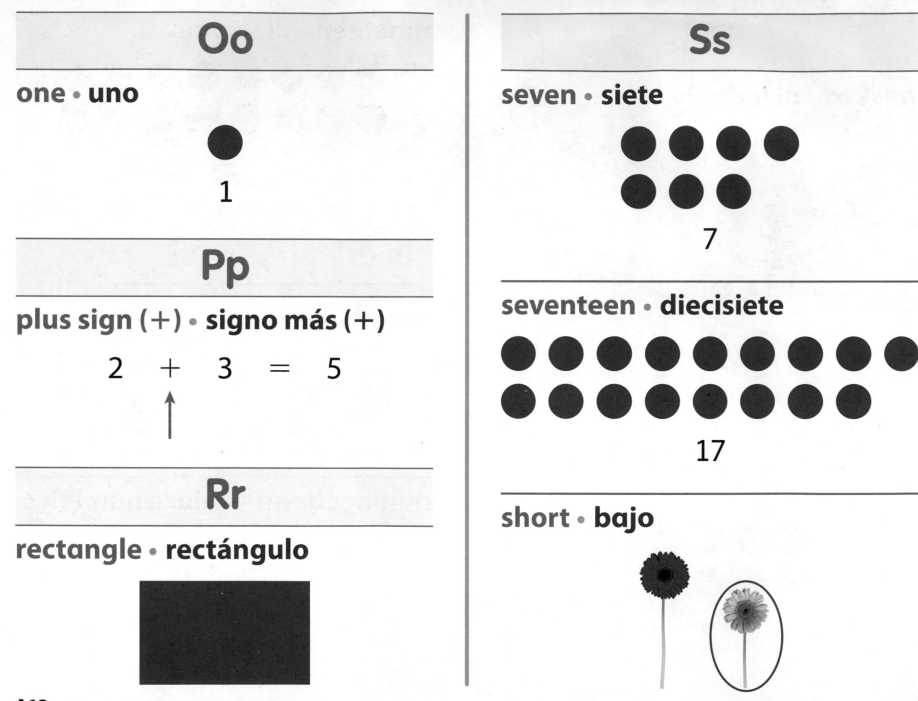

1

Pp

plus sign (+) • signo más (+)

2 + 3 = 5

Rr

rectangle • rectángulo

Ss

seven • siete

7

seventeen • diecisiete

17

short • bajo

shorter • más corto

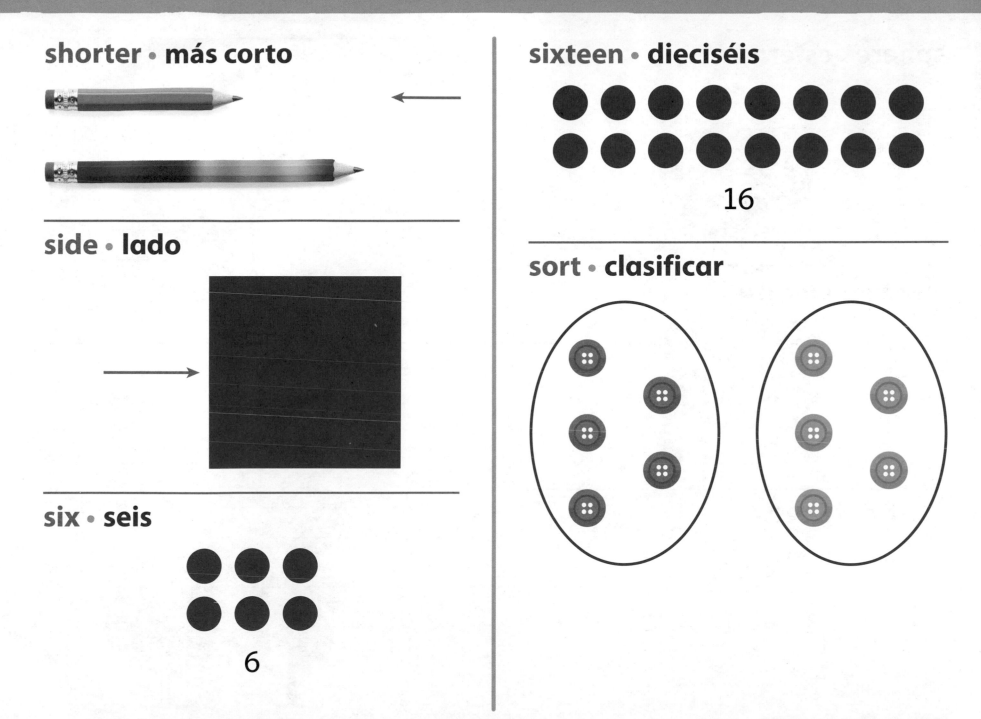

side • lado

six • seis

6

sixteen • dieciséis

16

sort • clasificar

sphere • esfera

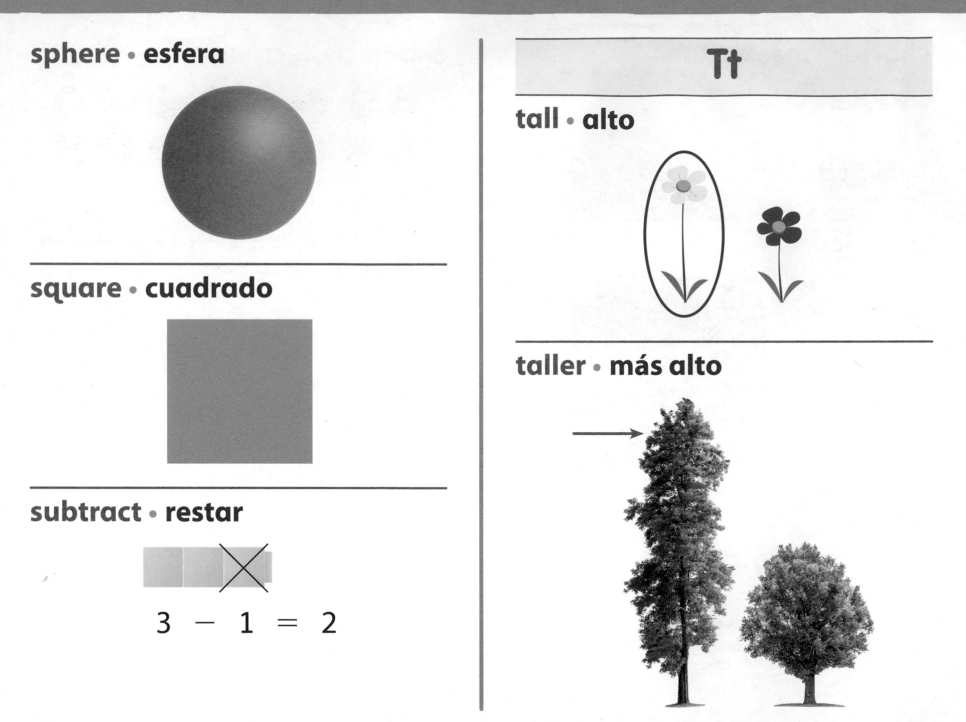

square • cuadrado

subtract • restar

3 − 1 = 2

Tt

tall • alto

taller • más alto

teen numbers • números del 11 al 19

| 11 | 12 | 13 | 14 | 15 | 16 | 17 | 18 | 19 |

ten • diez

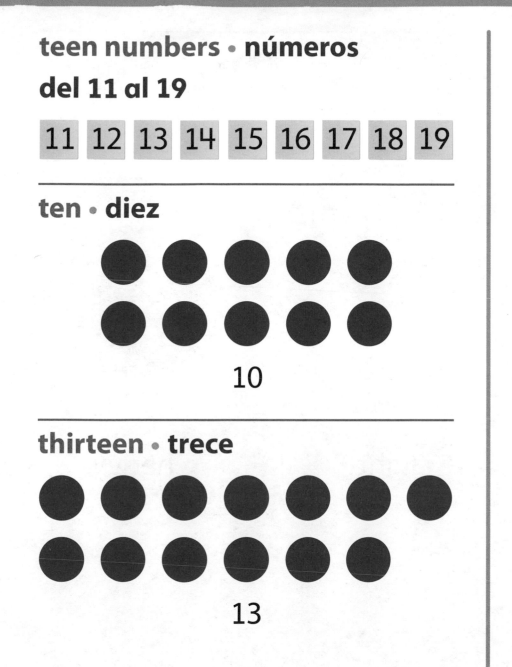

10

thirteen • trece

13

three • tres

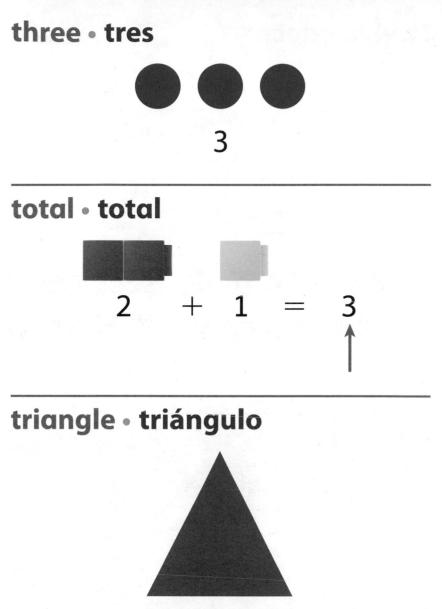

3

total • total

2 + 1 = 3

triangle • triángulo

twelve • doce

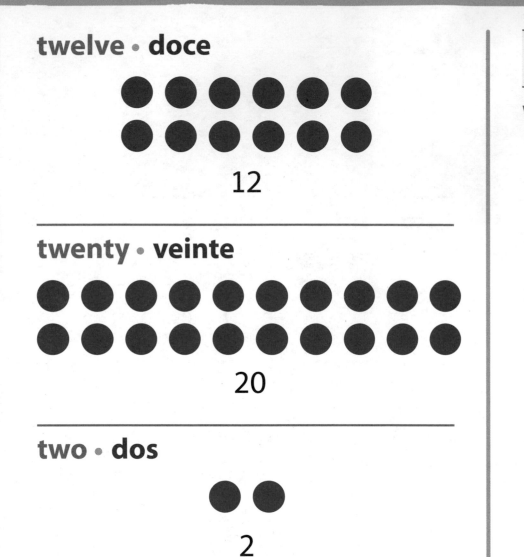

12

twenty • veinte

20

two • dos

2

Ww

weight • peso

light   heavy

Zz

zero • cero

0 fish

Acknowledgments

Common Core State Standards © 2010. National Governors Association Center for Best Practices and Council of Chief State School Officers. All rights reserved.

Photography Credits

United States coin images (unless otherwise indicated) from the United States Mint

Images used under license from **Shutterstock.com**.

Front Cover Danilaleo, Kamira, kool99, Robert Lessman; **vi** Ekaterina Abrosimova, Markus Mainka; **3** Yellow Cat, Dmitrij Skorobogatov, Triling Studio Ltd; **4** Jiang Hongyan, Elbud, LittleMiss; **5** Tom Gowanlock; **6** nuttakit; **8** SnapCraft; **20** Hong Vo, Anton Starikov, Mega Pixel; **39** Kostiantyn Fastov, smilewithjul; **40** Jiang Hongyan, Andrew Burgess, Roberaten; **45** Jajaladdawan; **50** Djmilic, r.classen, Enchanted_fairy; **51** Starikov, Mega Pixel, Insago; **52** Ruth Black; **55** BorisShevchuk; **59** HeinzTeh; **60** OnlyZoia; **65** Two over Two Studio; **72** KimHD, Preto Perola, Dmitrij Skorobogatov, FocusStocker, Iasha; **79** Photosync, Ispace, marssanya; **80** Wealthylady, showcake; **84** VanReeel; **85** Mardoz; **89** Kaspri; **99** Antpkr; **100** FocusStocker; **102** cynoclub, r.classen; **104** DenisNata; **105** Cynoclub, Prostock-studio, Picsfive; **106** artnLera, Vitaly Korovin, Smit, mhatzapa; **111** Zffoto; **115** artnLera, Africa Studio; **119** Smit; **123** mhatzapa, Eric Isselee, liskus; **124** r.classen; **125** mhatzapa, Anita Patterson Peppers, Butterfly Hunter, liskus; **126** Food Travel Stockforlife, Vitaly Zorkin, showcake; **127** Picsfive; **136–138** ntstudio; **141** artnLera, Ermolaev Alexander; **142** Anton Starikov, Africa Studio; **147** Smereka; **151** Monkeyoum; **159** Andrew Burgess **161** Tatyana Vyc; **162** AzriSuratmin; **166** stockcreations; **171** Passakorn Umpornmaha, Glass and Nature, Lightspring, Picsfive, Andrei Kuzmik, Mega Pixel, nehls16321, nelik, Africa Studio, Vorobyeva, oksana2010, Petr Malyshev, Chones; **172** cynoclub, Tatyana Vyc, Tim UR, Chones, bergamont, Lisa A. Svara, Eric Isselee, nelik, duangnapa_b; **173** Shebeko, bergamont, ntstudio, Nataliia K, kittipong kongwatmai, Tsveta Nesheva, Serg64, irin-k, Dora Zett, Natalia K, Eric Isselee, Lisa A. Svara; **174** HomeArt, pukach, Yellow Cat, Nata_Smilyk art, vipman's, Tim UR, bergamont, LZ Image, Danny Smythe, Jjustas Tim UR; **176** William Milner, BalancePhoto, Maksim Toome, Danny Smythe, EHStockphoto, Marisa Lia, Mtsaride, magicoven, Eric Isselee, Dimitris Leonidas, Anest; **177** Denis Pepin, Mega Pixel, aperturesound, Zhukovskaya Elena, Iasha, Vorotylin Roman, Andrei Kuzmik, Chones; **178** nattanan726, Eric Isselee, Glass and Nature, Butterfly Hunter, Passakorn Umpornmaha, Potapov Alexander, photomaster; **180** Preto Perola; **181** Yanugkelid; **182** Piyaset, Preto Perola, Africa Studio; **187** Chloe7992, **190** Charles Shapiro, Pixfiction, Chones, Utekhina Anna; **221** Eric Isselee; **224** oksana2010, DenisNata, Timothy Geiss; **228** Mega Pixel, Akugasahagy, Evannovostro, urfin, valdis torms, Chones, photogal, Denis Kovin, mhatzapa; **233** SomchaiP; **241** Mega Pixel, Tim UR, jeabsam, gmstockstudio, urfin, Chones, Resul Muslu, Brooke Becker, Mariyana M; **247** Handies Peak, SAPhotog, Ruslan Ivantsov, erashov, Sheila Fitzgerald, Fotoksa, Mega Pixel, Kletr, artnLera; **248** Abramova Elena, Sheila Fitzgerald; **253** Michelle Marsan; **254** VectorPic; **257** Brooke Becker, Matt Benoit, Sara van Netten, ColinCramm; **258** Mariyana M, Handies Peak, Kaspri, garyfox45114, Tim UR, Africa Studio, SAPhotog, Chones, jeabsam, baitong333, Mega Pixel; **259** de2marco, Vilaiporn Chatchawal, Michael Kraus, Mega Pixel, Maksym Bondarchuk, Sara van Netten, AzriSuratmin; **260** CHAIYARAT, Keith Bell, Diana Rich, magicoven, Fotoksa, Viktor1, valdis torms, Catinsyrup; **261** urfin; **262** Sergii Tverdokhlibov, urfin, Bennian, Eric Isselee, CharacterFamily Mega Pixel;

263 Bennian, Chones, Bluebloodbkk, nevodka, Maks Narodenko, Eric Isselee, Lisa A. Svara; **264** CharacterFamily, Dontree, J.Gatherum, Sergii Tverdokhlibov, Eric Isselee, nelik, Lightspring, Nejron Photo, Gts, oksana2010, Picsfive; **265** Bejim; **267** FocusStocker, Anton Starikov, Byggarn.se, Hank Shiffman, Mhatzapa; **268** Gts, Digipear, Lennon Schneider, mhatzapa; **273** Somporn Wongvichienkul; **281** Gts, Bennian, Maks Narodenko, Mariyana M, CharacterFamily; **287** Nenov Brothers Images, Marssanya; **288** Nonnakrit, BWFolsom; **293** Vovan; **301** Vadym Andrushchenko; **303** Beloborod; **305** Laborant, Monticello, Ugorenkov Aleksandr, pryzmat; **307** redstone; **308** Chones, Bejim; **313** Seregam, MrBright, Bergamont; **314** Hong Vo, Africa Studio; **320** Bergamont; **322** Utekhina Anna; **329** Le Do; **330** Nik Merkulov, AlenKadr, Irina Rogova; **335** dcwcreations; **340** Eric Isselee, Little Perfect Stoc, Olhastock, Lightspring, Butterfly Hunter, takoburito, DenisNata; **341** FocusStocker, n7atal7i, Valentina Razumova, stockphoto-graf; **342** Aleksey Stemme, Picsfive, bergamont, Maks Narodenko, SunshineVector; **343** bergamont, Butterfly Hunter, Lightspring, Picsfive; **344** bergamont, Lightspring, Butterfly Hunter, stockphoto-graf; **345** Aleksey Stemme, Yellow Cat, N7atal7i; **346** Tatyana Vyc, Topseller, bergamont, Dan Thornberg, FocusStocker; **349** Nejron Photo, Angeliki Vel; **350** MyImages – Micha, Lifestudio, Zeligen, Marssanya, Natasha Pankina; **356**, **358** Preto Perola; **365** Aleksey Troshin, Africa Studio, ExpressVectors; **366** Carolyn Franks, Palform, Blue67design, Pukach, Tatiana Popova; **371** Ntstudio; **380** Madlen, Aleksandr Bagri, Aleksey Troshin; **381** Preto Perola, Madlen, Aleksandr Bagri; **382** Danilaleo, Aleksey Troshin, Hurst Photo; **385** Ivonne Wierink, liskus; **386** Fotolotos, artnLera; **390** Mile Atanasov, artnLera; **399** xpixel, Eric Isselee; **402** Ivonne Wierink; **405** Africa Studio, Olllikeballoon; **406** Thomas Soellner, April Turner; **407** Natasha Pankina; **410** Africa Studio; **411** TigerStock's; **418** Oleksandr Lytvynenko, otsphoto, Rich Carey, StudioSmart, Tsekhmister, JIANG HONGYAN; **420** Tsekhmister, JIANG HONGYAN; **421** suns07butterfly, Kosarev Alexander, Kucher Serhii, Preto Perola; **424** Eric Isselee, absolutimages; **425** Dionisvera; **426** Nik Merkulov, Africa Studio; **431** acceptphoto; **444** Pixfiction; **445** Thitisan, liskus, Redchocolate; **446** photka, Drakuliren, primiaou; **451** Quang Vu; **457** Nitr, Africa Studio, Anna Kucherova, Eric Isselee, mexrix; **458** Miiisha, loskutnikov, Maslov Dmitr, Aksenova Natalya, Kapustin Igor, Tetiana Rostopira; **459** Picsfive; **460–461** Prostock-studio, photka, Picsfive; **462** Picsfive; **463** Eric Isselee; **465** nevodka, Petr Malyshev, Nik Merkulov, Apr-70, smilewithjul; **466** Nik Merkulov, Kelvin Wong, smilewithjul, Lalahouse; **471** Boumen Japet; **477** Benjawan phurit, Happymay; **478** Chones; **485** Fekete Tibor, Eric Isselee, liskus, Jody Ann; **486** Petr Malyshev, Apr-70, liskus; **490** Kaiskynet Studio, Volkova Anna; **491** suwatsilp sooksang; **500**; **505** Ivonne Wierink, liskus; **506** Picsfive, enchanted_fairy; **512** Prostock-studio, Mega Pixel, IB Photography; **527** xpixel, Gumenyuk Dmitriy, Wonderful Future World; **528** Marina Yesina, Bachkova Natalia, Nadisja, Zeligen; **530** Exopixel; **533** Stanislaw Mikulski; **539** Yellow Cat, Vorobyeva; **540** ecco, Bennian; **546** Africa Studio; **547** Mega Pixel, IB Photography; **548** mayakova, Graphic.mooi,

Illustration Credits

All Illustrations by **Tim Chi Ly**

olllikeballoon, Erica Truex; **567** EtiAmmos, Madlen; **568** Koosen, BravissimoS, liskus, marssanya; **569** chuchiko17; **570** klenger; **572** Revers; **573** David Franklin; **578** Studio DMM Photography, Design and Art; Designs & Art, EtiAmmos, Madlen; **579** EtiAmmos, Madlen, Goldnetz; **580** Pukach, Watchara Phochareung, Studio DMM Photography Design and Art; **587** Photosync, Lina_Lisichka, Balabolka; **588** Pakpoom Phummee, BLKstudio, gan chaonan, Ken StockPhoto, sarayuth3390; **589** Swill Klitch; **593–594** NumbSt; **607** Ravi; **608** Marques; **611** acceptphoto; **613** FabrikaSimf, Pixel B, Vorobyeva; **614** Yellow Cat, MichaelJayBerlin, Utekhina Anna, LightField Studios, Olizabet; **615** Evikka, Lucy Liu; **616** photastic; **618** Andrey Lobachev; **619** Andrey Myagkov; **622** Lineicons freebird; **623** andregric, Sergey Ash; **625** photastic, NARUDON ATSAWALARPSAKUN, sergign, Siyapath, cynoclub; **626** Africa Studio, SergiyN, urfin, Dora Zett; **628** nopporn0510, Zerbor, robotrecorder, Jiri Vaclavek; **629** QMTstudio, Richard Peterson, timquo, ESOlex; **630** ingret, Eric Isselee, Brooke Becker, Laboko; **632** Vorobyeva, gdvcom; **633** HeinzTeh, niwat chaiyawoot, Photo Melon, Potapov Alexander, Lano4ka, Mhatzapa; **634** MustafaNC, yauhenka, KK Tan, Little birdie, Zeligen, kostolom3000; **635** Chinnapong; **636** BlueRingMedia, Yellow Cat, Sondre Lysne; **638** pticelov, AVS-Images, Boltenkoff, 7th Son Studio; **639** Icosha; **645** Iakov Filimonov, topseller, Gts, pukach, kzww, Maks Narodenko, stockphoto-graf, Picsfive, FocusStocker, Valentina Razumova, 7th Son Studio; **646** kzww, Danilaleo, Ratikova, gts, MustafaNC, Sondre Lysne, Yellow Cat, Yarkovoy, Albo003, Keith Homan, csivasz, sergign; **647** Ladislav Berecz; **649** Mtsaride, Tim UR, Dan Thornberg, pukach, Keith Homan, topseller, Albo003, Picsfive, niwat chaiyawoot, kzww; **650** bergamont, Infinity T29, Iakov Filimonov, 7th Son Studio, sergign, Yellow Cat, Valentina Razumova, Ratikova, csivasz, Sondre Lysne, Danny Smythe, Gts; **651** JpeglonitaPhotographer; **652** Keith Homan; **653** Dionisvera, HomeArt; **654** Richard Peterson, cynoclub, ESB Professional; **655** Yellow Cat, Valentina Razumova, loskutnikov; **656** MustafaNC, cynoclub, urfin; **A1** urfin, Eric Isselee, Mega Pixel; **A2** urfin, Utekhina Anna, nopporn0510, Zerbor; **A3** MustafaNC, HomeArt; **A4**; **A8**; **A8** MustafaNC, HomeArt, Picsfive, nopporn0510; **A9** Eric Isselee, Mega Pixel, gdvcom, Picsfive, HomeArt; **A10** MustafaNC, HomeArt, Pixel B, FabrikaSimf; **A11** Utekhina Anna; **A12** Vorobyeva; **A13** photastic; **A14** nopporn0510, Zerbor; **A16** Picsfive, HomeArt; **A17** r. Classen

Student Handbook, appearing in Student Bookshelf and Teacher Guide only:
HBi ArtMari, Pixfiction, Rawpixel.com; **HB1** Pixfiction, Africa Studio, ArtMari; **HB2** iadams, ArtMari; **HB3** Palabra, ArtMari; **HB4** Tero Vesalainen, ArtMari; **HB5** Harvepino, ArtMari; **HB6–HB7** ArtMari **HB8** Chiyacat, ArtMari; **HB9** Kyselova Inna, Markus Mainka, ArtMari; **HB10** ArtMari